climate policy

■ **The leading international, peer-reviewed journal on responses to climate change**

VOLUME 8 ISSUE 2 2008

First published 2008 by
Earthscan

Published 2014 by Routledge
2 Park Square, Milton Park, Abingdon, Oxon OX14 4RN
711 Third Avenue, New York, NY, 10017, USA

*Routledge is an imprint of the Taylor & Francis Group,
an informa business*

© 2008 Earthscan

Climate Policy is editorially independent. The editorial
administration of the journal is supported by Climate
Strategies (a not-for-profit research network) and the
region *Ile de France/CNRS*.

Climate Policy is indexed in Thomson ISI Social Sciences
Citation Index.

Abstracting services which cover this title include:
Elsevier Scopus, Geobase, International Political
Science Abstracts and Econlit.

The Publishers acknowledge the generous support of
Shell Foundation and Climate Strategies for the
publication of this journal.

ISBN 13: 978-1-844-07641-3 (hbk)

Climate
Strategies

climate
policy

Aims and scope

Climate Policy presents the highest quality refereed research and analysis on the policy issues raised by climate change, and provides a forum for commentary and debate. It addresses both the mitigation of, and adaptation to, climate change, within and between the different regions of the world. It encourages a trans-disciplinary approach to these issues at international, regional, national and sectoral levels.

The journal aims to make complex, policy-related analysis of climate change issues accessible to a wide audience, including those actors involved in:

- research and the commissioning of policy-relevant research
- policy and strategy formulation/implementation by local and national governments;
- the interactions and impacts of climate policies and strategies on business and society, and their responses, in different nations and sectors;
- international negotiations including, but not limited to, the UN Framework Convention on Climate Change, the Kyoto Protocol, other processes.

Climate Policy thus aims to build on its academic base so as to inject new insights and facilitate informed debate within and between, these diverse constituencies.

Types of contribution

Climate Policy publishes a variety of contributions:

Peer reviewed articles
Peer reviewed articles present academic, evidence-based research on climate policy issues:

- **Research articles** (4–6000 words) present original high quality research
- **Synthesis articles** (6–8000 words) present a survey and syntheses of the state of knowledge and key issues in a particular area of relevance to climate policy, including scientific, economic, environmental, institutional, political, social or ethical issues.
- **Policy analysis articles** (1–3000 words) present evidence-based objective analysis of policy that is embedded within an existing literature and context.

Research and synthesis articles are subject to rigorous double-blind multiple academic peer review; policy analysis articles are also fully peer-reviewed.

Outlook
The Outlook section presents timely, relevant analysis and commentary, for a wide climate policy community, and includes:

- **Perspectives** from senior decisionmakers
- **Insights** from independent commentators on policy processes, positions, options and debates
- **Records** of important new agreements, legislation and other developments including analysis of key events
- **Feedback** on earlier material published in *Climate Policy*

Climate Policy Outlook contains both commissioned and submitted papers, subject to editorial and light external review, generally in the range 500-2500 words though longer pieces may be considered on an exceptional basis.

Climate Policy also carries **country studies** and **book reviews**, and publishes **special thematic issues** on particular topics.

Topics covered

Topics covered by *Climate Policy* include (but are not limited to):

- Analysis of mitigation or adaptation policies and strategies (at macro-, meso- and/or micro- scales)
- Studies of implementation and prospects in different countries and industrial sectors
- Sectoral options and strategies for meeting policy targets
- Studies on regional differences including North-South issues
- Policy and economic aspects of intergenerational and intragenerational equity
- Applications of integrated assessment to specific policy issues
- Policy and quantitative aspects of land-use and forestry
- Design of the Kyoto mechanisms and their implications
- Analysis of corporate strategies for climate change
- Socio-political analysis of prospects for the UNFCCC system
- Economic and political aspects of developing country policy formation, action and involvement
- Social studies of climate change, including public perception, where policy implications are derived
- Local resilience, adaptation and insurance measures: extreme events and gradual change
- National and international adaptation and coping with impacts, including migration, natural resource allocation and use, etc.
- Policy formulation processes, including negotiation, public consultation, political processes and 'bottom-up' approaches

Authors' charter

This journal is committed to maintain the highest editorial standards and continuous improvement. As part of moving to an online submission system, we are implementing an Authors' Charter (see www.climatepolicy.com) to make our procedures and policies explicit and to help authors understand the editorial process and what to expect. As part of maintaining the highest standards, *Climate Policy* asks all authors, editors and reviewers to disclose any relationship (e.g. financial, economic or institutional) that could be perceived as affecting the integrity of the scientific process.

climate
policy

■ editorial

Integrating development and climate policies

BERT METZ*, MARCEL KOK

Netherlands Environmental Assessment Agency, Bilthoven, The Netherlands

Social and economic development is strongly related to climate change. It is now well established that climate change and its impacts can have a very negative influence on people and their economies, for example on agriculture or in areas vulnerable to droughts and floods. The livelihoods of the poor, young and elderly will be most seriously undermined by extreme events (e.g. droughts, floods, epidemics) as well as more subtle changes (e.g. different disease vectors, heat stress, changes in growing season). The global effort to fight poverty, confirmed again with the adoption of the Millennium Development Goals, will be seriously hampered if mitigation and adaptation to climate change are not addressed.

Paradoxically, social and economic development is the very driver of climate change. The way in which human societies have transformed the land over the past centuries to produce food, timber and fuel, and the use of coal, oil and natural gas to fuel our economies are directly responsible for the strong increase in GHG concentrations in the atmosphere. The trends in exploitation of natural resources and the use of fossil fuel are not changing. Projections into the future show a further decline in the forests and natural vegetation and a further increase in greenhouse gas emissions, exacerbating climate change. The question is how to reconcile the development aspirations of countries with the challenges posed by human-induced climate change.

The complex relationship between development and climate change necessitates a two-way approach, embracing:

■ The influence of climate change and (climate change) policy/strategy/action on development.
■ The influence of development policies, strategies and decisions on climate change. This applies to development strategies that reduce vulnerability to climate change ('climate-safe' development or 'climate-proofing' development) as well as 'climate-friendly' or 'low-carbon' development strategies.

Both perspectives are important in order to engage effectively with the projected change in the climate. However, dealing with these aspects independently is not enough. Given the interconnectedness of development and climate change, only an integrated approach could work. Such an integrated approach moves towards what is normally called 'sustainable development'. Integrating (or mainstreaming) climate change is what needs to be done, for both industrialized and developing countries.

This looks like an obvious idea and has been embraced widely in policy debates. Who can be against sustainable development? However, when it comes to specific issues, the same people who strongly support sustainable development for example object on the grounds of cost, and they

■ *Corresponding author. E-mail: Bert.Metz@mnp.nl

CLIMATE POLICY 8 (2008) 99–102

doi:10.3763/cpol.2008.0523 © 2008 Earthscan ISSN: 1469-3062 (print), 1752-7457 (online) www.climatepolicy.com

argue that combating climate change shifts essential financial resources away from promoting development. In other words, at the practical level, both nationally and internationally, there is an enormous 'disconnect' between the general support of sustainable development and the practical implementation of moving in that direction by integrating climate change into development decisions.

Scientific studies have been exploring this relationship between development and climate change for some time. In the Third Assessment Report of the IPCC, the issue was discussed at a more generic level. The Fourth Assessment Report, building on a much bigger body of literature, treats the issues of development and climate much more prominently, with all chapters paying attention to this connection and a whole chapter devoted to the link with sustainable development in both in the report on adaptation and mitigation. The messages from the latest IPCC report are:

- many opportunities for synergies exist between pursuing development and dealing with climate change
- much better insight has been created for understanding the trade-offs that in some cases have to be made.

These trade-offs relate to aspects of sustainable development where compromises may have to be made when giving attention to climate change. The findings apply to reducing vulnerability by making the right development choices as well as to ways of combining development with a low-GHG-emissions economy. However, the literature is still predominantly of a generic nature. It does not answer the many questions that arise when trying to implement integrated sustainable development at local, national or international levels. In other words, the literature makes the case for doing it, but provides little help to practitioners with the question of how to do it. However, cutting-edge work is now emerging on these questions; see, for example, the recent *Climate Policy* special issue 'Integrating Climate Change Actions into Local Development' (volume 7, number 4, 2007).

This special issue therefore focuses on new literature that goes deeper into the matter, by identifying options for action, i.e. how development strategies, policies and decisions can be made more sustainable by integrating climate change, and how to overcome the barriers that hinder implementation. This is sometimes called the 'development-first' approach. It considers three levels:

- The local and national level, where the basis for sustainable development strategies lies.
- The scaling-up of national experiences to large-scale initiatives or to other countries, making it possible to have a meaningful impact on the climate change problem as a whole.
- The level of international agreements, which can create the incentives for sustainable development at the local and national levels.

The latter directly relates to the negotiations on a post-2012 climate change agreement, especially the financial and technological support for developing countries' contributions to limiting GHG emissions and to the adaptation issues. It is obvious that this goes beyond what is contained within the Framework Convention on Climate Change. In that sense this special issue explores directions for the catalytic role the Convention can play for both adaptation and mitigation that are specifically mentioned in the Bali Action Plan.

Most of the articles emerged from a workshop on Development and Climate that was held in Paris in September 2006.[1] This meeting brought together a number of the leading researchers in this field and policy stakeholders (government, business, non-governmental organizations). The science policy debate that took place contributed significantly to improved insights into what really matters for implementing integrated development and climate policies. It helped the authors of the scientific papers to improve their analysis, along with this journal's subsequent independent double-blind peer-review, editorial processes and the authors' subsequent revisions. Outcomes of the meeting have been presented to the UNFCCC's 'Long-term Dialogue on Cooperative Action'.

Kok, Metz, Verhagen and van Rooijen provide an overview of the issues and an assessment of what we can currently say, based on scientific studies, about how to implement integrated development and climate strategies at the three levels mentioned above. Winkler, Höhne and den Elzen explore the concept of sustainable development policies and measures (SD-PAMs) at the international level. This approach focuses on policies and measures that are firmly within the national sustainable development priorities of developing countries. Formal recognition in an international agreement could be given either by listing countries in an Annex to the Convention, or by including the pledged policies in a dedicated register. Regular reporting on the sustainable development and climate benefits of SD-PAMs could take place through national communications or a separate reporting mechanism. Incentives for SD-PAMs could come from both climate and non-climate funding.

Energy investment is fundamental to development and is capital-intensive, but access to finance is not equally available across countries and for different types of investments. Two articles address the finance issues. Miller signals that the context for the financing of climate change mitigation is evolving rapidly, with significant implications for climate policy. The policy challenge lies in making financing available, commensurate with the scale and urgency of addressing climate change. Targeted financing programmes will most probably be inadequate for this purpose. Instead, policy makers need to focus on creating adequate signals that climate change will be an important and continuing factor in government policies for the foreseeable future, in order to affect investor expectations of relative risk and reward. If this is done, financing will follow. Tirpak and Adams focus on trends in development assistance funding for energy and the implications for mitigating climate change. Their analysis suggests that there has been somewhat of a shift away from fossil fuel to lower greenhouse-gas-emitting projects. The increases in funding and shifts to low-greenhouse-gas technologies are, however, fragile. Both articles show that the continuing evolution of modalities of development finance for project-based activities needs to be supplemented with macro-economic and sector-wide assistance, targeted at promoting policy reforms, institutional change, and capacity building.

The next three articles address vulnerability and adaptation. Jerneck and Olsson argue that adaptation needs to be facilitated, promoted and achieved in the local context, where vulnerability to climate change is perceived and experienced, especially among the poorest populations. But the international community needs to realize that adaptation must be addressed at all levels from the local to the global. There is also a need for policy renewal in other international regimes that are central to adaptation, such as environment, human rights, development and trade. Drawing upon illustrative case studies in six developing countries, Agrawala and van Aalst examine the synergies and trade-offs involved in integrating adaptation to climate change in development cooperation activities. Key barriers facing such integration are identified, and an agenda is proposed for enhancing development efforts by mainstreaming climate risk management. O'Brien, O'Keefe, Meena, Rose and Wilson argue that poverty alleviation is the main policy driver for poor nations, although changes in livelihood strategies are driven by a range of factors. Using a case study, direct and indirect adaptation is examined with reference to the specific livelihoods of the Chagga people of Tanzania. The authors conclude that the starting point for adaptation in the developing world must be poverty alleviation, based on a rights-based approach.

Halsnæs, Shukla and Garg provide an overview of national case studies related to climate change mitigation in the energy and transportation sector and studies related to the infrastructure sector and water supply. They find that, in most cases, existing development policies will not lead to a sustainable development pattern, since they do not sufficiently deal with climate change. However, there are several examples of good opportunities in many countries for integrated policies that can achieve development goals while dealing with climate change. For the energy and transportation sector, studies identified many alternative national low-cost policies with much lower GHG emissions than the business-as-usual policy. For infrastructure and water supply, studies identified opportunities for alternative national development policies that will lead to much higher resilience against climate variability and future climate change. Ribeiro and Abreu analyse four public policy initiatives in the Brazilian transport sector: the adoption of flex-fuel technology, the National Biodiesel Programme, the National Vehicle Efficiency Programme, and the Rio de Janeiro State Light Vehicle Inspection and Maintenance Programme. High oil prices and poor air quality in urban areas are the dominant factors that motivated these policies to emerge. Economic and environmental impacts in terms of cutting consumption of petroleum products are analysed. Significant CO_2 emission reductions are demonstrated as a co-benefit of these policies. Lessons from these initiatives for domestic and international policy are presented.

This special issue presents important material for reconciling development needs with an effective policy to address climate change; one of the big challenges of the coming decade for national governments and the international community. We hope it will trigger a further policy action as well as further research in how to make things work in practice.[2]

Notes

1. The workshop was organized by the Netherlands Environmental Assessment Agency, together with Wageningen University and Research, Plant Research International, The Netherlands; the French Institute for Sustainable Development and International Relations (IDDRI); the University of Cape Town, South Africa; the Institute for Global Strategies (IGES), Japan; and the UNEP Risoe Centre for Energy, Climate and Sustainable Development.
2. A research agenda is identified in the article by Kok, Metz, Verhagen and van Rooijen.

References

Agrawala, S., van Aalst, M., 2008, 'Adapting development cooperation to adapt to climate change', *Climate Policy* 8(2), 183–193.

Bizikova, L., Robinson, J., Cohen, S. (eds), 2007, *Integrating Climate Change Actions into Local Development*, Special Issue, *Climate Policy* 7(4).

Halsnæs, K., Shukla, P.R., Garg, A., 2008, 'Sustainable development and climate change: lessons from country studies', *Climate Policy* 8(2), 202–219.

Jerneck, A., Olsson, L., 2008, 'Adaptation and the poor: development, resilience and transition', *Climate Policy* 8(2), 170–182.

Ribeiro, S.K., Abreu, A.A. de, 2008, 'Brazilian transport initiatives with GHG reductions as a co-benefit', *Climate Policy* 8(2), 220–240.

Kok, M., Metz, B., Verhagen, J., van Rooijen, S., 2008, 'Integrating development and climate policies: national and international benefits', *Climate Policy* 8(2), 103–118.

Miller, A.S., 2008, 'Financing the integration of climate change mitigation into development', *Climate Policy* 8(2), 152–169.

O'Brien, G., O'Keefe, P., Meena, H., Rose, J., Wilson, L., 2008, 'Climate adaptation from a poverty perspective', *Climate Policy* 8(2), 194–201.

Tirpak, D., Adams, H., 2008, 'Bilateral and multilateral financial assistance for the energy sector of developing countries', *Climate Policy* 8(2), 135–151.

Winkler, H., Höhne, N., den Elzen, M., 2008, 'Methods for quantifying the benefits of sustainable development policies and measures (SD-PAMs)', *Climate Policy* 8(2), 119–134.

climate policy

■ synthesis article

Integrating development and climate policies: national and international benefits

MARCEL KOK[1]*, BERT METZ[1], JAN VERHAGEN[2], SASCHA VAN ROOIJEN[1]

[1] Netherlands Environmental Assessment Agency, Bilthoven, The Netherlands
[2] Plant Research International, Wageningen University and Research, The Netherlands

What lessons for policy makers at national and international level can be drawn from the growing experiences of reconciling development and climate change? The key to achieving this is to approach the problem from the development perspective, since that is where in most countries the priority lies. Current knowledge on how to realize the benefits of such an integrated approach is assessed. The focus is on the main national development priorities, such as poverty reduction, disaster reduction, rural development, energy supply and transportation. Barriers and promising approaches are identified, based on the experience gained in several countries. The potential is explored for enhancing the global impact of such integrated approaches through replication of national experiences, supported by international organizations. Opportunities for large-scale initiatives are considered at national or regional level. The role of international agreements in fostering integrated development and climate policies is analysed, showing opportunities for achieving large co-benefits for addressing climate change by making use of existing policy frameworks for development and going beyond the UNFCCC framework.

Keywords: climate change vulnerability; development; disaster reduction; mainstreaming; policy formation; poverty reduction; sustainable development; synergy

Quelles sont les leçons que les décideurs peuvent tirer au niveau national et international pour multiplier les expériences de réconciliation entre développement et changement climatique? La solution est d'aborder le problème selon la perspective du développement, vu que c'est là où se situe la priorité pour la plupart des pays. Les connaissances actuelles sur la façon de réaliser les avantages d'une telle approche intégrée sont analysées. L'accent est mis sur les priorités nationales de développement principales, telles que la réduction de la pauvreté, la réduction des catastrophes, le développement rural, l'approvisionnement et le transport de l'énergie. Les obstacles et les approches prometteuses sont identifiés, sur la base d'une expérience obtenue dans plusieurs pays. Le potentiel pour améliorer l'impact global de telles approches intégrées est étudié par la reproduction d'expériences nationales, avec le soutien d'organisations internationales. Les opportunités pour les initiatives à grande échelle sont envisagées aux niveaux nationaux et internationaux. Le rôle des accords internationaux à l'intégration des politiques sur le développement et sur le climat est analysé, montrant comment, en employant les cadres de politiques existants pour le développement et en allant au-delà du cadre de la CCNUCC, de grandes synergies peuvent s'ouvrir en faveur de la lutte contre le changement climatique.

Mots clés: développement; développement durable; formation de politiques; intégration; lutte contre la pauvreté; lutte contre les catastrophes naturelles; synergie; vulnérabilité au changement climatique

■ *Corresponding author. E-mail:* marcel.kok@mnp.nl

CLIMATE POLICY 8 (2008) 103–118

doi:10.3763/cpol.2007.0436 © 2008 Earthscan ISSN: 1469-3062 (print), 1752-7457 (online) www.climatepolicy.com

1. Introduction: the relation between development and climate change

Development efforts will be seriously hampered by the risks of climate change if these are not tackled. Reduced economic growth due to climate change damages, threatened or under-performing investments, and lower food production due to maladaptation to a changing climate, are examples of the influence of climate on development (Murphy, 2006; Schipper and Pelling, 2006; IPCC, 2007a; UNDP, 2007). Development that does not take climate change into account is unsustainable, as it will create societies that are vulnerable to climate change and can lead to high emissions of greenhouse gases from energy, transport and land use that will exacerbate climate change (Sathaye et al., 2007; Yohe et al., 2007). So there is a need to align and integrate policies on development and climate change.

The 'development first' approach, which starts from development priorities and integrates climate change vulnerability and greenhouse gas emissions considerations, provides a framework for reconciling development and climate concerns (Beg et al., 2002; Davidson et al., 2003; Heller and Shukla, 2003; Agrawala, 2005; Bradley and Baumert, 2005; CCAP, 2006; Srinivasan, 2006; Halsnæs et al., 2008; O'Brien et al., 2008; Ribeiro and Abreu, 2008). The resulting climate-inclusive policies aim at development with low vulnerability to climate change and development with low greenhouse gas emissions. They look for synergies and for a rational consideration of possible trade-offs between the different dimensions of sustainability.

The focus of this article is on exploring this integrated approach for developing countries. However, it is just as relevant for industrialized countries, where tensions between economic growth, job creation, and other socio-economic concerns with climate change have led to huge increases in the emissions of greenhouse gases and subsequent changes of the global climate (Robinson et al., 2006).

The objective of this article is to assess the current understanding on how to integrate development and climate policies so that mutual benefits are created at national and international levels. In other words, what lessons for policy at the national and international level can be drawn from the growing experiences in trying to reconcile development and climate change? The article therefore presents a comprehensive assessment of the relevant literature to draw a synthetic picture of key issues, major barriers and promising solutions.

2. Benefits of integration

Several countries have already demonstrated the benefits of an integrated development and climate strategy. Such benefits include reduced poverty, increased employment opportunities, and improvements in health, energy and food security, and infrastructure, as well as climate benefits (Halsnæs et al., 2008; O'Brien et al., 2008; Ribeiro and Abreu, 2008).

The alcohol fuel programme in Brazil, for instance, has created a cost-effective way to substitute for fossil fuels. Labour-intensive sugarcane production systems provide opportunities for income and job generation for hundreds of thousands of poor smallholder families in the Brazilian northern and north-eastern regions. In doing so, the economy has become less vulnerable to changes in oil prices while generating income for the rural population. The programme has helped to reduce its import dependency from oil, has saved about US$52 billion (January 2003 US$) between 1975 and 2002 in foreign exchange, has created 900,000 relatively well-paid jobs, and has considerably reduced local air pollution in the cities as well as decreasing greenhouse gas emissions (Moreira et al., 2005; Lebre la Rovere et al., 2006).

In Senegal, the pressure on land is increasing with the growing population. Climate change poses an additional stress, which increases the vulnerability of forest and agricultural systems. To stabilize agricultural production levels, the restoration of soil fertility is a key factor. Agroforestry assists agricultural development and addresses climate change by providing a local energy supply for the rural poor, rehabilitating degraded lands, and sequestering carbon from the atmosphere (Sokona et al., 2003; Sow and Saint Sernin, 2005).

In many cases there is not a pure win–win situation. Trade-offs often have to be made between certain aspects of development and addressing climate change. In fact, the intention of making development more sustainable by bringing in the climate dimension might be at odds with other dimensions of sustainability. Promoting large-scale bioenergy production is a prime example of a policy where trade-offs between food security, biodiversity and climate change have to be made (see further below). Higher costs of clean energy systems have to be weighed against social and economic benefits.

3. Implementing integrated policies at the national and sub-national level

Country experiences show that integration of development and climate policies, or mainstreaming, can be most effectively occur at the national or sub-national level. This article therefore starts with an assessment of national experiences. This is followed by investigating the possibilities for scaling-up national experiences and, finally, the international context for such national approaches is discussed.

3.1. Key barriers to implementation

Although some national governments and international organizations have begun to mainstream climate policy in other policy areas, integrated development and climate strategies are not widely implemented for a variety of reasons (Agrawala, 2005; Sow and Saint Sernin, 2005; Mitchell et al., 2006; Schipper and Pelling, 2006; Hellmuth et al., 2007; Kok and de Coninck, 2007; Agrawala and van Aalst, 2008).

Climate change has, for a long time, not been recognized as an important issue for development, despite the fact that it is already starting to negatively impact development efforts. In addition, the costs and benefits of an integrated approach are not always clear, and attribution to single actions or policies is difficult. There are also reasons that have to do with how governments work and the lack of human and institutional capacity and lack of coordination and cooperation. Lack of joint decision making between different national ministries is a major constraint. Developing countries feel the pressure, especially from the international donor community, to mainstream various interrelated aspects into their core development policies; not only climate change, but also gender, HIV/AIDS, biodiversity and other issues. The OECD (Agrawala, 2005) calls that mainstreaming 'fatigue' or 'overload'. And last, but not least, there is a poor understanding of how to deal with scientific uncertainties amongst stakeholders.

3.2. Poverty alleviation

Poverty alleviation is a core objective for national governments in developing countries. At the international level, realization of the Millennium Development Goals (MDGs) is the most prominent issue on the development agenda at the moment. Climate change is threatening the realization of these policy objectives, because the poor are among the most vulnerable to climate change. Improved access to clean energy will help local development and reduce health problems from indoor air pollution caused by traditional fuel use. So, poor people can benefit most from mainstreaming climate change into development policy (see also Jerneck and Olsson, 2008; O'Brien et al., 2008).

The challenge is to make better use of the core instruments of poverty reduction policies, such as the Poverty Reduction Strategies (IMF/World Bank, 2005) and sector-wide approaches that are vital to get access to multilateral and bilateral assistance. Practically, this can be achieved through 'climate proofing' poverty reduction policies, i.e. systematically evaluating development strategies, policies and projects on their climate dimension. This means checking whether climate vulnerability is reduced, GHG emissions are minimized, parallel climate change decision-making structures are avoided, affected communities are involved, and traditional knowledge and coping strategies are being used. Promising results are shown by the Danish Development Assistance Programme (Danida, 2005; Klein et al., 2007; Agrawala and van Aalst, 2008).

3.3. Rural development and land use

One opportunity for integrated development and climate policies in rural areas comes from the emerging bioenergy market. Bioenergy crops not only generate income for farmers, they can also improve the rural renewable energy supply and national energy security, and they have potential as an export commodity. However, there are possible trade-offs with food production. On the one hand, investments in bioenergy crops could be mutually reinforcing, since market and transport conditions and inputs for productive and efficient biofuel and food production systems are similar. Farmers' income could increase, and better agricultural policies to deal with drought and erosion will directly influence the food security of the poor. On the other hand, competition for land and labour could have a negative effect on local food production and food prices, and increase dependency on food imports, especially when large-scale bioenergy markets emerge. In that case, biodiversity also becomes a concern (UNDP, 2000; Sow and Saint Sernin, 2005; Hunt and Sawin, 2006; IPCC, 2007b). Current scenarios for biofuel production up until 2030, however, do not require more than 4% of the world's arable lands (IEA, 2006). Experience from several countries shows that national biofuel policies could benefit from careful analyses of the local circumstances regarding problems with food, labour and biodiversity, better regional market integration to allow bioenergy cash crops to reach the relevant markets, and improved coordination between agricultural and energy policies (Dubash and Bradley, 2005; Sow and Saint Sernin, 2005; Dufey, 2007; Shukla, 2007).

3.4. Disaster reduction

There is a great potential for linking existing disaster reduction and prevention, on the one hand, and climate change adaptation, on the other, to reduce vulnerability to weather-related disasters. Both approaches reduce risks. A primary condition for this is that disaster-reduction and climate-change communities within governments, private sector, civil society and science in countries need to cooperate. Involving the people and institutions at the local level is important. Better information on upcoming extreme weather events is crucial, requiring capacity for early warning and climate predictions. Combined actions could help to shift attention from relief to prevention and preparedness through better land-use planning, and improved quality of houses and other building structures. A problem with preventive actions is that they are not always possible, such as in high-population-density areas in poor countries where people are forced to live in flood-prone areas. They are also less visible, and therefore often less attractive to politicians and donors (Schipper and Pelling, 2006).

3.5. Energy

Energy security and improving access to energy are very important for local and national economic development. This can be realized in ways that also reduce health risks (through reduction of indoor and outdoor air pollution), and mitigating climate change through lower emissions of CO_2.

Shifts from coal to natural gas and domestic renewable energy supply (bioenergy, wind power, hydropower) lead to a more diverse and cleaner energy supply. Even in countries with large coal reserves, such as China, there are possibilities to do this, given the air pollution problems caused by coal, logistical problems to move coal in sufficient quantities to power stations, and the opportunities created by energy system reform (Heller and Shukla, 2003; Heller, 2006; Winkler, 2006; Sathaye et al., 2007; Victor and Heller, 2007). Applying clean coal technologies (including CO_2 capture and storage, and provisions to limit air pollution) would be a possibility to make coal use sustainable, but additional costs are still a major obstacle (IPCC, 2005).

Efficiency in energy supply and in the end-use sectors plays a key role in realizing development benefits, such as reducing energy costs, making production more competitive, improving availability of electricity supply, increased energy security, and employment opportunities (Ng and Schipper, 2005; Jiang et al., 2006; Shukla, 2006; Winkler, 2006). Achieving energy efficiency, however, is faced with many economic, institutional and market barriers. Financing renewable energy and energy efficiency is still problematic in many countries (Dave et al., 2005; KfW Development Bank, 2005). In countries with a large share of renewable electricity, maintaining that share in the future is a challenge. The private sector plays a key role in energy supply and use in many countries and therefore needs to be closely involved in mainstreaming climate change into energy policy (Heller, 2006; Victor and Heller, 2007).

3.6. Transport

In the area of transportation, development priorities are focused on increased mobility, creating new infrastructure, and on health, air pollution and security of oil supply. Both development and climate can benefit by changing fuels (biofuel or natural gas), introducing more efficient vehicles, promoting public transportation and bicycles, and adapting city models (Ng and Schipper, 2005). Well-maintained public transportation systems, such as busses, can make a large contribution to increasing social well-being through improved convenience, less congestion, cleaner air and social contacts. Excellent examples exist in Bogota and other Latin American mega-cities (Hidalgo, 2003; WRI/EMBARQ, 2006). Avoiding lock-in into a car infrastructure is a prerequisite for such a public transport policy. This means that better integration of city planning, urban transport and environmental policy is a key condition to achieve these benefits.

The Brazilian bioethanol and biodiesel experience (Moreira et al., 2005; Ribeiro and Abreu, 2008) shows the importance of consistent government policies, a sizeable scale of production, and the introduction of flexible fuel vehicles by the automobile industry, as key success factors for the introduction of biofuels. Major obstacles to moving towards a sustainable transport system are the complexities of securing sustainable biofuel production in many countries (i.e. avoiding the massive use of subsidies to support unsustainable solutions), lack of political will to give priority to the large part of the population without cars, and the up-front investments in good public transport systems.

3.7. General conclusions

Several general conclusions can be drawn on effective ways of integrating climate change into different policy areas at a national level and making implementation happen:

■ Take the evolving political and economic conditions in the country as the point of departure, and concentrate on the main policies and programmes that form the core of development planning. This means involvement of all relevant players.

- Acknowledge the importance of the sub-national level for implementation of, in particular, measures to reduce vulnerability. Local level solutions are key. Without the involvement of decentralized institutions, local development planning, and use of participatory approaches, policy implementation is not likely to be successful.
- Develop shared strategies between relevant ministries and governmental bodies and allocate responsibilities in a coordinated manner. National development strategies, sector and environmental strategies, poverty reduction strategy papers, and the planning and budgeting process offer opportunities to mobilize coordinated efforts. It is not primarily a matter for the Ministry of Environment; action has to come from the Ministries of Economic Affairs, Finance, Planning, Agriculture, and Energy, where the core decisions on development are taken.
- Promote a risk-management approach in public and private decision making, so that stakeholders will take uncertainties on climate change and its impacts into account. An important contribution can be made by the scientific community in communicating these climate change risks to all stakeholders in the development process in terms that relate to everyday practice.
- Consider climate change as a cross-cutting issue in development assistance. This implies moving away from a situation in which the topic is dealt with by climate experts in a special division. Integrate climate change with other development policy areas such as agriculture, trade, forestry, infrastructure and technology.
- Focus on facilitating national governments in their process to mainstream development and climate. Capacity building and capacity utilization will be key factors.
- Show realism in dealing with synergies and trade-offs. Synergies are not always possible, especially when markets are imperfect. Low energy prices due to heavy subsidies can, for instance, be a major obstacle to improving energy efficiency.

4. Enhancing the global impact of national experiences

The second part of this article looks at the scaling-up of national approaches. In order to have a global impact there is a need to:

- Replicate promising approaches of integrated development and climate policies in other countries, with assistance from international organizations;
- Increase the scale of development activities within countries that have a positive influence on reducing vulnerability or keeping GHG emissions low.

The key question is how this scaling-up process could be realized through international initiatives.

International organizations, (such as the FAO, UNDP, UNEP, UN Regional Commissions, the World Bank, Regional Development Banks, OECD, the Red Cross) as well as new public–private partnerships (such as the Global Village Energy Partnership, the Renewable Energy Policy Network 21), do already play a facilitating role in implementing integrated development and climate strategies in many countries. They can provide a forum for further development of these approaches, share good practices, build adequate human and social capacities, initiate new partnerships and regional collaboration, set standards and guidelines, and provide reliable data. However, differences between countries and regions are very important, and replication is therefore not the same as copying. Approaches need to be tailored to specific needs and circumstances, along with available resources (Red Cross, 2003; Burton and van Aalst, 2004; UNDP, 2004).

4.1. Poverty reduction

A critical issue for scaling-up is financing the mainstreaming of climate change into poverty reduction strategies (O'Brien et al., 2008).There is a tendency in the development assistance communities to rely on additional climate funding to realize this mainstreaming. However, the inherent risks of climate change to poverty eradication strategies (as a significant proportion of development assistance is sensitive to climate change) warrant the use of core development funding for this purpose (Greene, 2004; Brouwer and Aerts, 2006; Murphy, 2006). This would require integration of climate change risks in the national poverty reduction and development plans of developing countries. Given the magnitude of the climate change risks, increasing overall funding through leveraging non-ODA funding remains critical.

A second important issue for scaling-up is creating the right conditions in developing countries – with assistance from bilateral and multilateral organizations – for mainstreaming climate change in poverty reduction policies. A good example is the Poverty and Climate Change Initiative (African Development Bank et al., 2003). A large number of bilateral and multilateral donors agreed on an approach on how to mainstream and integrate adaptation to climate change into poverty reduction efforts. Local livelihoods, human capacities, and technologies serve as the starting point. Creating access to resources and markets to build coping capacities is important. Data on vulnerabilities can be provided by international organizations. Partnerships between the public and private sector at community, national and international levels, such as the Poverty and Environment Partnership (UNDP, 2005a), are effective vehicles for disseminating best practices. Implementation of the MDG agenda will provide a strong incentive for such partnerships (Rockström et al., 2005).

4.2. Rural development and land use

For land-use systems, where large differences exist in local conditions, scaling-up integrated development and climate policies has to be adapted to local circumstances. Efforts are needed to provide reliable land-use data, practical standards and guidelines to both national policy makers and local communities. This requires a coordinated effort between national governments and international organizations. The FAO Food Security and Nutrition and Vulnerability-related Information and Mapping System (FIVIMS) is an example of such information systems for agricultural development (FAO, 2007).

Biofuel production is one of the prime candidates for scaling-up integrated agriculture and climate strategies. Coordination of UN activities in promoting sustainable bioenergy programmes and partnerships is assisted through the International Bioenergy Platform (FAO, 2006a) and the Global Bioenergy Partnership (FAO, 2006b). Since many countries are not able to generate the necessary investment and the required institutional support, the assistance of financial institutions is important. An interesting development in this field is the recent announcement of a biodiesel production programme in Senegal, financially supported by Brazil, India and the West-African Bank for Investment and Development (Africa Research Bulletin, 2007). Improving international trade opportunities in biofuels, as discussed by the WTO, can be significant for rural development (Dufey, 2007).

4.3. Disaster reduction

Scaling-up integrated disaster reduction and climate change adaptation policies seems very promising, especially by making use of the UN ISDR Hyogo Framework for Action 2005–2015 (UNISDR, 2006). Climate change risks have already been recognized, and integration in disaster preparedness and prevention is being discussed at international and national levels (Sperling and Szekely, 2005). Implementation of the agreed actions is on a voluntary basis, but is supported by intergovernmental processes to develop guidelines, monitoring tools and data, with encouragement by national platforms. Improvement in mapping vulnerable areas, effective prevention approaches and early warning systems is a key concern. Resources for national implementation have to come from national budgets, which make disaster prevention vulnerable to the setting of priorities. Climate change may help to better integrate disaster reduction policies in development planning. What is needed is practical action at the national level on mainstreaming of climate risks in the disaster reduction and development agenda, with the support of the international processes (Thomalla et al., 2006).

4.4. Energy

Scaling-up in the energy sector can follow two different routes. One focuses on future large-scale energy projects. The other refers to the many small-scale initiatives that are needed in many countries for improving energy efficiency and the implementation of renewable energy.

Large-scale shifts to natural gas in the power sector are realistic options for China and India. As indicated above, considerations of air pollution and logistics, combined with opportunities for importing LNG (liquefied natural gas), do make this attractive for China. In India, regional cooperation in importing natural gas from the Central Asian Republics and Iran would create similar opportunities although the current political instability will unfortunately make this difficult. From studies in China, it can be seen that an important success factor seems to be the alignment of the interests of provincial and local government, the business sector, and the national government. Understanding the political power structure and the local conditions is vital in such circumstances (Heller and Shukla, 2003; Heller, 2006; Victor and Heller, 2007). For clean coal technologies (including CO_2 capture and storage), international cooperation is needed in order to overcome the financial and technical barriers in developing countries (IPCC, 2005). A scale-up opportunity for Africa would be the building of a large hydropower-based electricity network in southern Africa (WEC, 2007).

Replication of national success stories is effective for energy efficiency and renewable energy. Partnerships such as the Renewable Energy Network 21 and the Global Village Energy Partnership have proved to be effective in mobilizing national initiatives and sharing experiences. Enhanced energy access, another top development priority, is not in conflict with integrated energy and climate policies, because it will only marginally influence total energy consumption (Wang et al., 2006; Sathaye et al., 2007).

The role of international organizations is important in knowledge transfer on energy efficiency, renewable energy and clean fossil energy (IEA, 2006), but also in leveraging the financial means for sustainable energy investments. The recently published World Bank strategy for clean energy and sustainable development, in response to a G8 initiative, is a good example of the latter (World Bank, 2006a; Miller, 2008). The Clean Development Mechanism may be a supplemental source of financing clean energy, but capital flows are small compared with the financing needs (Tirpak et al., 2007; Miller, 2008; Tirpak and Adams, 2008).

4.5. Transport

Since transportation greatly depends on local conditions, the replication of successful integrated transport and climate policies is difficult. The Brazilian successes with biofuels and flex vehicles (see Ribeiro and Abreu, 2008) might not be easily replicable elsewhere. The lack of international organizations, partnerships and programmes focusing on sustainable transport systems make it even more challenging. One of the few examples is the EMBARQ programme (WRI/EMBARQ, 2006), which represents an attempt to learn lessons about sustainable urban transport from different cities around the world. What is needed is a combination of documentation of case studies, development of guidelines for monitoring and measuring the effects of sustainable transport programmes, facilitation of regional cooperation and, most important, integration of these experiences in infrastructure investment, both nationally and within international development financing.

5. Mainstreaming climate change in international frameworks and agreements

The third element of this article is the influence of international frameworks and agreements on the mainstreaming of climate change into development policy. Realizing climate benefits at the national level can be facilitated or hindered by international policy frameworks and agreements. Existing international frameworks and agreements are usually not designed to promote integration between different policy areas, and institutional structures often complicate such integration. So the question is, what opportunities are there to make better use of existing policy frameworks to realize development and climate benefits, and how to design future frameworks and agreements in such a way that they facilitate the implementation of integrated development and climate policies at national level. This obviously means there is a need to go beyond the Framework Convention on Climate Change and to broaden the climate agenda (Kok and de Coninck, 2007; Drexhage et al., 2007; Jerneck and Olsson, 2008). In that sense it is important that the Bali Action Plan for post-2012 climate agreements identifies the need to explore the catalytic role of the Convention.

5.1. Adaptation

There is general consensus that it is important to strengthen the adaptation component under the UNFCCC when designing post-2012 agreements (Aerts et al., 2005). But how can this be done to facilitate integrated development and climate approaches to deal with climate variability and change? One possibility is to create a close link at the level of a post-Kyoto agreement with the ISDR Hyogo Framework for Action 2005–2015 that is already integrating climate change risks into national and local disaster preparedness and risk reduction plans (UNISDR, 2006). The same could be done regarding existing and future bilateral and multilateral development assistance and poverty reduction programmes (African Development Bank et al., 2003; WRI, 2005; World Bank, 2006b), for instance by establishing formal reporting requirements. A very different possibility is to make use of the provisions of the Human Rights Convention for the protection of refugees to deal with possible forced migration as a consequence of climate change impacts (UN Security Council, 2007). Furthermore, linking insurance mechanisms to a new agreement, drawing on international platforms such as the UNEP Finance Initiative, would help the mainstreaming. Last, but not least, it would make sense to create links with the UN Convention on Combating Desertification, which deals with adaptation to drought. An additional advantage of integrating implementation of various international frameworks and agreements is the simplification of the administrative burden in developing countries.

5.2. Technology development and diffusion

The development and deployment of technologies that are climate-friendly call for a combined 'push and pull' approach. All climate-friendly technologies will be needed to manage climate change risks (IPCC, 2007b). Both a 'push' via government-funded research and development and a 'pull' via regulations, taxes, subsidies and tradable quotas will be needed to make those technologies available. It must be kept in mind that the development of technologies for the longer term is not sufficiently triggered by short-term cap-and-trade systems alone. Research and development support and price signals (at least until 2020) will be important (Barker et al., 2007). In that respect the recent decisions by the European Union to reduce GHG emissions unilaterally to 20% below 1990 levels is a promising first step (European Commission, 2007). Diffusion of technology to developing countries is crucial in achieving the MDGs and supporting sustainable development. Investment by the private sector, facilitated by the UNFCCC Clean Development Mechanism, carbon funds of private and development banks, and adequate enabling conditions in developing countries, is the main driver for this technology diffusion (IPCC, 2000). Investment incentives and institutional enabling conditions for technology transfer need to be applied across the economy. Therefore it is important not to single out climate-relevant technologies, but to focus on general innovation and modernization policies (Tirpak et al., 2007).

One important way to create incentives through international frameworks and agreements is a strengthening of international cooperation in research and development of low-carbon technologies. There are existing arrangements within the IEA; in addition, several partnerships on hydrogen, fuel cells and CO_2 capture and storage are operational. De Coninck et al. (2007), in their analysis of Technology Oriented Agreements, point to the modest role of both information-sharing and cost-sharing agreements in bringing about significant emission reductions. It is not yet clear how best to reinforce these arrangements (Tirpak et al., 2007).

In terms of promoting the diffusion of clean technologies, facilitating conditions in recipient countries is essential. The current UNFCCC provisions are inadequate to make sufficient progress, because they are not based on the mainstreaming of climate-friendly technology diffusion into the regular innovation and investment frameworks of developing countries. Exchanging best practices, capacity-building, and public–private partnerships can all contribute (IPCC, 2000). A potentially effective approach to enhance technology diffusion could be agreements on technology mandates (standards, implementation), as discussed by de Coninck et al. (2007). Within a post-Kyoto agreement, this might be placed under the umbrella of Policies and Measures in the form of sector agreements or sustainable development policies and measures (see below). Longer-term emission goals could also create useful incentives (Tirpak et al., 2007). Given the central role of investment patterns for diffusion of technology, a lot will depend on new financing instruments (see below). The involvement of the real decision makers is essential, and the problem of the current UNFCCC technology transfer and financing framework is that these stakeholders are often not represented there.

5.3. Finance

Financing climate-safe and climate-friendly development requires large additional funds, which are not available through the UNFCCC financial mechanisms. Although CDM is now generating capital flows in the order of several billions of dollars per year, and GEF has spent several billions of dollars over the past 10 years (Tirpak et al., 2007; Tirpak and Adams, 2008), this is still a small amount compared with the additional US$100–200 billion that is estimated to be needed per year to invest in clean energy, improved energy access, and making development less vulnerable to climate change (World Bank, 2006a; UNFCCC, 2007a). The UNFCCC adaptation fund, to be filled by a 2% surcharge on CDM project financing, is not likely to generate capital flows of this magnitude either. The main contribution needs to come from development financing and private investments, both domestic and international (Sussman and Helme, 2004; Miller, 2008). The World Bank's clean energy and the sustainable development framework is a first attempt to generate such a leveraging mechanism (World Bank, 2006a).

Apart from the problem of additional funding, there is also the issue of access to basic investment capital. This may not be an issue for large energy projects, since these are mostly located in countries with good access to investment capital and attractive conditions for FDI (foreign direct investment). But for small-scale energy-efficiency initiatives, access to financing is more frequently a barrier, even when it has excellent economic, social and environmental benefits. Solving this problem requires national solutions that involve the banking system as well as government involvement. Institutions such as the International Finance Corporation (IFC) and the European Bank for Reconstruction and Development (EBRD) have developed such lending programmes. Positive experiences can be replicated, but the lack of international frameworks or partnerships is a major barrier (KfW Development Bank, 2005; World Bank, 2006c; Miller, 2008).

5.4. Sustainable development and emission reduction

The notion of linking GHG emission reduction in developing countries to the development agenda is now widely accepted as necessary for the broadening of the international efforts to deal with climate change. The question of how international frameworks and agreements could be designed to facilitate integrated development and climate policies leading to lower GHG emissions is being addressed in the context of the UNFCCC discussions on post-2012 agreements (Tirpak et al., 2007; UNFCCC, 2007b).

A promising idea is to look at local sustainable development policies and measures (SD-PAMs) in developing countries, as part of a system with different stages of commitments for countries, depending on their development stage. For developing countries that are not yet ready to participate in absolute emission reduction efforts, a system of voluntary or mandatory obligations to implement policies and measures to make development more sustainable could be created. That would lead to co-benefits in terms of limiting GHG emissions and reducing vulnerability to climate change (Baumert and Winkler, 2005; Winkler et al., 2007, 2008). This thinking may indeed appeal to large developing countries (CCAP, 2006; Gao, 2006). Proposals on expanding the UNFCCC Clean Development Mechanism to allow for sectoral CDM programmes (Figueres, 2005; Sterk and Wittneben, 2006) show some similarities, but the main difference is that sustainable development policies and measures would be built on domestic development policies and would therefore not be fully dependent on additional climate financing, as is the case with CDM. Discussions are, however, still at an early stage. Many questions remain unanswered, such as on quantification of the emission effects, whether it should be strictly voluntary or have a more mandatory character to make country efforts comparable, if it can be connected to the carbon market and the manageability of a system of SD-PAMs. A possible barrier is the baseline issue: the current CDM system only applies to measures that achieve a deviation from the baseline. If SD-PAMs change that baseline, it may interfere with CDM (UNDP, 2005b; Miller, 2008). Further elaboration of these questions is necessary to help negotiators make use of these ideas.

6. Conclusions and the need for further study

Over the last few years, progress towards integrating development and climate policies in several countries has been observed. Mutual understanding is increasing between different actors in this field and benefits have been demonstrated in several countries. Experiences show that integrated development and climate policies can be most effectively integrated at the national or sub-national level. This requires commitment of all relevant ministries and government bodies. Using a risk-management approach in decision making facilitates the mainstreaming of climate change issues, provided that the scientific information is presented in a practical manner. The development assistance community can make a major contribution by making 'climate proofing' of programmes a centrepiece. However, significant barriers exist that hamper implementation. In various sectors, promising approaches have been identified to overcome these barriers.

Successfully multiplying and replicating promising experiences, facilitated by international organizations, programmes and networks, is crucial to enhance the global impact of the integrated approach. Replicating successful approaches in other countries, as well as aiming at activities at country level with large impacts, are both needed. Starting from evolving political and economic priorities in development planning is core to the approach. Promising approaches are viable in sectors such as poverty alleviation, rural development, disaster reduction, energy and transport. International organizations have an important role to play that needs to be targeted to the specific circumstances of individual countries. Especially in the energy and transport sectors, strong private-sector involvement is needed.

Multilateral frameworks and agreements can be used to create the right conditions for mainstreaming climate change at the national level. Good opportunities in that respect exist in the context of the ongoing discussions about new agreements and mechanisms to follow the Kyoto Protocol. Using existing agreements, frameworks and partnerships outside the climate domain, such as those for disaster reduction, combating desertification, human rights, trade, technology development and finance, has a large potential.

Obviously there is a need for further work, in particular on:

- More intense exchanges between development and climate communities, with the strong involvement of the private sector
- More in-depth analyses of barriers to integrated development, and climate approaches and possible solutions at both national and international level
- Further exploring of 'large emitter deals' (clean coal, coal to gas, avoiding deforestation, peatland conservation) and 'replication mechanisms' (adaptation, efficiency) and their relation to processes and organizations at different levels
- Further exploration on how development and climate approaches fit into new international frameworks and regime architectures
- Implementation of a series of 'action-oriented' demonstration projects.

References

Aerts, J.C.J.H., Berkhout, F.G.H., Biermann, F.H.B., Bouwer, L.M., Bruggink, J.J.C., Gerlagh, R., Gupta, J., Hisschemoller, M., Kuik, O.J., Tol, R.S.J., Verhagen, J., 2005, *Post-2012 Climate Policy: Assessing the Options*, Institute for Environmental Studies, Amsterdam.

African Development Bank (AfDB), ADB, DFID, DGIS, DGDev, BMZ, OECD, UNDP, UNEP, World Bank, 2003, *Poverty and Climate Change: Reducing the Vulnerability of the Poor through Adaptation*, Department for International Development (DFID), London.

Africa Research Bulletin, 2007, 'Biofuel production: Senegal', *Africa Research Bulletin: Economic, Financial and Technical Series* 43(11), 17203A–17203B.

Agrawala, S. (ed.), 2005, *Bridge over Troubled Water: Linking Climate Change and Development*, OECD, Paris.

Agrawala, S., van Aalst, M., 2008, 'Adapting development cooperation to adapt to climate change', *Climate Policy* 8(2), 183–193.

Barker, T., Bashmakov, I., Alharthi, A., Amann, M., Cifuentes, L., Drexhage, J., Duan, M., Edenhofer, O., Flannery, B., Grubb, M., Hoogwijk, M., Ibitoye, F.I., Jepma, C.J., Pizer, W.A., Yamaji, K., 2007, 'Mitigation from a cross sectoral perspective', in: B. Metz, O. Davidson, P. Bosch, R. Dave, L. Meyer (eds), *Climate Change 2007: Mitigation. Contribution* of *Working Group III to the Fourth Assessment Report of the Intergovernmental Panel on Climate Change*, Cambridge University Press, Cambridge, UK.

Baumert, K., Winkler, H., 2005, 'Sustainable development policies and measures and international climate change agreements', in: R. Bradley, K.A. Baumert (eds), *Growing in the Greenhouse: Protecting the Climate by Putting Development First*, World Resources Institute, Washington, DC.

Beg, N., Corfee Morlot, J., Davidson, O., Afrane-Okesse, Y., Tyani, L., Denton, F., Sokona, Y., Thomas, J.P., Lebre la Rovere, E., Parikh, J.K., Parikh, K., Rahman, A.A., 2002, 'Linkages between climate change and sustainable development', *Climate Policy* 2, 129–144.

Bradley, R., Baumert, K.A., (eds), 2005, *Growing in the Greenhouse: Protecting the Climate by Putting Development First*, World Resources Institute, Washington, DC.

Brouwer, L.M., Aerts, C.J.H., 2006, 'Financing climate change adaptation', *Disasters* 30, 49–63.

Burton, I., van Aalst, M.K., 2004, *Look Before You Leap: A Risk Management Approach for Climate Change Adaptation in World Bank Operations*, World Bank, Washington, DC.

CCAP (Center for Clean Air Policy), 2006, *Greenhouse Gas Mitigation in Brazil, China, and India: Scenarios and Opportunities through 2025*, CCAP, Washington, DC.

de Coninck, H.C., Fischer, C., Newell, R., Ueno, T., 2007, *International Technology-oriented Agreements to Address Climate Change*, Discussion Paper DP 06-50, Resources for the Future, Washington, DC.

Danida, 2005, *Danish Climate Change and Development Action Programme: A Toolkit for Climate Proofing Danish Development Cooperation*, Ministry of Foreign Affairs, Copenhagen.

Dave, R., Heller, T., Kok, M.T.J., Shukla, P.R., 2005, *Financing Integrated Development and Climate Strategies*, Report 500019002, Netherlands Environmental Assessment Agency, Bilthoven [available at www.mnp.nl/bibliotheek/rapporten/500019002.pdf].

Davidson, O., Halsnaes, K., Huq, S., Kok, M., Metz, B., Sokona, Y., Verhagen, J., 2003, 'The development and climate nexus: the case of Sub-Saharan Africa', *Climate Policy* 3(S1), S97–S113.

Drexhage, J., Murphy, D., Brown, O., Cosbey, A., Dickey, P., Parry, J.-E., Van Ham, J., Tarasofsky, R., Darkin, B., 2007, *Climate Change and Foreign Policy: An Exploration of Options for Greater Integration*, International Institute for Sustainable Development, Winnipeg, Canada.

Dubash, N.K., Bradley, R., 2005, 'Pathways to rural electrification in India: are national goals also an international opportunity?', in: R. Bradley, K.A. Baumert (eds), *Growing in the Greenhouse: Protecting the Climate by Putting Development First*, World Resources Institute, Washington, DC, 69–93.

Dufey, A., 2007, *International Trade in Biofuels: Good for Development? And Good for Environment?* International Institute for Environment and Development, London.

European Commission, 2007, *An Energy Policy for Europe*, SEC(2007)12, 10 January 2007, European Commission, Brussels.

FAO, 2006a, *Introducing the International Bioenergy Partnership*, FAO, Rome.

FAO, 2006b, *Global Bioenergy Partnership*, FAO, Rome [available at www.fao.org/newsroom/en/news/2006/1000405/index.html].

FAO, 2007, *Food Security and Nutrition Vulnerability Related Information and Mapping System (FIVIMS)*, FAO, Rome [available at www.fivims.net/static.jspx?lang=en&page=fivims].

Figueres, C., 2005, 'Sectoral CDM: opening the CDM to the yet unrealized goal of sustainable development', *International Journal of Sustainable Development Law and Policy* 2(1).

Gao, G., 2006, *Policies and Measures of China on Climate Change Mitigation under the Framework of Sustainable Development*, presentation at the 2nd Workshop on the Dialogue on Long-term Cooperative Action, UNFCCC, Bonn, Germany [available at http://unfccc.int/files/meetings/dialogue/application/vnd.ms-powerpoint/061115_cop12_dial_3.pps].

Greene, W., 2004, 'Aid fragmentation and proliferation: can donors improve the delivery of climate finance?', *IDS Bulletin* 35, 66–75.

Halsnæs, K., Shukla, P.R., Garg, A., 2008, 'Sustainable development and climate change: lessons from country studies', *Climate Policy* 8(2), 202–219.

Heller, T., 2006, 'Diversifying power generation in China', in: M. Colombier, J. Loup (eds), *Bringing Developing Countries into the Energy Equation*, IDDRI Analyses, No. 2, Paris.

Heller, T.C., Shukla, P.R., 2003, 'Development and climate: engaging developing countries', in: J.E. Aldy et al. (eds), *Beyond Kyoto: Advancing the International Effort Against Climate Change*, Pew Center on Global Climate Change, Arlington, VA.

Hellmuth, M.E., Moorhead, A., Thomson, M.C., Williams, J. (eds), 2007, *Climate Risk Management in Africa: Learning from Practice*, International Research Institute for Climate and Society (IRI), Pallisades, NY.

Hidalgo, D., 2003, 'The backbone of the mobility strategy of Bogota TransMilenio', *Public Transport International* 52, 28–30.

Hunt, S.C., Sawin, J.L., 2006, 'Cultivating renewable alternatives to oil', in: L. Starke (ed.), *The State of the World 2006*, Worldwatch Institute, Washington, DC.

IEA (International Energy Agency), 2006, 'The outlook for biofuels', in: *World Energy Outlook 2006*, IEA, Paris, 385–417.

IMF/World Bank, 2005, *2005 Review of the Poverty Reduction Strategy Approach: Balancing Accountabilities and Scaling Up Results – Synthesis*, IMF/World Bank, Washington, DC.

IPCC, 2000, *Special Report on Technological and Methodological Issues of Technology Transfer*, B. Metz, O. Davidson, J.W. Martens, S.N.M. van Rooijen., L. Van Wie McGrory (eds), Cambridge University Press, Cambridge, UK.

IPCC, 2005, *Carbon Dioxide Capture and Storage*, B. Metz, O. Davidson, H. de Coninck, M. Loos, L. Meyer (eds), Cambridge University Press, Cambridge, UK.

IPCC, 2007a, *Climate Change 2007: Impacts, Adaptation and Vulnerability. Contribution of Working Group II to the Fourth Assessment Report of the Intergovernmental Panel on Climate Change*, M.L. Parry, O.F. Canziani, J.P. Palutikov, C.E. Hanson, P.J. van der Linden (eds), Cambridge University Press, Cambridge, UK.

IPCC, 2007b, *Climate Change 2007: Mitigation. Contribution of Working Group III to the Fourth Assessment Report of the Intergovernmental Panel on Climate Change*, B. Metz, O. Davidson, P. Bosch, R. Dave, L. Meyer (eds), Cambridge University Press, Cambridge, UK.

Jerneck, A., Olsson, L., 2008, 'Adaptation and the poor: development, resilience and transition', *Climate Policy* 8(2), 170–182.

Jiang, K., Hu, X., Liu, Q., 2006, 'China's energy sector', in: K. Halsnaes, A. Garg (eds), *Sustainable Development, Energy and Climate: Exploring Synergies and Trade-offs*, UNEP Risoe Centre, Roskilde, Denmark.

KfW Development Bank, 2005, *Financing Renewable Energy: Instruments, Strategies, Practice Approaches*, KfW Development Bank, Frankfurt am Main, Germany.

Klein, R.J.T., Eriksen, S.E.H., Naess, L.O., Hammill, A., Tanner, T.M., Robledo, C., O'Brien, K.L., 2007, *Portfolio Screening to Support the Mainstreaming of Adaptation to Climate Change into Development Assistance*, Tyndall Centre Working Paper 102.

Kok, M.T.J., de Coninck, H.C., 2007, 'Widening the scope of policies to address climate change: directions for mainstreaming', *Environmental Science and Policy* 10, 587–599.

Lebre la Rovere, E., Santos Pereira, A., Felipe Simoes, A., 2006, 'Brazil country studies', in: K. Halsnaes, A. Garg (eds), *Sustainable Development, Energy and Climate: Exploring Synergies and Trade-offs*, UNEP Risoe Centre, Roskilde, Denmark.

Miller, A.S., 2008, 'Financing the integration of climate change mitigation into development', *Climate Policy* 8(2), 152–169.

Mitchell, T., Tanner, T., Wilkinson, E., 2006, *Overcoming the Barriers: Mainstreaming Climate Change Adaptation in Developing Countries*, Tearfund Climate Change Briefing Paper 1, Tearfund, Teddington, UK.

Moreira, J.R., Horta Nogueira, L.A., Parente, V., 2005, 'Biofuels for transport, development and climate change: lessons from Brazil', in: R. Bradley, K.A. Baumert (eds), *Growing in the Greenhouse: Protecting the Climate by Putting Development First*, World Resources Institute, Washington, DC.

Murphy, M. (ed.), 2006, *Africa- Up in Smoke: 2*, Second Report on Africa and Global Warming from the Working Group on Climate Change and Development, New Economics Foundation, London.

Ng, W., Schipper, L., 2005, 'China motorization trends: policy options in a world of transport challenges', in: R. Bradley, K.A. Baumert (eds), *Growing in the Greenhouse: Protecting the Climate by Putting Development First*, World Resources Institute, Washington, DC, 48–67.

O'Brien, G., O'Keefe, P., Meena, H., Rose, J., Wilson, L., 2008, 'Climate adaptation from a poverty perspective', *Climate Policy* 8(2), 194–201.

Red Cross, 2003, *Preparedness for Climate Change: A Study to Assess the Future Impact of Climatic Changes upon the Frequency and Severity of Disasters and the Implications for Humanitarian Response and Preparedness*, prepared by the International Federation of Red Cross and Red Crescent Societies in cooperation with the Netherlands Red Cross [available at www.icrc.org/Web/eng/siteeng0.nsf/htmlall/5XRFZB/$File/ClimateChange_Report_FINAL_ENG.pdf].

Ribeiro, S.K., Abreu, A.A. de, 2008, 'Brazilian transport initiatives with GHG reductions as a co-benefit', *Climate Policy* 8(2), 220–240.

Robinson, J., Bradley, M., Busby, P., Connor, D., Murray, A., Sampson, B., Soper, W., 2006, 'Climate change and sustainable development: realizing the opportunity', *Ambio* 35, 2–8.

Rockström, J., Nilsson Axberg, G., Falkenmark, M., Lannerstad, M., Rosemarin, A., Caldwell, I., Arvidson, A., Nordström, M., 2005, *Sustainable Pathways to Attain the Millennium Development Goals: Assessing the Key Role of Water, Energy and Sanitation*, Stockholm Environment Institute, Stockholm.

Sathaye, J., Najam, A., Cocklin, C., Heller, T., Lecocq, F., Llanes Regueiro, J., Pan, J., Petschel-Held, G., Raymer, S., Robinson, J., Schaeffer, R., Sokona, Y., Swart, R., Winkler, H., 2007, 'Sustainable development and mitigation', in: B. Metz, O. Davidson, P. Bosch, R. Dave, L. Meyer, (eds), *Climate Change 2007: Mitigation. Contribution of Working Group III to the Fourth Assessment Report of the Intergovernmental Panel on Climate Change*, Cambridge University Press, Cambridge, UK.

Schipper, L., Pelling, M., 2006, 'Disaster risk, climate change and international development: scope for, and challenges to, integration', *Disasters* 30, 19–38.

Shukla, P.R., 2006, 'Integrating sustainable development and climate policies: case studies of the energy sector in India', in: K. Halsnaes, A. Garg (eds), *Sustainable Development, Energy and Climate: Exploring Synergies and Trade-offs*, UNEP Risoe Centre, Roskilde, Denmark.

Shukla, P.R., 2007, *Biomass Energy Strategies for Aligning Development and Climate Goals in India*, MNP Report No. 500101002, Netherlands Environmental Assessment Agency, Bilthoven, The Netherlands [available at www.mnp.nl/ en/publications/2007/BiomassenergystrategiesforaligningdevelopmentandclimategoalsinIndia.html].

Sokona, Y., Thomas, J.-P., Touré, O., 2003, *Country Study: Senegal*, Environnement et Développement du Tiers Monde (ENDA-TM), Dakar, Senegal [available at www.developmentfirst.org/publications.htm].

Sow, B., Saint Sernin, E., 2005, *Rural Development: The Roles of Food, Water and Biomass – Opportunities and Challenges*, Workshop Report, ENDA TM, Dakar, Senegal [available at www.developmentfirst.org/publications.htm].

Sperling, F., Szekely, F., 2005, *Disaster Risk Management in a Changing Climate*, Discussion Paper prepared for the World Conference on Disaster Reduction on behalf of the Vulnerability and Adaptation Resource Group (VARG), Washington, DC.

Srinivasan, A. (ed.), 2006, *Asian Aspirations for Climate Change beyond 2012*, Institute for Global Environmental Studies, Hayama, Japan.

Sterk, W., Wittneben, B., 2006, 'Enhancing the clean development mechanism through sectoral approaches: definitions, applications and ways forward', *International Environmental Agreements* 6, 271–287.

Sussman, H., Helme, N., 2004, *Harnessing Financial Flows from Export Crediting Agencies for Climate Protection*, Center for Clean Air Policy, Washington, DC.

Thomalla, F., Downing, T., Spanger-Siegfried, E., Han, G., Rockström, J., 2006, 'Reducing hazard vulnerability: towards a common approach between disaster risk reduction and climate adaptation', *Disasters* 30, 39–48.

Tirpak, D., Adams, H., 2008, 'Bilateral and multilateral financial assistance for the energy sector of developing countries', *Climate Policy* 8(2), 135–151.

Tirpak, D., Gupta, S., Burger, N., Gupta, J., Höhne, N., Boncheva, A.I., Kanoan, G.H., Kolstad, C., Kruger, J., Michaelowa, A., Murase, S., Pershing, J., Saijo, T., Sari, A., 2007, 'Policies, instruments and co-operative arrangements', in: B. Metz, O. Davidson, P. Bosch, R. Dave, L. Meyer, (eds), *Climate Change 2007: Mitigation. Contribution of Working Group III to the Fourth Assessment Report of the Intergovernmental Panel on Climate Change*, Cambridge University Press, Cambridge, UK.

UNDP, 2000, *Bioenergy Primer: Modernized Biomass Energy for Sustainable Development*, UNDP, New York [available at www.undp.org/energy/publications/2000/2000b.htm].

UNDP, 2004, *Meeting the Climate Change Challenge: Sustaining Livelihoods*, UNDP, New York [available at www.undp.org/ gef/05/documents/publications/climate_change_brochure2004.pdf].

UNDP, 2005a, *Sustaining the Environment to Fight Poverty and Achieve the MDGs: The Economic Case and Priorities for Action*, UNDP, New York [available at www.undp.org/pei/pdfs/Synthesis_Paper_Final.pdf].

UNDP, 2005b, *MDG Carbon Facility: Mobilizing Carbon Finance for the Millennium Development Goals*, UNDP, New York [available at www.undp.org/mdgcarbonfacility/docs/BookletMDGCarbonFacility.pdf].

UNDP, 2007, *Human Development Report*, UNDP, New York.

UNFCCC, 2007a, *Investment and Financial Flows to Address Climate Change*, UNFCCC, Bonn, Germany [available at http://unfccc.int/files/cooperation_and_support/financial_mechanism/application/pdf/background_paper.pdf].

UNFCCC, 2007b, *Bali Action Plan*, Bonn, Germany [available at http://unfccc.int/files/meetings/cop_13/application/ pdf/cp_bali_action.pdf].

UNISDR, 2006, *Words Into Action: Implementing the Hyogo Framework for Action*, UNISDR, Geneva.

United Nations Security Council, 2007, *5663rd Meeting, Tuesday 17 April 2007*, United Nations, New York.

Victor, D., Heller, T., 2007, *The Political Economy of Power Sector Reform*, Cambridge University Press, Cambridge, UK.

Wang, Z.Y., Gao, H., Zhou, D., 2006, 'China's achievements in expanding electricity access for the poor', *Energy for Sustainable Development* 10, 5–16.

WEC (World Energy Council), 2007, *How to make the Grand Inga Hydrower Project Happen for Africa?*, WEC, London.

Winkler, H. (ed.), 2006, *Energy Policies for Sustainable Development in South Africa*, Energy Research Centre, Capetown, South Africa.

Winkler, H., Howells, M., Baumert, K., 2007, 'Sustainable development policies and measures: institutional issues and electrical efficiency in South Africa', *Climate Policy* 7(3), 212–229.

Winkler, H., Höhne, N., den Elzen, M., 2008, 'Methods for quantifying the benefits of sustainable development policies and measures (SD-PAMs)', *Climate Policy* 8(2), 119–134.

World Bank, 2006a, *Clean Energy and Development: Towards an Investment Framework – A Progress Report*, Report DC 2006-0012, World Bank, Washington, DC.

World Bank, 2006b, *Managing Climate Risk: Integrating Adaptation into World Bank Group Operations*, World Bank, Washington, DC.

World Bank, 2006c, *Proceedings of the Energy Efficiency Investment Forum: Scaling Up Financing in the Developing World*, World Bank, Washington, DC.

WRI (World Resources Institute), 2005, *Mainstreaming Climate Change Considerations at the Multi-lateral Development Banks*, World Bank, Washington, DC.

WRI/EMBARQ, 2006, *Sustainable Mobility*, Vol. 1, World Resources Institute, Washington, DC.

Yohe, G.W., Lasco, R.D., Ahmad, Q.K., Arnell, N., Cohen, S.J., Hope, C., Janetos, A.C., Perez, R.T., 2007, 'Perspectives on climate change and sustainability', in: M.L. Parry, O.F. Canziani, J.P. Palutikof, C.E. Hanson, P.J. van der Linden (eds), *Climate Change 2007: Impacts, Adaptation and Vulnerability. Contribution of Working Group II to the Fourth Assessment Report of the Intergovernmental Panel on Climate Change*, Cambridge University Press, Cambridge, UK.

climate policy

■ research article

Methods for quantifying the benefits of sustainable development policies and measures (SD-PAMs)

HARALD WINKLER[1]*, NIKLAS HÖHNE[2], MICHEL DEN ELZEN[3]

[1] Energy Research Centre, University of Cape Town, South Africa
[2] ECOFYS Energy and Environment Cologne, Eupener Strasse 59, 50933 Cologne, Germany
[3] MNP Netherlands Environmental Assessment Agency, PO Box 303 3720 AH Bilthoven, The Netherlands

How can the concept of sustainable development policies and measures (SD-PAMs) be operationalized in a multilateral climate regime? The strategic approach is to focus on policies and measures that are firmly within the national sustainable development priorities of developing countries but which, through the inclusion in an international climate framework, recognize, promote and support means of meeting these policy priorities on a lower-carbon trajectory. The concept of SD-PAMs is further elaborated in two ways: (1) possible methods for quantifying SD-PAMs and (2) policy design. An important step in operationalizing the concept of SD-PAMs is the examination of available methods to quantify their benefits. Four ways to quantify the effect of SD-PAMs on development and emissions are identified: (1) case studies, (2) national energy modelling, (3) analysis of sectoral data and (4) inclusion of policies in global emission allocation models. Each of the methodological approaches has its strengths and weaknesses, but these approaches are demonstrated as being capable of quantifying the effect of SD-PAMs on development and emissions. Formalizing the commitment of SD-PAMs could be aided by more fully elaborating these methodologies. Formal recognition could be given either by listing countries in an Annex to the Convention or by including the pledged policies in a dedicated register. Regular reporting on the sustainable development and climate benefits of SD-PAMs could take place through national communications or a separate reporting mechanism. Incentives for SD-PAMs could come from both climate and non-climate funding. Development funding through other agencies could also be mobilized. International finance will be critical, as will the mobilization of domestic investment.

Keywords: co-benefits of mitigation; developing countries; methodologies; policies and measures; post-2012 architecture; sustainable development

Comment le concept des politiques et mesures de développement durable (SD-PAMs) peut-il être opérationnalisé dans un régime climatique multilatéral? L'approche stratégique est de se concentrer sur les politiques et mesures étant fermement ancrées dans les priorités nationales de développement durable des pays en développement, mais surtout dans leur inclusion dans un cadre climatique international qui reconnaît, encourage et soutient les efforts à dessein de satisfaire ces priorités politiques selon une trajectoire sobre en carbone. Le concept des SD-PAMs est davantage élaboré de deux manières: méthodes possible de quantification des SD-PAMs et forme des politiques. Une étape importante d'opérationnalisation du concept des SD-PAMs est l'examen des méthodes disponibles au calcul de leurs bénéfices. Quatre moyens ont été identifiés pour quantifier l'effet des SD-PAMs sur le développement et les émissions: études de cas, modélisation énergétique nationale, analyse de données sectorielles et inclusion des politiques dans les modèles d'allocation d'émissions à l'échelle mondiale. Bien que chacune des approches méthodologiques ait ses forces et faiblesses, la capacité de ces approches à quantifier l'effet des SD-PAMs sur le développement et les émissions est démontré. Une mise au point plus complète de ces méthodologies aiderait à formaliser l'engagement aux SD-PAMs. Une reconnaissance formelle pourrait être attribuée ou bien en inscrivant les pays dans une annexe à la Convention, ou bien en incluant les engagements aux politiques dans un registre dédié. Un rapport régulier des bénéfices des SD-PAMs pour le développement durable et le climat pourrait s'effectuer par le biais des communications nationales ou bien par un mécanisme de rapport séparé. L'appui aux SD-PAMs pourrait

■ *Corresponding author. E-mail: Harald.Winkler@uct.ac.za

CLIMATE POLICY 8 (2008) 119–134
doi:10.3763/cpol.2007.0433 © 2008 Earthscan ISSN: 1469-3062 (print), 1752-7457 (online) www.climatepolicy.com

provenir de financement climatique ou autre. Un financement pour le développement provenant d'autres agences pourrait aussi être mobilisé. La finance internationale sera essentielle, comme le sera la mobilisation de l'investissement domestique.

Mots clés: architecture de l'Après 2012; co-bénéfices de l'atténuation; développement durable; méthodologies; pays en développement; politiques et mesures

1. Introduction

Negotiations under the United Nations Framework Convention on Climate Change (UNFCCC) and its Kyoto Protocol seek to build an effective and equitable multilateral response to climate change. Several elements will be essential to ensure a successful outcome (IISD, 2005a), critically balancing the need for climate protection and sustainable development.

To achieve the objective of the Convention, deeper emission reductions will be required in all developed countries, but the growth of emissions in developing countries also needs to slow rapidly. Meaningful participation by developing countries may take several forms. This article explores an approach for developing countries that starts from sustainable development – which is part of the UNFCCC objective – rather than climate targets.

Sustainable development policies and measures (SD-PAMs) are an approach to stimulating action on climate change mitigation in developing countries. Instead of starting from explicit climate targets, the approach deliberately sets out to start from development objectives. This strategic approach taps into the primary motivation for developing countries, namely development (Winkler et al., 2002b).

Previous work has focused on SD-PAMs as a strategic approach (Winkler et al., 2002b) and case studies to illustrate its viability (Bradley et al., 2005; Winkler et al., 2007). This article briefly revisits the concept of SD-PAMs, its basis in the Convention (Section 2), and analyses the type of commitment (Section 3). Section 4 outlines four methods that are available to specify the implications of SD-PAMs, ranging from bottom-up case studies, through national modelling, to international models. Broader questions of policy design are addressed in Section 5, which asks how SD-PAMs could be formalized within the UNFCCC system.

2. Starting from development: the basis of SD-PAMs

The challenge of integrating greenhouse gas (GHG) considerations into national development programmes is recognized in the very objective of the Convention, namely the:

> stabilization of greenhouse gas concentrations in the atmosphere at a level that would prevent dangerous anthropogenic interference with the climate system. Such a level should be achieved within a time frame sufficient to allow ecosystems to adapt naturally to climate change, to ensure that food production is not threatened, and to enable economic development to proceed in a sustainable manner (UNFCCC, 1992, Art. 2).

The oft-forgotten second sentence of this objective codifies the environmental, social and economic dimensions of sustainable development. Development is a key priority for decision makers in developing countries; climate policy tends to have lower priority. The contribution that alternative development paths can make to mitigation is increasingly recognized (Sathaye et al., 2007).

Sustainable development is critical in delivering improved basic services such as energy, housing, transport, health, food security, ecoservices and others. Socio-economic development and poverty eradication are the first and overriding priorities of developing country Parties. Making development more sustainable can significantly reduce greenhouse gas emissions, compared with what they would otherwise have been.

One of the underlying principles of the Convention is that Parties have a right to, and should, promote sustainable development (Art. 3.4). The Delhi Ministerial Declaration on Climate Change and Sustainable Development (Decision 1/CP.8) outlined the importance of linking climate change and sustainable development in both directions – contributing to mitigation through action in key development sectors such as energy, transport, industry, health, agriculture, biodiversity, forestry and waste management, but also taking climate change considerations into account in national sustainable development strategies.

Defining more sustainable pathways to meet given development objectives has significant climate co-benefits. These co-benefits have been widely reported in the literature (IPCC, 2001; Winkler et al., 2002a, 2006; Baumert and Winkler, 2005; Bradley et al., 2005; IISD, 2005b; Munasinghe and Swart, 2005; Szklo et al., 2005; Robinson et al., 2006; Sathaye et al., 2007); the question is how to capture these benefits in the multilateral climate regime. A new strategic approach for developing countries is needed, and SD-PAMs offer one possible approach.

The co-benefits of making development more sustainable are well-recognized in the IPCC's Fourth Assessment Report (Sathaye et al., 2007) and its Special Report on Emission Scenarios (SRES). Figure 1 shows four of the families of scenarios from the SRES. Each of the striped scenario families represents a different storyline of how global emissions might evolve in future. The SRES scenarios deliberately

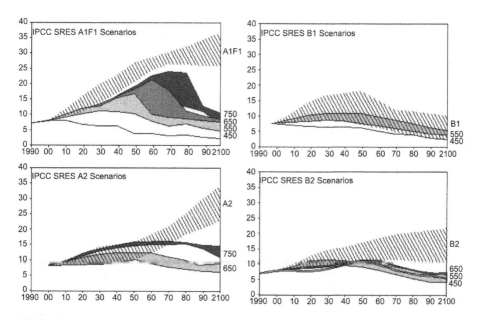

FIGURE 1 Comparison of SRES reference emissions scenarios (without climate policy) and 'post-SRES' climate change mitigation scenarios.

Source: Morita and Robinson (2001, p. 151, Fig. 2.14).

do not consider policies explicitly aimed at combating climate change. The striped reference scenarios shown in Figure 1 do not include climate policy and are shown together with mitigation scenarios resulting in stabilization of atmospheric concentrations of CO_2 ranging from 450 to 750 ppmv.

Choosing a sustainable development path means that the baseline – or reference – GHG emissions are lower than in other possible futures. Put differently, a more sustainable development path has lower emissions, *even without* any explicit climate policy. The IPCC's Third Assessment Report found this choice of future 'world' more important than the drivers determining GHG emissions (Morita and Robinson, 2001, p. 142). Future worlds are not chosen as a whole, but through multiple decisions affecting drivers such as GDP, population, technology, equity and others.

The corollary is also true – development objectives can be met in more or less emission-intensive ways. Beginning with one or more future development ambitions, it would be possible to describe paths towards those goals (Metz et al., 2002; Winkler et al., 2002a; Sathaye et al., 2007). The selected scenarios show clearly that to reach the same atmospheric concentrations, significantly less effort is required if reference emissions are low (in the B family) than if the future world had higher emissions (in the A scenarios). The difference in emissions between the reference case in A1FI and 550 ppmv is much larger than the corresponding difference between B1 reference emissions and a path stabilizing at the same level.

The use of USD-PAMs as an approach builds on existing commitments by developing countries. Under Article 4.1 of the Convention, all countries made the commitment to 'take climate change considerations into account, to the extent feasible, in their relevant social, economic and environmental policies and actions' (Art. 4.1f). Developing countries' commitments under the Kyoto Protocol specify that mitigation programmes 'would, *inter alia*, concern the energy, transport and industry sectors as well as agriculture, forestry and waste management' (Art. 10b(i)).

Clearly, the co-benefits of pursuing sustainable development can make a meaningful contribution to mitigating climate change. The challenge considered in this article is to turn the conceptual link between sustainable development and climate change into a workable approach.

3. What are SD-PAMs?

The SD-PAMs commitment would be to *implement* sustainable development policies. The voluntary pledge would be to implement and accelerate national sustainable development plans.

The commitment is based on choosing a development path that results in lowered emissions, rather than an explicit climate target, i.e. targets to reduce or limit GHG emissions. The approach starts by considering a country's own long-term development objectives. Next, policies and measures are identified that would make the development path more sustainable. These SD-PAMs aim to encompass large-scale policies and measures – not only projects, as in the Clean Development Mechanism (CDM). Each country would define what it means by making development more sustainable, but when registering SD-PAMs the international community would have to accept that the policy constitutes sustainable development. The housing policy discussed below is an example of a large-scale policy, another would be cross-cutting measures such as air quality standards – both are not neatly packaged as projects in the current CDM architecture. Both climate and non-climate funding can be mobilized to implement SD-PAMs (see Section 5). Progress in achieving both the local sustainable development benefits and climate co-benefits is monitored through national institutions, but is also reviewed internationally. Acknowledgment for the contribution of SD-PAMs could be achieved by recording them in a registry maintained by the UNFCCC Secretariat. How the approach could be formalized is considered further in Section 5.

A wide variety of approaches to future climate action have been identified (see reviews in, e.g., Bodansky et al., 2004; den Elzen and Berk, 2004; Höhne and Lahme, 2005; Gupta et al., 2007).

Some approaches have a more bottom-up approach like SD-PAMs, for example sectoral CDM or Triptych approaches. Sectoral CDM proposes extending the mechanism beyond projects to sectors in various ways (Sterk and Wittneben, 2006), while the Triptych approach (Phylipsen et al., 1998) develops mitigation options focused on three broad sectors – the power, energy-intensive industry and domestic sectors. Like any other approach, using SD-PAMs has its strengths and weaknesses. The greatest strength of the approach is its alignment with the national priority of most developing countries, namely development. It makes the approach attractive to developing countries, and also gives greater certainty about the actions taken. This strength also leads to its main weakness, that the environmental effectiveness of the approach is not clear. The climate implications of SD-PAMs depend on the number and scale of policies actually implemented. Avoided emissions might be offset by other policies, not registered as SD-PAMs. Similarly, another strength is that the development-focused approach allows for non-climate, development-related funding sources. At the same time, this distances SD-PAMs from the efficiency of market-based instruments and the carbon markets, seen by many as key sources of future climate funding.

Some analyses on future climate action have suggested architectural elements or options for approaches to building on the Kyoto Protocol (Baumert et al., 2002, ch. 1; Bodansky et al., 2004; Höhne, 2005). Table 1 develops its own set of elements and summarizes the SD-PAMs approach to those elements.

TABLE 1 Summary of SD-PAMs approach to key architectural elements and options. Adapted from den Elzen and Berk (2004)

Element of climate architecture or option	SD-PAMs
Type of commitment	Commitment to implement sustainable development policies
Objectives and target-setting	Objectives framed in terms of development, rather than climate; targets set in SD units, GHG emission reductions reported as co-benefits
Legally binding nature of commitments	Voluntary agreement in multilateral regime
Top-down allocation or bottom-up pledge	Pledge-and-review
Accountability procedures	Reporting, monitoring and review, no compliance system
Environmental effectiveness	Depends on SD-PAMs pledged and implemented
Sensitivity to national circumstances	By design based on national policies and measures
Timing and triggers	Available to all developing countries without an entire new climate regime
Finance	Can mobilize climate and development funding; domestic and international
Market-based mechanisms	Not linked to carbon markets, avoiding issues of additionality and baselines
Technology commitments	Sustainable development requires technology innovation and diffusion
Forum	UNFCCC, but synergies with forums and agencies focused on sustainable development
Differentiation	Developing countries only
Complementarity with other approaches	Can be combined with other approaches in multi-stage schemes (and could become mandatory at agreed stages); important first step in creating a climate of trust

Table 1 provides a shorthand summary of the SD-PAMs approach. Critical to the definition of the approach, however, is the quantification of both sustainable development and climate benefits.

Hence, it will be important to establish methodologies to quantify the benefits of SD-PAMs, both for local sustainable development and climate co-benefits. The 'commitment' would be measured not only in GHG emissions units but primarily in sustainable development units ('SD units') – for instance, building 100,000 energy-efficient homes – rather than a specified reduction in tonnes of CO_2 emissions. Section 4 examines a range of different methodologies.

4. Methodologies for quantifying SD-PAMs

Methodologies are needed to quantify, firstly, the local sustainable development benefits and, secondly, the GHG co-benefits of SD-PAMs. Four methodologies are explored in this article:

1. Case studies of sustainable development policies
2. National energy modelling of policies and measures
3. Analysis by sectoral data
4. Global emission allocation models to investigate the implications of SD-PAMs within a multilateral agreement.

The first two of these methods focus on the national or subnational level in quantifying results. Case studies, by their nature, focus on a specific context, while energy modelling quantifies results (for energy and often also emissions) as a partial analysis of a national economy. Method 4 has a more global focus, being designed for the purpose of comparing international emission allocation schemes. Method 3 bridges the national/global divide by collecting fairly detailed data from countries (for selected sectors), but allowing international projections.

In the literature on SD-PAMs to date, the methodological approaches have tended to be bottom-up (Dubash and Bradley, 2005; Moreira et al., 2005; Szklo et al., 2005; Wei-Shiuen and Schipper, 2005; Winkler, 2006b). The approach itself starts from national development goals and, correspondingly, analysis has looked at detailed case studies and national energy models to illustrate the impacts of SD-PAMs.

Top-down methodologies could be explored, in particular, to answer questions about the environmental effectiveness – relating to climate change mitigation – of SD-PAMs. The quantification of GHG emissions avoided is not the primary driver of the strategic approach, but methodological tools to address this concern could include analysis of efficiency improvements and analysis of global emission allocation models.

A combination of bottom-up and top-down methods seems most likely to yield useful information for decision makers. Which method is most applicable would depend on the purpose or result that is of interest – to quantify specific policies with sensitivity to national circumstances or to compare implications in the multilateral context. Each of the four methods is illustrated in the following sections.

4.1. Method 1: Case studies
The first method – the use of case studies – has been reported the most extensively in the literature on SD-PAMs to date. Case studies can be used to quantify specific policies through a bottom-up approach. Case studies lend themselves to SD-PAMs, since the approach starts from specific national circumstances and can report on their own SD units. Some examples of existing case studies are summarized below.

Rural electrification in India seeks to empower the 56% of households that are still without an electricity supply. The development challenge is that 500–600 million people remain without access to electricity. Three paths were examined in one study (Dubash and Bradley, 2005):

1. A *grid first* approach, which has little chance of meeting electrification targets
2. A strategic approach of *diesel first*, which raises concerns about the cost of oil imports, security of supply and local air pollution
3. *Renewables first*, which provides benefits, contributing to rural electrification, but at significant incremental capital costs (Dubash and Bradley, 2005).

Given the concerns raised about the grid and diesel technologies, there are important reasons for India to prefer renewable energy on domestic policy grounds. Renewables already play an important role in rural electrification (measured in percentage of the population with access) and continue to contribute without adding to dependence on imports. The diesel scenario, by contrast, adds some $21 billion per year to India's import bill (as a share of total, this could be the SD units reported). Favouring renewable energy sources brings significant CO_2 emission savings: between 14 and 100 million tonnes of CO_2 compared with using the grid (Dubash and Bradley, 2005).

Other case studies include energy-efficient, low-cost housing in South Africa as one example of a SD-PAM, with the potential to remove the housing backlog while reducing emissions compared with a coal-fired grid (Winkler et al., 2002c; Spalding-Fecher et al., 2003). Avoided emissions come together with substantial local sustainable development benefits – household energy savings (Rand/ household/month), reduced indoor air pollution (another SD unit), improved health, and increased levels of comfort. Experience at the project level has quantified some of these benefits – not only a level of thermal comfort at 21°C (as the SD unit was defined in this case), but less active space heating that reduces energy bills by some R625 (ca. $100) per household per year (SSN, 2004).

If implemented at larger scale – e.g. applied through policy to all housing, not just a single project – avoided emissions might range between 0.05 and 0.6 Mt CO_2-eq if implemented as policy (Winkler et al., 2005). The climate co-benefits are relatively small, since poor households use less energy than richer ones; the savings, at most, account for a reduction of 7% of residential CO_2 emissions or 0.2% of national emissions (Winkler et al., 2002b).

Case studies as a method illustrate both the local sustainable development benefits and the climate co-benefits of nationally specific actions. Further examples of the use of case studies in China's energy sector (Kejun et al., 2006), include China's efforts to reduce air pollution in the process of motorization (Wei-Shiuen and Schipper, 2005). In the case of Brazil (Moreira et al., 2005; La Rovere et al., 2006), the ethanol programme, which produces approximately one-third of Brazil's transport fuel, has saved $100 billion in foreign currency expenditure, has created over 1 million rural jobs, and has climate co-benefits estimated at 574 million tCO_2 over the lifetime of the programme. These measures suggest that these may be meaningful SD units in Brazil. Without the biofuels programme, Brazil's cumulative emissions of CO_2 from 1975 to the present would have been 10% higher (Moreira et al., 2005). A report combining case studies of India, China and Brazil found the potential for reductions below business-as-usual in 2020 totalling more than 625 Mt CO_2 per year – the equivalent of avoiding the construction of more than 150 coal-fired power plants (CCAP, 2006). Case studies on climate and development are not limited to large developing countries but have also considered electrification in rural Bangladesh (Rahman et al., 2006) and the impact of power sector reform in Senegal (Thiam, 2006).

Case studies, by their nature, are rooted in national circumstances. They can be used in any country. However, results from case studies are not always easily comparable, since the underlying assumptions and the results reported may not be consistent across studies. Guidelines might be needed for basic parameters that should be reported in SD-PAMs case studies.

4.2. Method 2: National energy modelling

The second methodology considered is to use national energy models to investigate the local sustainable development and climate implications of energy policies. In South Africa, emissions from energy supply and use account for almost 80% of total GHG emissions (van der Merwe and Scholes, 1998; RSA, 2004).

Studies on energy policies for sustainable development in South Africa have used this tool (Winkler, 2006a). The study considered a range of potential future energy policies, using the least-cost optimizing Markal energy modelling framework. On the demand side, the policy options modelled covered the industry, commerce, residential and transport sectors; on the supply side, they covered electricity and liquid fuels. The types of policy instruments investigated included both economic and regulatory instruments. Assessments against indicators of sustainable development were conducted to provide a sound means for policy makers to identify synergies and trade-offs between options, and to evaluate their economic, social and environmental dimensions.

In brief, the study showed that the combined effect of these energy policies could *reduce* total energy system costs over the period by about R16 billion (approx. US$2.3 billion) relative to base case. The cost savings are small in percentage terms (0.27%), since the costs on the whole system over the full 25-year period (2000–2025) are very large. The increased costs of a lower-carbon electricity supply were offset by the savings made through energy efficiency. At the same time, local air pollutants such as NMVOC (non-methane volatile organic compounds), NO_x, SO_2 and carbon monoxide were reduced. The climate co-benefits of the combined policies were avoided CO_2 emissions of 142 Mt CO_2 for 2025, or 24% lower than in the base case (Winkler, 2006a).

Over the 25-year study period, energy efficiency makes the greatest impact when seen against indicators of sustainable development. Industrial efficiency, in particular, shows significant savings in energy and costs, with reductions in air pollution. Energy efficiency in the commercial sector shows a similar pattern, although at a slightly smaller scale. Residential energy efficiency is particularly important for social sustainability. Even small energy savings can be important for poorer households. In the short term – the decade 2006–2015 – it was concluded that energy efficiency will be critical to making South Africa's energy development more sustainable (Winkler, 2006a).

In the longer term – the next several decades – transitions which include the supply side will become increasingly important. To achieve greater diversity, there will need to be a combination of policies, since single policies on their own will not change the share of coal in total primary energy supply (TPES) by very much. The various alternative electricity supply options show potential for significant emission reductions and improvements in local air quality. However, they will require a policy of careful trade-offs in relation to energy system costs, energy security and diversity of supply.

As a method, national energy modelling allows a range of policies and measures in the energy sector to be analysed together. With an appropriate model choice, the dynamics of the energy system are taken into account. For example, the reduced energy demand due to energy efficiency measures is passed through to electricity supply, so that emission reductions from lower-carbon power stations are not overestimated. National energy models are often used as a basis for energy planning as well, providing a means to mainstream climate mitigation into energy policy.

Höhne and Moltmann (2008) have compared the results of national energy modelling studies in several developing countries (Brazil, China, India, Mexico, South Africa and South Korea) and found, as a general result, that the policies considered in these analyses can reduce emissions 10–20% below reference emission in 2020 but, as such, would only slow the growth and not reverse the trend.

Clearly, the energy modelling method is appropriate only for the energy sector. It would be most useful in those developing countries whose GHG emissions derive mainly from the energy sector. A methodological approach for SD-PAMs in the LULUCF (land use, land-use change and forestry) sector would also be required for a more comprehensive approach. Methods for estimating emissions from LULUCF are complex, and the challenge of developing tools useful across countries is non-trivial.

4.3. Method 3: Analysis of sectoral data

The analysis of sectoral data can be used to compare GHG intensities. While the analysis in studies to date has focused on the energy sector, the approach differs from modelling in that the focus is on a comparison across countries. Höhne et al. (2006a) considered the electricity production, iron and steel, cement, pulp and paper, refineries, and transport sectors in this way.

With this method, the emission reduction potential of a country can be assessed on an aggregated scale in order to understand the order of magnitude of reductions that could be achieved with policies and measures, be they motivated by sustainable development or by climate change goals. Detailed data collected from the available literature includes activity data (in tonnes of product/ output by economic sector), value added (in monetary terms), and energy use by fuel type. This data allows the calculation of both energy and GHG intensities. On the latter, the focus is mainly on CO_2 from the energy sector. It also allows a comparison of the GHG intensities between countries. Future scenarios can be generated, assuming production growth and improvements in efficiency.

The original purpose of this work was to analyse the implications of a possible sectoral approach as a post-2012 climate mitigation regime, but the insights can also be used to quantify the possible effect of SD-PAMs. The study found that large differences in energy efficiency and GHG indices can be observed between countries. There is also substantial variation in these indices between different sectors in the same country. By bringing together data in sectors that contribute to GHG emissions, the approach forms the basis for further analysis of particular policies that would make development more sustainable and would reduce emissions.

The effect of a set of policies was considered by Höhne et al. (2006a) in future scenarios, where the GHG indices of all countries converge to best-available-technology (BAT) by 2020 or 2030. The study found that large emission reduction potentials could be realized if countries were to use BAT. Together with ambitious Annex I reductions, global emissions could then stabilize by 2020 (Höhne et al., 2006a).

This is relevant in the context of SD-PAMs, as moving to the best-practice technology would be in the interest of developing countries improving their energy efficiency and reducing their dependency on fossil fuels.

Sectoral data analysis as a method has the advantage of comparability across countries, but compromises on country-specific details. Scenarios for the future can be developed although, by definition, for sectors rather than the whole economy.

4.4. Method 4: Global emission allocation models

The fourth method is analysis of SD-PAMs in global emission allocation models. Models such as the Framework to Assess International Regimes (FAIR) model (den Elzen and Lucas, 2005) and Evolution of Commitments (EVOC) model (Höhne et al., 2006b) are designed to allocate a given global greenhouse gas emissions budget across countries under different multilateral agreements. They could be used as a top-down approach to analysing the climate implications of SD-PAMs, even though the latter are, in principle, bottom-up approaches. The key motivation for doing so would be to illustrate the environmental effectiveness in terms of climate change mitigation of SD-PAMs. The method allows comparison of levels of efforts of countries through SD-PAMs.

These analyses place the SD-PAMs approach in the context of multi-stage approaches. Such approaches are based on participation and differentiation rules that come into play when a country moves from one stage to another (see, for example, Gupta, 1998; Berk and den Elzen, 2001; den Elzen, 2002; Criqui et al., 2003; Höhne et al., 2003; Ott et al., 2004). In Höhne et al. (2003), the progression is as follows. Stage 1 – no commitments: countries with a low level of development, i.e. the least developed countries, participate in this stage; Stage 2 – enhanced sustainable development: countries commit in a clear way to sustainable development by implementing SD-PAMs or no-lose targets; Stage 3 – emission limitation targets; and Stage 4 – absolute reduction targets. Annex I countries start at Stage 4. SD-PAMs are an option at Stage 2, which provides developing countries with incentives to start acting on mitigation. SD-PAMs might eventually become mandatory for countries at agreed stages.

Stage 2 is qualitatively described in terms of sustainable development requirements, e.g. improved energy efficiency and energy conservation, inefficient equipment being phased out, switching to low-carbon fuels. Studies have so far not quantified this explicitly, and have simply assumed that the emissions for the countries at Stage 2 are reduced by 10–15% below the reference emissions level (e.g. den Elzen et al., 2007) This value is consistent with the findings of Höhne and Moltmann (2008), as summarized in Table 15 of their study. This method, however, does not quantify sustainable development co-benefits.

A more sophisticated quantification of SD-PAMs depends on the detailed specification of a sufficient number of policies for several developing countries. A key constraint on this method is that data on policies and measures in key developing countries are not yet publicly available.

One approach would be to use results generated from national energy modelling (Method 2) to analyse the effect of detailed SD-PAMs. Results from these models could then be incorporated into models such as FAIR and EVOC. A more detailed quantification of the climate implications of sustainable development policies has been conducted by Höhne and Moltmann (2008). They illustrate the link between national climate and sustainable development policies for Brazil, China, India, South Africa, Indonesia, South Korea and Mexico and the international climate regime post-2012. Drawing on such a national analysis, an assessment could be conducted of SD-PAMs in the global context, and analysis of emissions avoided, compared against projections of both global and country emissions and other proposals or allocation approaches such as the Brazilian proposal (Brazil, 1997) or Multi-stage approaches.

In this context, Höhne and Moltmann (2008) consider what contributions developing countries could make to the global climate regime post-2012 that are in line with their national objectives and circumstances. Sustainable development objectives examined include energy security, sustainable economic development, technology innovation, job creation, local environmental protection, and enhancement of adaptive capacity to climate change impacts.

Their paper puts the impact of a set of SD-PAMs in the energy sectors of the seven developing countries (mentioned above) into a broader international context. The policies differ by country, from Annex-I-like commitments to moderate supported emission reductions (Table 1 in Höhne and Moltmann, 2008). Roughly speaking, the non-Annex I countries achieve around 10–20% reductions in CO_2 emissions, compared with the reference case, until 2020.

These policies are analysed with the following further assumptions:

1. *Reference scenario:* An assumed reference case of the IPCC's A1B scenario (IPCC, 2000) for all countries till 2020; CO_2 only.
2. *Annex I reduces:* Annex I emission reductions of 30% below the 1990 level by 2020, except for the USA, which returns to the 1990 level.

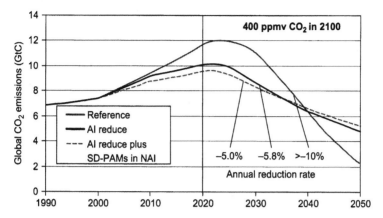

FIGURE 2 Alternative global CO$_2$ emission pathways leading to a CO$_2$ concentration of 400 ppmv in 2100 for a reference case, Annex I countries' reductions and additional non-Annex I countries' reductions.

Source: Höhne and Moltmann (2008).

3. *Annex I reduces plus SD-PAMs for non-Annex I:* In addition to the above reduction of Annex I countries, the non-Annex I countries achieve the 10–20% reductions in CO$_2$ emissions through SD-PAMs until 2020; constant LULUCF emissions at 1 GtC between 2000 and 2020; after 2020, for all three cases, global CO$_2$ emissions (all sources and countries together) decline so that CO$_2$ concentration in 2100 is below 400 ppmv (although the concentration first overshoots till 430–460 ppmv in around 2040). For details, see Höhne and Moltmann (2008).

The results in Figure 2 show that SD-PAMs in the energy sector from the seven countries reduce emissions to a lower level than Annex I reductions alone. To get from the A1B reference case in 2020 to the chosen stabilization level of 400 ppmv CO$_2$, emissions would have to decline by more than 10% per year after 2020. The assumed Annex I reductions reduce this to 5.8% per year; still a very demanding task. Adding sustainable development policies and measures in the energy sectors of seven larger developing countries reduces the required rate of reduction to 5% per year. Together with stringent reductions of Annex I countries, the combined package might be sufficient to keep global average temperature increase below 2°C, but only if followed by substantial global reductions of the order of 5–10% per year after 2020 (Höhne and Moltmann, 2008). In addition, meeting a 2°C target also depends critically on assumed contributions of other GHGs and the uncertainty range of the climate sensitivity.

For SD-PAMs to make a contribution to the overall effort, the approach would need to be formalized in the multilateral system. Ways would need to be found to give recognition to actions by developing countries through the Convention and its instruments.

5. How can SD-PAMs be formalized in the multilateral system?

Formalizing the pledged commitment could take two possible forms:

1. The initial register could simply be a list of countries that wish to record their existing contribution through sustainable development and pledge further implementation. This

could be recorded, for example, in a new Annex to the Convention. It has the advantage of simplicity and of giving recognition. By choosing to join Annex III, developing countries would no longer be defined by what they are not ('non-Annex I').

2. Another option would be a register of pledged policies and programmes. This approach has the advantage of specifying in more detail the actions to which countries are committing.

The two approaches are not mutually exclusive – there could be an initial list of countries, with a register of SD-PAMs maintained, for example, by the UNFCCC Secretariat.

A more detailed description of other aspects of formalizing SD-PAMs has been elaborated elsewhere (Winkler et al., 2007), but the issue of financing of SD-PAMs bears some restatement and elaboration.

To realize the potential of SD-PAMs, the appropriate incentives are needed. A major advantage of SD-PAMs is that they could access both climate and non-climate funding. Bradley and Pershing (2005) suggested that SD-PAMs can offer more *rigour* and *flexibility* than the present system: rigour by establishing quantifiable commitments towards which financial resources can meaningfully be directed, and flexibility by not separating climate funding from non-climate funding. Incentives for developing countries could include funding from development agencies, which have an interest in funding sustainable development, beyond climate change.

SD-PAM funding should be able to come from a wide range of sources: international financial institutions, bilateral aid agencies, the GEF, multilateral development banks, export credit agencies, the private sector, domestic sources, State and local communities, among others. Some funders – host governments, development banks and aid agencies – would be primarily concerned with alleviating poverty or otherwise boosting economic development. Since SD-PAMs implement national development objectives, significant amounts of domestic funding should be mobilized for the non-incremental costs. The real challenge is to instil carbon considerations into the broader set of international capital flows, only some of which are climate-specific.

Climate funding might instead be made available through expedited access to existing mechanisms, including the Global Environment Facility and climate investments by international financial institutions. Existing mechanisms include grants from the public sector, leveraging of investment by the private sector, as well as risk mitigation instruments. New mechanisms, such as a clean energy vehicle, might be particularly appropriate for SD-PAMs focused on energy development, while a clean energy support fund is more directly linked to emission reductions (World Bank and IMF, 2006).

A potentially large source of funding would be carbon markets, notably the CDM. Linking SD-PAMs to carbon markets initially would make it similar to CDM, accompanied by the complexities of additionality and project baselines.[1] To avoid these problems and to distinguish the approach (e.g. from programmatic or sectoral CDM), it is proposed not to link SD-PAMs to markets, at least initially.

Beyond the institutional arrangement proposed in previous work (Winkler et al., 2007), this article also suggests that the multilateral system could provide further support to SD-PAMs through elaborating and formalizing methodologies. The methodological approaches sketched in this article could be investigated and elaborated more fully, perhaps by the Consultative Group of Experts (CGE) or a sub-committee of the CGE. The Secretariat could be asked to prepare compilation and synthesis reports on the implementation of SD-PAMs.

6. Conclusions

SD-PAMs provide a strategic approach for capturing the climate co-benefits of developing countries' pursuit of sustainable development as one element of a future international climate regime. They offer the potential for a less confrontational approach between industrialized and developing countries, and a means to address developing-country emissions by promoting rather than threatening their development.

Sustainable development policies and measures are not a panacea. In particular they do not change the need for industrialized countries to lead with explicit action to mitigate their own GHG emissions. By itself, the approach may not guarantee a particular environmental outcome – although this would depend on the number and ambition level of the policies implemented. The approach, however, is aimed at mobilizing action, by turning climate change from a 'threat' to development into genuine opportunity to make development sustainable for developing countries. The approach does not require an entire new Protocol or mechanism, but 'only' a decision by the COP.

An important step in operationalizing the concept of SD-PAMs is to examine methods available to quantify the benefits of SD-PAMs. This article has identified four ways to quantify the effect of SD-PAMs on development and emissions.

The first method, case studies, has as its main aim to provide detailed examples of what SD-PAMs are and how they might work in a particular context. They are very specific to national circumstances. This strength also is a weakness of the method, in that results from different case studies might not be comparable, unless guidelines are developed for the parameters that need to be reported.

National energy modelling is the second method examined, a key strength of which is that it provides a link to energy policy and planning. While capable of providing an overview of emission from fuel combustion, no comparable method for LULUCF is available.

The third method draws on the analysis of sectoral data across countries. This allows comparative studies of energy and GHG intensity across countries, although setting up comparable indices limits the extent to which national circumstances can be taken into account. It combines detailed analysis at the national level for selected sectors with international projections.

Global emission allocation models potentially provide a comprehensive overview of the implications of SD-PAMs. Models such as FAIR and EVOC also allow comparison of the SD-PAMs approach with others. The key constraint is data availability to represent national policies and measures in sufficient detail. Combining this method with national energy modelling might provide both detail and comprehensive assessment.

The article suggests that formalizing the commitment of SD-PAMs could be aided by more fully elaborating the methodologies initially outlined here. Establishing the pledged commitment within the UNFCCC could take two possible forms – a new Annex to the Convention or a dedicated register of pledged policies. Confidence could be built through regular reporting of both the local sustainable development gains and the climate co-benefits of implementing SD-PAMs. Incentives for SD-PAMs could come from both climate and non-climate funding. Article 12.4 of the convention provides the means for countries to propose projects for climate financing (UNFCCC, 1992). Development funding through other agencies could also be mobilized.

SD-PAMs could be important as one approach among others to build trust between countries in enhancing the climate regime. This article has elaborated the concept and has begun to outline some methods for operationalizing SD-PAMs. Sustainable development policies and measures, implemented through technology, enabled by finance, in balance with adaptation, could be an important package of options to take us beyond 2012.

Note

1. For a detailed comparison of SD-PAMs with CDM and other approaches, see Baumert and Winkler (2005).

References

Baumert, K., Winkler, H., 2005, 'SD-PAMs and international climate agreements', in: R. Bradley, K. Baumert, J. Pershing (eds), *Growing in the Greenhouse: Protecting the Climate by Putting Development First*, World Resources Institute, Washington, DC, 15–23.

Baumert, K., Blanchard, O., Llosa, S., Perkaus, J.F. (eds), 2002, *Building on the Kyoto Protocol: Options for Protecting the Climate*, World Resources Institute, Washington, DC [available at http://climate.wri.org/pubs_pdf.cfm?PubID=3762].

Berk, M.M., den Elzen, M.G.J., 2001, 'Options for differentiation of future commitments in climate policy: how to realise timely participation to meet stringent climate goals?', *Climate Policy* 1(4), 465–480.

Bodansky, D., Chou, S., Jorge-Tresolini, C., 2004, *International Climate Efforts beyond 2012*, Pew Center on Global Climate Change, Arlington, VA [available at www.pewclimate.org].

Bradley, R., Pershing, J., 2005, 'Introduction to sustainable development policies and measures', in: R. Bradley, K. Baumert, J. Pershing (eds), *Growing in the Greenhouse: Protecting the Climate by Putting Development First*, World Resources Institute, Washington, DC, 1–14.

Bradley, R., Baumert, K., Pershing, J. (eds), 2005, *Growing in the Greenhouse: Protecting the Climate by Putting Development First*, World Resources Institute, Washington, DC [available at http://pubs.wri.org/pubs_description.cfm?PubID=4087].

Brazil, 1997, *Proposed Elements of a Protocol to the UNFCCC*, presented by Brazil in response to the Berlin mandate, FCCC/AGBM/1997/MISC.1/Add.3, UNFCCC, Bonn, Germany.

CCAP (Center for Clean Air Policy), 2006, *Greenhouse Gas Mitigation in Brazil, China and India: Scenarios and Opportunities through 2025*, CCAP. Washington, DC [available at www.ccap.org].

Criqui, P., Kitous, A., Berk, M.M., den Elzen, M.G.J., Eickhout, B., Lucas, P., van Vuuren, D.P., Kouvaritakis, N., Vanregemorter, D., 2003, *Greenhouse Gas Reduction Pathways in the UNFCCC Process up to 2025*, Technical Report B4-3040/2001/325703/MAR/E.1 for the DG Environment, CNRS-IEPE, Grenoble, France.

den Elzen, M., 2002, 'Exploring climate regimes for differentiation of future commitments to stabilise greenhouse gas concentrations', *Integrated Assessment* 3(4), 343–359.

den Elzen, M.G., Berk, M.M., 2004, *Bottom-up Approaches for Defining Future Climate Mitigation Commitments*, MNP-Report 728001029, Environmental Assessment Agency (MNP), Bilthoven, The Netherlands [available at www.mnp.nl/en].

den Elzen, M., Lucas, P., 2005, 'The FAIR model: a tool to analyse environmental and costs implications of climate regimes', *Environmental Modeling and Assessment* 10(2), 115–134.

den Elzen, M., Höhne, N., Brouns, B., Winkler, H., Ott, H.E., 2007, 'Differentiation of countries' future commitments in a post-2012 climate regime: an assessment of the "South–North Dialogue" proposal', *Environmental Science and Policy* 10, 185–203.

Dubash, N., Bradley, R., 2005, 'Pathways to rural electrification in India: are national goals also an international opportunity?', in: R. Bradley, K. Baumert , J. Pershing (eds), *Growing in the Greenhouse: Protecting the Climate by Putting Development First*, World Resources Institute, Washington, DC.

Gupta, J., 1998, *Encouraging Developing Country Participation in the Climate Change Regime*, Institute for Environmental Studies, Free University Amsterdam, Amsterdam.

Gupta, S., Tirpak, D.A., Burger, N., Gupta, J., Höhne, N., Boncheva, A.I., Kanoan, G.M., Kolstad, C., Kruger, J.A., Michaelowa, A., Murase, S., Pershing, J., Saijo, T., Sari, A., 2007, 'Policies, instruments and co-operative arrangements', in: B. Metz, O.R. Davidson, P.R. Bosch, R. Dave, L.A. Meyer (eds), *Climate Change 2007: Mitigation. Contribution of Working Group III to the IPCC Fourth Assessment Report*, Cambridge, UK, Cambridge University Press, 745–807.

Höhne, N., 2005, *What is next after the Kyoto Protocol? Assessment of options for international climate policy post 2012*, PhD thesis, Utrecht University, The Netherlands.

Höhne, N., Lahme, E., 2005, *Types of Future Commitments under the UNFCCC and the Kyoto Protocol post-2012*, Worldwide Fund for Nature, Gland, Switzerland.

Höhne, N., Moltmann, S., 2008, *Linking National Climate and Sustainable Development Policies with the Post-2012 Climate Regime: Proposals in the Energy Sector for Brazil, China, India, South Africa, Indonesia, South Korea and Mexico*, Draft version, November 2006, Ecofys, Cologne, Germany.

Höhne, N., Galleguillos, C., Blok, K., Harnisch, J., Phylipsen, D., 2003, *Evolution of Commitments under the UNFCCC: Involving Newly Industrialized Economies and Developing Countries*, Federal Environmental Agency (Umweltbundesamt), Berlin, Germany.

Höhne, N., Moltmann, S., Lahme, E., Worrell, E., Graus, W., 2006a, CO_2 *Emission Reduction Potential under a Sectoral Approach Post 2012*, prepared for the Netherlands Environmental Assessment Agency (MNP), No. DM70210, Ecofys, Cologne, Germany.

Höhne, N., Phylipsen, D., Moltmann, S., 2006b, *Factors Underpinning Future Action*, Ecofys, Cologne, Germany [available at www.fiacc.net/data/Factors_underpinning_future_action.pdf].

IISD (International Institute for Sustainable Development), 2005a, *Action on Climate Change: Elements of an International Approach*, IISD, Winnipeg, Canada.

IISD (International Institute for Sustainable Development), 2005b, 'Which Way Forward? Issues in Developing an Effective Climate Regime after 2012', IISD, Winnipeg, Canada.

IPCC (Intergovernmental Panel on Climate Change), 2000, *Special Report on Emissions Scenarios: A Special Report of Working Group III of the IPCC*, Cambridge, UK, Cambridge University Press.

IPCC (Intergovernmental Panel on Climate Change), 2001, *Summary for Policymakers: Climate Change 2001: Mitigation. Contribution of Working Group III to the Third Assessment Report*. Accra.

Kejun, J., Xiulan, H., Qiang, L., 2006, 'China's energy sector', in: K. Halsnaes, A. Garg (eds), *Sustainable Development, Energy and Climate Change: Methodological Issues and Case Studies from Brazil, China, India, South Africa, Bangladesh and Senegal*, UNEP Risø Centre, Roskilde, Denmark, 21–26.

La Rovere, E.L., Pereira, A.S., Simões, A.F., 2006, 'Brazil country studies', in: K. Halsnaes, A. Garg (eds), *Sustainable Development, Energy and Climate Change: Methodological Issues and Case Studies from Brazil, China, India, South Africa, Bangladesh and Senegal*, UNEP Risø Centre, Roskilde, Denmark, 15–20.

Metz, B., Berk, M., den Elzen, M., de Vries, B., van Vuuren, D., 2002, 'Towards an equitable global climate change regime: compatibility with Article 2 of the Climate Change Convention and the link with sustainable development', *Climate Policy* 2(2–3), 211–230.

Moreira, J.R., Nogueira, L.A.H., Parente, V., 2005, 'Biofuels for transport, development and climate change: lessons from Brazil', in: R. Bradley, K. Baumert, J. Pershing (eds), *Growing in the Greenhouse: Protecting the Climate by Putting Development First*, World Resources Institute, Washington, DC.

Morita, T., Robinson, J., 2001, 'Greenhouse gas emission mitigation scenarios and implications', in: IPCC (ed.), *Climate Change 2001: Mitigation. Contribution of WG III to the Third Assessment Report of the IPCC*, Intergovernmental Panel on Climate Change, Cambridge, UK, Cambridge University Press, 115–166.

Munasinghe, M., Swart, R., 2005, *Primer on Climate Change and Sustainable Development: Facts, Policy Analysis and Applications*, Cambridge, UK, Cambridge University Press.

Ott, H.E., Winkler, H., Brouns, B., Kartha, S., Mace, M., Huq, S., Kameyama, Y., Sari, A.P., Pan, J., Sokona, Y., Bhandari, P.M., Kassenberg, A., La Rovere, E.L., Rahman, A., 2004, *South–North Dialogue on Equity in the Greenhouse: A Proposal for an Adequate and Equitable Global Climate Agreement*, Gesellschaft für Technische Zusammenarbeit, Eschborn, Germany [available at www.wupperinst.org/uploads/tx_wiprojekt/1085_proposal.pdf].

Phylipsen, D., Bode, J.W., Blok, K., Merkus, H., Metz, B., 1998, 'A Triptych sectoral approach to burden differentiation: GHG emissions in the European bubble', *Energy Policy* 26(12), 929–943.

Rahman, A.A., Sharif, M.I., Alam, M., 2006, 'Rural electrification in Bangladesh', in: K. Halsnaes, A. Garg (eds), *Sustainable Development, Energy and Climate Change: Methodological Issues and Case Studies from Brazil, China, India, South Africa, Bangladesh and Senegal*. UNEP Risø Centre, Roskilde, Denmark, 43–48.

Robinson, J., Bradley, M., Busby, P., Connor, D., Murray, A., Sampson, B., Soper, W., 2006, 'Climate change and sustainable development: realizing the opportunity', *Ambio* 35(1), 2–8.

RSA (Republic of South Africa), 2004, *South Africa: Initial National Communication under the United Nations Framework Convention on Climate Change*, submitted at COP-9. Pretoria, South Africa [available at http://unfccc.int/resource/docs/natc/zafnc01.pdf].

Sathaye, J., Najam, A., Cocklin, C., Heller, T., Lecocq, F., Llanes-Regueiro, J., Pan, J., Petschel-Held, G., Rayner, S., Robinson, J., Schaeffer, R., Sokona, Y., Swart, R., Winkler, H., 2007, 'Sustainable development and mitigation', in: B. Metz, O.R. Davidson, P.R. Bosch, R. Dave, L.A. Meyer (eds), *Climate Change 2007: Mitigation. Contribution of Working Group III to the IPCC Fourth Assessment Report*, Cambridge, UK, Cambridge University Press, 691–743.

Spalding-Fecher, R., Mqadi, L., Oganne, G., 2003, 'Carbon financing for energy efficient low-cost housing', *Journal of Energy in Southern Africa* 14(4), 128–134.

SSN (SouthSouthNorth), 2004, *Project Design Document for the Kuyasa Project*, submitted to the Executive Board of the Clean Development Mechanism, SouthSouthNorth Project, Cape Town, South Africa [available at http://cdm.unfccc.int and www.southsouthnorth.org].

Sterk, W., Wittneben, B., 2006, 'Enhancing the Clean Development Mechanism through sectoral approaches: definitions, applications and ways forward', *International Environmental Agreements: Politics, Law and Economics* 6, 271–287.

Szklo, A.S., Schaeffer, R., Schuller, M.E., Chandler, W., 2005, 'Brazilian energy policies side-effects on CO_2 emissions reduction', *Energy Policy* 33, 349–364.

Thiam, N., 2006, 'Development impacts of electricity sector reforms in Senegal', in: K. Halsnaes, A. Garg (eds), *Sustainable Development, Energy and Climate Change: Methodological Issues and Case Studies from Brazil, China, India, South Africa, Bangladesh and Senegal*, UNEP Risø Centre, Roskilde, Denmark, 49–52.

UNFCCC, 1992, *United Nations Framework Convention on Climate Change*, United Nations, New York [available at http://unfccc.int/essential_background/convention/items/2627.php].

van der Merwe, M.R., Scholes, R.J., 1998, *South African Greenhouse Gas Emissions Inventory for the Years 1990 and 1994*, National Committee on Climate Change, Pretoria, South Africa.

Wei-Shiuen, N., Schipper, L., 2005, 'China motorization trends: policy options in a world of transport challenges', in: R. Bradley, K. Baumert, J. Pershing (eds), *Growing in the Greenhouse: Protecting the Climate by Putting Development First*, World Resources Institute, Washington, DC.

Winkler, H. (ed.), 2006a, *Energy Policies for Sustainable Development in South Africa: Options for the Future*, Energy Research Centre, Cape Town, South Africa [available at www.iaea.org/OurWork/ST/NE/Pess/assets/South_Africa_Report_May06.pdf].

Winkler, H., 2006b, *Energy policies for sustainable development in South Africa's residential and electricity sectors: implications for mitigating climate change*, PhD thesis, Energy Research Centre, University of Cape Town, South Africa.

Winkler, H., Spalding-Fecher, R., Mwakasonda, S., Davidson, O., 2002a, 'Sustainable development policies and measures: starting from development to tackle climate change', in: K. Baumert, O. Blanchard, S. Llosa, J.F. Perkaus (eds), *Building on the Kyoto Protocol: Options for Protecting the Climate*, World Resources Institute, Washington, DC, 61–87.

Winkler, H., Spalding-Fecher, R., Mwakasonda, S., Davidson, O., 2002b, 'Sustainable development policies and measures: tackling climate change from a development perspective', in: O. Davidson, D. Sparks (eds), *Developing Energy Solutions for Climate Change: South African Research at EDRC*, Energy and Development Research Centre, University of Cape Town, Cape Town, South Africa, 176–198.

Winkler, H., Spalding-Fecher, R., Tyani, L., Matibe, K., 2002c, 'Cost–benefit analysis of energy efficiency in urban low-cost housing', *Development Southern Africa* 19(5), 593–614.

Winkler, H., Howells, M., Baumert, K., 2005, *Sustainable Development Policies and Measures: Institutional Issues and Electrical Efficiency in South Africa*, Center for Clean Air Policy, Washington, DC [available at www.ccap.org/international/oct05.htm].

Winkler, H., Mukheibir, P., Mwakasonda, S., 2006, *Electricity Supply Options, Sustainable Development and Climate Change: Case Studies for South(ern) Africa*, Draft, Energy Research Centre, University of Cape Town, South Africa.

Winkler, H., Howells, M., Baumert, K., 2007, 'Sustainable development policies and measures: institutional issues and electrical efficiency in South Africa', *Climate Policy* 7, 212–229.

World Bank and IMF (World Bank and International Monetary Fund), 2006, *An Investment Framework for Clean Energy and Development: A Progress Report*. Paper for Meeting on 29 August of the Development Committee (Committee of the Whole), SecM2006-0360, World Bank, Washington, DC.

climate
policy

■ research article

Bilateral and multilateral financial assistance for the energy sector of developing countries

DENNIS TIRPAK[1,2]*, HELEN ADAMS[2]

[1] World Resources Institute and International Institute for Sustainable Development, Washington DC, USA
[2] Tyndall Centre for Climate Change Research, School of Environmental Sciences, University of East Anglia, UK

This article examines trends in development assistance funding for energy and the implications for mitigating climate change. It presents financial data from bilateral and multilateral donors during 1997–2005, a period that begins with the agreement on the Kyoto Protocol under the United Nations Framework Convention on Climate Change. During this period, aid for energy totalled over US$64 billion or 6–10% of all development assistance. Annual energy assistance was virtually stagnant at approximately US$6–7 billion from 1997 to 2005, but preliminary evidence indicates that some efforts are being made to fill the resource gap and to mitigate climate change. Analysis suggests that there has been somewhat of a shift away from fossil fuel to lower greenhouse-gas-emitting projects. However, the increases in funding and shifts to low greenhouse gas technologies are fragile. Analysis also suggests that, unless development assistance for energy increases in the coming years, the influence of multilateral banks will diminish and their ability to encourage sustainable energy projects will decline. It should be noted that funding levels for projects do not tell the whole story. There is a continuing evolution of aid modalities under way, as development financing for project-based activities is supplemented with macro-economic and sector-wide assistance targeted at promoting policy reforms, institutional change and capacity building. Several challenges will need to be met in the future: to increase funding for the MDBs by finance ministers; to 'green' private sector funds to ensure that investments made today do not pollute tomorrow; and to overcome the lack of a common reporting format by standardizing the collection and reporting of data on investments for energy.

Keywords: climate change; development assistance; finance; energy; multilateral development banks

Cet article examine les tendances dans le financement de l'assistance au développement énergetique et leurs conséquences pour l'atténuation du changement climatique. L'article présente des données financières de bailleurs bilatéraux et multilatéraux de 1997 à 2005, période qui débute avec les accords sur le protocole de Kyoto sous la Convention Cadre des Nations Unies sur le Changement Climatique. Pendant cette période, le montant de l'aide à l'énergie s'élevait au-dessus de US$ 64 milliards ou bien 6–10% de la totalité de l'aide au développement. L'aide annuelle à l'énergie stagnait pratiquement aux alentours de US$ 2–7 milliards de 1997 à 2005, mais l'évidence préliminaire indique que des efforts ont été effectués pour combler le manque de ressources et amorcer la lutte contre le changement climatique. L'analyse suggère qu'une forme de transfert au loin de projets fossiles vers des projets plus sobres en émissions de gaz a effet de serre a eu lieu. Cependant, l'augmentation du financement et le transfert vers les technologies sobres en gaz à effet de serre sont précaires. L'analyse suggère aussi qu'à défaut de l'augmentation de l'aide au développement énergetique dans les prochaines années, l'influence des banques multilatérales diminuera ainsi que leur capacité à favoriser des projets d'énergie durable. Il est à noter que le degré de financement des projets ne révèle pas toute l'affaire. Les modalités de l'aide continuent d'évoluer en conséquence à l'augmentation du financement aux projets de développement, par une assistance macro-économique et sectorielle visant la promotion de réformes des politiques, le changement institutionnel, et le renforcement des capacités. Plusieurs défis devront être affrontés à l'avenir: l'augmentation du financement aux Banques Multilaterales de Developpement (MDBs) par les ministres des finances: pour verdir les fonds du secteur privé et assurer que les investissements faits aujourd'hui ne pollueraient pas demain, pour surmonter le manque de format commun de reporting en standardisant la collecte et le rapport des données sur les investissements énergetiques.

Mots clés: assistance au développement; banques multilatérales de développement; changement climatique; énergie; finance

■ *Corresponding author. E-mail: dennis@tirpak.com

CLIMATE POLICY 8 (2008) 135–151

doi:10.3763/cpol.2007.0443 © 2008 Earthscan ISSN: 1469-3062 (print), 1752-7457 (online) www.climatepolicy.com

1. Introduction

In his book titled *The White Man's Burden: Why the West's Efforts to Aid the Rest have Done So Much Ill and So Little Good*, Easterly (2006) examines why there have been so few improvements in the lives of poor people, after spending US$2.3 trillion in aid over 50 years. Nearly a decade earlier Kozloff (1995) asked a similar question with regard to bilateral development assistance for renewable electric power. Drawing on lessons from individual assistance projects, he noted that bilateral energy assistance has been erratic over the period 1979–1991, with renewables (mainly hydro and geothermal projects) constituting only 3% of total bilateral energy assistance. During that period, World Bank records indicate that it was focusing on improving economic efficiency and financial stability by encouraging least-cost planning, marginal-cost pricing, international accounting standards, and international competitive bidding, and that lending for the power sector in developing countries up until 1991 was about US$40 billion. The World Bank (1993) and Tharakan et al. (2007) noted that during the 1990–1997 period, reductions in official development assistance (ODA) for energy, combined with reduced private investments in energy projects, significantly affected the development of energy resources in developing countries.

The entry into force of the United Nations Framework Convention on Climate Change (UNFCCC) in 1994 created a new stimulus for the promotion of development assistance for energy projects. Articles 4.3 and 4.5 of the Convention both call for developed countries to provide new and additional financial resources to meet the agreed costs of developing countries in complying with their obligations under the Convention, including implementing measures to mitigate climate change by addressing anthropogenic emissions by sources – for example energy sources – and removals by sinks. In addition, Article 11.5 stipulates that developing countries may avail themselves of financial resources related to the implementation of the Convention through bilateral, regional and other multilateral channels. More specifically, the Convention established a new financial mechanism (the Global Environment Facility (GEF)) for the provision of financial resources on a grant or concessional basis. Articles 10(c) and 11(a) of the Kyoto Protocol reiterated and further reinforced the requirements of the Convention when it was adopted in 1997.[1] Subsequent to the entry into force of the UNFCCC and its Kyoto Protocol, the United Nations formulated Millennium Development Goals (MDGs)[2] and, while energy was not listed specifically, the Millennium Project recognized that the provision of sustainable energy services is an essential requirement if poverty is to be reduced among the world's poorest countries (Modi et al., 2005). Scaling-up energy services to address poverty will be required of energy sources, but the challenge is to provide those services in a sustainable way that makes the fulfilment of this requirement compatible with the objectives of the UNFCCC.

Therefore, bilateral and multilateral assistance programmes which aim to expand sustainable energy services in developing countries must now aim to achieve multiple goals. However, this article attempts to address a narrower question relating to climate change; namely, what has been bought with over US$60 billion in financial assistance for energy projects since the Kyoto Protocol came into existence? Put another way: has the mix of investments for energy projects in developing countries changed in recognition of the Convention, the Protocol, and the need for a more sustainable energy development path? In assessing the data on development assistance for energy, we also seek to identify critical issues that need to be addressed by bilateral donors and multilateral banks (MDBs) in the future.

2. Methods and data

This article uses official development assistance (ODA) data from the Creditor Reporting System (CRS) database of the Organisation for Economic Cooperation and Development (OECD).

The original data were reported by bilateral donors who include the 22 members of the OECD's Development Assistance Committee (DAC) and the European Commission (OECD, 2007). The objective of the CRS is to create a comparable reporting basis for all DAC members through the use of common guidelines and definitions. Data from multilateral organizations were obtained directly from those institutions, since they are not obliged to report to the OECD.

This article does not cover aid activity comprehensively. Not all donors supply data to the OECD. The coverage of donors' activities varies over time, although activity data have been more complete since 1999. Reporting of data may be influenced by staff changes in aid agencies, and may often be subjective, despite adherence to the guidelines. The major gaps in coverage post-1999 in official bilateral development assistance reporting come from Japan and the European Commission. The former does not report technical cooperation activities, while the latter does not report activities financed through the budget of the European Commission. Information on data quality indicators and a list of DAC members can be found in the CRS online User's Guide.[3]

Within the CRS database, aid activities are recorded on the basis of commitments according to a 'marker' system that identifies the purpose of the aid. For DAC purposes, grants and 'soft' loans are recorded on the face value of the activity at the date a grant or loan agreement is signed with the recipient. Cancellations and reductions of previous years' agreements are not included in the database. This article reports bilateral assistance using the markers for all energy generation, including coal, oil and gas development. Energy efficiency projects are not readily captured by the DAC marker system, hence the total amounts reported for energy efficiency from bilateral sources may be somewhat of an underestimate.

We had hoped to provide data on funding from multilateral agencies using the same set of markers, but data were not available at the same level of detail. Data from multilateral institutions are reported in a simplified format using categories drawn from the approach used by the World Bank Group to classify energy projects. While energy efficiency data are reported, such projects present a particular challenge in their classification. For example, a transmission line project may be reported by some organizations either as an expansion of the grid or an improvement in efficiency.

To keep the analysis manageable, this article mainly includes projects over US$1 million. This leads to the exclusion of many valuable projects aimed at building capacity, training, feasibility studies, planning, enabling activities and, in some cases, small projects aimed at reforming the market. These types of project are essential to filling the 'project pipeline' with high-quality projects. We estimate that approximately one-third of all projects may fall into this category, but we have made no attempt to estimate the level of funding for these activities. We have also grouped together approved loans and grants. While most projects are supported through loans (for example, in the case of bilateral projects, loans account for 83% of all projects), grants play a special role by reducing the risks associated with new technologies which may not otherwise be deployed. We have also excluded loan guarantees, make no attempt to account for leveraging – that is, the extent to which projects are co-funded with private sector funds – and have not attempted to reconcile disbursements against approved loans and grants.

3. General trends in foreign direct investment (FDI) and official development assistance (ODA)

Over the period 1997–2005, ODA for all purposes totalled approximately US$490 billion. This has risen from the low levels observed in 1997 (US$60 billion) to US$106.8 billion in 2005, the highest level ever in both real and nominal terms. The increase was exceptionally high due to the Paris

Club's debt relief effort for Nigeria and Iraq, which accounted for nearly 20% of the total. However, tsunami relief and other humanitarian needs also contributed to the increase. In the next one or two years, official development assistance (ODA) is expected to decrease slightly as debt relief efforts taper off. Over a slightly longer period, aid donors will have to increase funding in order to fulfil their commitments to increase aid to $130 billion and double aid to Africa by 2010 (OECD, 2006).

During the same period (1997–2005), inflows of all foreign direct investment (FDI) to developing countries totalled over US$2 trillion. Inflows of FDI to developing countries were US$267, 164 and 334 billion in 2000, 2002 and 2005, respectively, with FDI nearly three times higher than ODA in 2005. FDI therefore tends to rise and fall with financial cycles and be risk-averse (UNCTAD, 2006). It is also selective – it will only flow to those countries where relatively strong enabling conditions for investment exist. These include stable political environments, strong legal systems, macro-economic stability, readily available skilled labour, and good institutions. Since many of the poorest countries do not have these basic governance conditions, ODA remains an important source of funding for technology transfer for these countries (Ellis et al., 2007).

In recent years, strong economic growth has reduced demands for aid from large and medium-sized Asian countries. For example, India's net ODA receipts fell below US$1 billion, the lowest level since the 1970s, as it repaid loan principal of US$1.8 billion in 2003. Net aid to China also fell by two-thirds from its level in the early 1990s as it increased its repayments in 2003. As a result, ODA is increasingly being concentrated on the most needy countries, with sub-Saharan Africa receiving more than one-third of country-allocable ODA in 2002/2003. At the same time, the war on terrorism has boosted aid flows to some countries, for example Iraq.[4]

4. Bilateral assistance for energy development

Bilateral energy development assistance represents approximately 31% of the funding of all aid for energy, totalling over US$20 billion during the period 1997–2005. Funding was at its highest in 1997, reaching nearly US$4 billion, and was at its lowest in 2000 (approximately US$1.3 billion), before recovering in more recent years, during which it has averaged slightly more than US$2 billion annually (see Table 1).

The overall percentage of bilateral aid for energy has averaged approximately 2% of total development assistance for the period 1997–2005. Japan, having provided over two-thirds of all bilateral aid for energy during the period 1997–2005, is the most significant donor, out-distancing by far the next most important donors, namely Germany (12.0%) and France (3.4%). These countries, particularly Japan and Germany, have an opportunity through their cooperation with developing countries to influence the type of technologies being diffused to developing countries. Assuming they continue to be the most important donors, they have a great opportunity as they work together with developing countries to ensure that the lowest greenhouse-gas-emitting technologies are transferred to those countries. However, it is not clear why bilateral assistance for energy has remained static while ODA in general has increased, even accounting for debt relief. One answer may reside in the form of development assistance; that is, some countries provide multi-sector funds and general programme assistance which may incorporate or obscure support for energy activities. While more efficient for donors and more flexible for recipient countries, assistance of this type could limit the ability of donors to promote and track energy policy reforms (OECD, 2006).

Figure 1 identifies bilateral development assistance by sector by year and Figure 2 identifies total funding over the period 1997–2005 for different energy categories. Expanding or upgrading electrical transmission lines and power projects have both received approximately US$4.4 billion

TABLE 1 Bilateral assistance to all energy sectors in the period 1997–2005 from major donors (US$ million)

	1997	1998	1999	2000	2001	2002	2003	2004	2005	Country total 1997–2005 (million USD)	% of grand total 1997–2005 (million USD)
Japan	3,068.3	1,746.2	1,204.7	803.9	888.5	1,332.9	2,151.8	1,666.5	1,035.6	13,918.4	69.2
Germany	367.2	316.7	298.6	81.9	229.5	100.9	188.0	319.8	496.5	2,419.1	12.0
France	94.1	187.2	66.9	27.0	25.8	38.9	77.1	80.5	82.3	679.7	3.4
Spain	166.0	54.5	62.4	112.6	14.2	75.4	36.3	0.5		521.9	2.6
Italy	24.1	4.2	9.1	13.1	13.2	29.5	53.3	22.6	273.4	442.7	2.2
United Kingdom	-8.4	58.1	45.8	69.3	48.7	43.8	48.7	73.2	1.8	407.9	2.0
United States	6.6	10.1	17.6	59.6	46.9	148.5	15.0	8.1	69.0	381.4	1.9
Norway	55.7	45.2	20.9	34.0	60.4	23.7	30.1	19.1	23.3	312.5	1.6
Denmark	31.4	30.3	15.4	18.6	5.1	55.0	24.6	40.4	64.3	285.3	1.4
Netherlands	23.7	23.7	12.2	29.2	24.6	44.6	14.8	3.5	9.4	185.8	0.9
Canada	66.6	19.3	33.1	11.3	0.2	11.1	9.4	3.1	6.6	160.5	0.8
Sweden	9.1	13.2	14.4	20.3	8.0	13.3	29.5	19.1	23.4	150.2	0.7
Finland	2.1	2.7	5.6	0.5	0.4	4.7	15.0	12.0	33.3	76.1	0.4
Belgium	1.8	1.0	6.5	3.9	1.1	6.4	3.2	14.3	6.0	44.3	0.2
Switzerland	0.7			1.3		0.4	26.7	10.9		40.1	0.2
Australia	-6.1	8.2	3.5	5.0	2.2	2.1	0.0	0.3		37.4	0.2
Austria	0.9	1.9	4.1	3.1	2.5	16.6	0.7	1.0	4.2	35.0	0.2
New Zealand						1.0	0.8	0.4	1.8	4.0	0.0
Portugal				0.0	0.4	0.9	1.0	0.5	0.2	3.1	0.0
Luxembourg					0.4				0.4	0.8	0.0
Greece						0.1	0.0	0.1	0.2	0.4	0.0
Ireland				0.1	0.1	0.1		0.0		0.3	0.0
Total	3,932.8	2,522.6	1,820.8	1,294.6	1,372.4	1,950.1	2,725.8	2,295.9	2,131.8	20,106.880	100.0

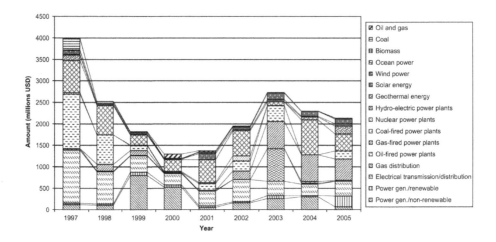

FIGURE 1 Bilateral development assistance by sector by year from 1997–2004 in US$ million.

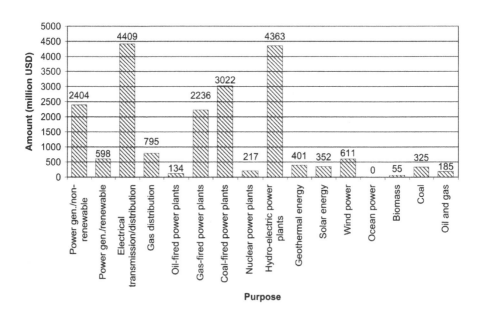

FIGURE 2 Total bilateral assistance for energy by category over the 9-year period from 1997 to 2005 by sector in US$ million.

(22% for each). Funding for these two categories has been relatively stable throughout the period. Coal-fired power plants received approximately US$3.0 billion (15%), but most of this funding occurred in the first two years of the period. Funding for gas power plants has increased, particularly in the last three years, averaging approximately US$590 million annually during those years.

Total support for all renewables (excluding hydropower) was approximately US$2 billion (10%) over the period, with wind energy receiving the most support (over US$600 million). The increase in spending on solar power was due to a large increase in spending by Germany in 2001, followed by an increase (albeit smaller) in spending by Spain in 2003. The increase in spending on wind power can be attributed to two years in which Japan made large contributions (2002 and 2003), and also to Germany, which has been gradually increasing its spending on wind power since 2002. Over the period examined, the number of renewable projects per year has doubled from approximately 100 to 200, while the number of non-renewable projects has remained nearly static at approximately 50. This may reflect the larger size of coal, oil and gas projects and the relatively small size of many renewable projects.

In general, there is an apparent shift to less greenhouse-gas-intensive energy systems through bilateral assistance programmes, but the variability and low levels of funding suggest that this trend is fragile and not well established as an existing policy among donors, or is not supported strongly among recipient countries. Consequently, there appear to be ample reasons for all donors to assess their assistance for energy projects, given the goals of the UNFCCC, while working cooperatively with, and respecting the priorities of, the recipient countries.

The top 20 recipients of bilateral development assistance for energy are listed in Table 2. These recipients include 14 Asian countries, 3 African countries and 2 Latin American countries. While China and India are among the recipients who received the largest amount of bilateral assistance over the time period covered (that is, 33%), they also emitted approximately 52% of developing-country CO_2 emissions from fossil fuel combustion in 2005. Their relative proportion of aid is thus somewhat high, but their rapid growth over the last decade seems to warrant higher assistance. Assistance to other developing countries, particularly those undergoing rapid growth, is also warranted because collectively they account for 48% of developing-country emissions (IEA, 2007).

However, the listing in Table 2 does not reflect the growing influence and market power of China and India. As of 2006, the two richest energy entrepreneurs in the world were Tulsi Tanti – Suzlon (India) and Zhengrong Shi – Suntech Power (China); the largest wind power company by capitalization is Suzlon (India), and the largest recipients of venture capital money were the USA and China.[5]

There is also anecdotal information indicating that India and China have recently begun to reverse the direction of development assistance by providing support for projects in Asia and Africa. The total level of aid from these countries for all purposes is small relative to bilateral and multilateral sources (in the range of US$3 billion). Data on aid for energy projects is not available. It is yet to be determined whether these countries will promote the same standards and consideration for the environment that OECD countries and the multilateral banks have come to adopt over time (Miller, 2008).[6] It is also difficult to say whether the emergence of energy entrepreneurs and the transformation of these countries into lenders reflect a success story for development assistance programmes, but two things appear to be clear. First, the growing economic power of these countries and their strategic interests in ensuring adequate raw material supplies is enabling them to emerge as 'players' capable of influencing the development, including energy development, of poorer developing countries. Secondly, any future development assistance to large developing countries will need to be carefully focused on areas where market forces are not already working and where further economic reforms are needed to match the strategic interests of OECD countries, such as ensuring open access to markets. Recently, the 'Group of Eight' industrial nations (G8), in its communiqué, encouraged the emerging economies as well as developing countries to associate themselves with the values and environmental standards contained in these OECD guidelines (G8, 2007).

TABLE 2 Top 20 Recipients of bilateral development assistance for energy (US$ million) and the percentage of aid for renewables during the period 1997–2005

	Total 1997–2005	Percentage of all bilateral assistance (%)	Percentage for renewables* (%)
India	2,433.7	17.6	30
Indonesia	2,418.6	17.5	11
China	2,146.4	15.5	28
Viet Nam	1,960.6	14.2	33
Malaysia	1,087.3	7.9	14
Azerbaijan	585.0	4.2	0
Sri Lanka	453.7	3.3	59
Thailand	363.5	2.6	0
Philippines	356.8	2.6	47
Peru	204.0	1.5	2
Uzbekistan	199.2	1.4	0
Armenia	192.0	1.4	0
Egypt	159.6	1.2	73
Pakistan	158.0	1.1	78
Kenya	154.9	1.1	100
Morocco	152.4	1.1	0
Costa Rica	137.3	1.0	100
Mongolia	85.3	0.6	0
Iran	69.5	0.5	100
Bosnia-Herzegovina	57.0	0.4	0

* Renewables includes power generation, hydropower, geo-thermal, solar, wind, ocean and biomass.

5. Multilateral assistance for energy development

Data on energy projects funded by the multilateral institutions[7] are generally available only in an aggregated format, with the exception of the GEF. The categories used for the compilation of multilateral development assistance generally reflect those of the World Bank Group. Refer to Table 3 for a description of these categories (World Bank, 2007).

Funding for energy projects has exceeded US$44 billion over the period 1997–2005; however, levels of funding have been virtually stagnant, despite demands for energy to alleviate poverty, increase economic growth and address climate change (see Table 4). The reasons for this are undoubtedly complex and may include: shifting donor and developing country priorities, competition with emergency humanitarian needs, the long process of identifying and implementing high-quality projects, and the abundance of and ease of access to private-sector capital in some large countries. However, many small countries, such as those in Africa, cannot easily access capital and tend to rely on bilateral and multilateral institutions to help launch many projects. Stagnant funding therefore represents a real challenge to their development goals. Nevertheless,

TABLE 3 Categories used for compilation of multilateral development assistance

Power	Includes generation, collection, transmission, and distribution of electric energy for sale to household, industrial and commercial users.
Renewable energy	Hydro, wind, geothermal, biomass, solar for electricity production and for thermal applications.
Energy efficiency	Includes efficiency improvements in energy supply and demand and improvements in district heating.
Coal	Includes support for mine rehabilitation and mine closing and coal, lignite, and peat mining.
Oil and gas	Includes crude oil and natural gas liquids (NGLs), fuel quality, gas distribution, oil and gas pipelines, liquefied natural gas (LNG) plant, liquid fuels, including liquefied petroleum gas (LPG), manufactured gases, natural gas and its fuel products, refineries.
General energy sector	Classification used if no other energy sector category is appropriate, or for activities that span more than five sectors.

there is evidence that the situation is changing. The World Bank's Clean Energy and Development Investment Framework (World Bank, 2007) highlights the need to address poverty reduction (particularly in Africa), low-carbon growth strategies for key developing countries, diffusion of clean energy technologies, and other climate change issues. It reports on efforts to scale-up investment in these areas and to enhance coordination among multilateral development banks.

The World Bank Group has been the largest source of multilateral funds, contributing nearly 39% of all funding, including bilateral funds. Support for the power sector, while down from earlier years, has dominated energy funding. Funds for the oil and gas category have been relatively constant, while support for energy-efficiency measures and renewables has been variable, despite efforts since the early 1990s to expand both portfolios. Collectively, the power, coal, oil and gas categories account for 75% of all funding (Table 5).

One question that arises when examining the data is: 'Why did World Bank support for the power sector decline during the mid-1990s?' Bayliss and McKinley (2007) suggest that, during this

TABLE 4 Multilateral and bilateral funding for energy during the period 1997–2005 (US$ million)

	Multilateral and Bilateral Support for Energy Projects									
Source	1997	1998	1999	2000	2001	2002	2003	2004	2005	Total
Bilateral Development Assistance	3,992	2,522	1,820	1,294	1,372	1,950	2,726	2,296	2,132	20,104
World Bank Group	3,633	3,833	2,258	2,643	2,642	2,817	2,450	1,828	2,794	24,898
EBRD	357	357	357	597	620	680	667	768	766	5,168
GEF	136	113	83	113	134	97	120	134	124	1,054
Asian Development Bank	824	400	699	1,042	663	927	654	707	677	6,593
Inter-American Development Bank	1,131	1,261	464	1,172	1,188	184	379	152	1,056	6,987
Total	10,073	8,486	5,681	6,851	6,619	6,655	6,996	5,885	7,548	64,794

period, the hopes for privatization were so high that donor spending on infrastructure fell, in the expectation that the private sector would take up the slack. For example, World Bank lending for infrastructure investment declined by 50% between 1993 and 2002 – with much of the remaining amount directed towards preparing firms for privatization. During the period 1993–1997, the World Bank Group increased its support for private investment in utilities through its International Finance Corporation and its Multilateral Investment Guarantee Agency.

These authors go on to argue that this has largely been a failure and that the Bank needs to revert to much greater investment in public utilities. This is confirmed by the World Bank, which notes that private flows fell from a peak of US$50 billion in 1997 to US$7 billion in 2002. The bank attributes this to difficulties in sustaining reforms to place the power sector on a commercial footing in some countries, a wide reduction in investments flows in emerging markets, and a withdrawal of investors (World Bank, 2003, 2004).

However, the WBG is the largest single source of funds for both renewables and energy efficiency projects and is committed to increasing support for renewable energy and energy efficiency by 20% per year between 2005 and 2009 (World Bank, 2006a). The exact level of support for the energy-efficiency projects is particularly hard to estimate, due to ambiguities in the classification of projects. For example, in some cases, a transmission line upgrade might be classified as an efficiency project, while in other cases it may have been classified as a power project. With regard to renewables, some of the funds for renewable energy come from the GEF, which often co-finances projects with the WBG (see Annex 3 in World Bank, 2006a).

The regional development banks individually provide less than one-quarter of the funding provided by the World Bank Group. However, they play a unique role in meeting the special energy needs of their regions. They generally do not have an explicit mandate to address climate change, but their collective influence through energy programmes is important (see Table 6). Among the regional banks, the EBRD has focused the most on energy efficiency, including the upgrading of heat and power systems, the refurbishment of power plants in Eastern Europe, and on the need to diversify sources of oil and gas in an effort to promote energy security. EBRD countries of operations use up to seven times the amount of energy it takes to produce each unit of GDP, relative to Western Europe. These countries also emit more greenhouse gas per unit of GDP consumed than do Western European countries – 30 times more in some cases. Businesses and governments in the region are starting to see that the highly inefficient use of energy undermines their competitiveness in global markets. To underline the importance of energy

TABLE 5 World Bank Group support for energy during the period 1997–2005 by category (US$ million) (World Bank 2007)

World Bank Group	1997	1998	1999	2000	2001	2002	2003	2004	2005	Total	Percent of total
Power	2,685	1,613	1,026	1,179	1,589	1,861	1,257	705	1,064	12,979	52%
Renewable energy	351	477	239	765	26	350	342	273	666	3,488	14%
Energy efficiency	56	356	26	295	193	67	168	67	243	1,469	6%
Coal	255	902	254	51	116	194	75	160	234	2,239	9%
Oil and gas	283	412	462	178	544	292	438	494	462	3,565	14%
General energy sector	3	74	251	176	175	55	170	128	125	1,157	5%
Total	3,633	3,833	2,258	2,643	2,642	2,817	2,450	1,828	2,794	24,898	

efficiency, the Bank has adopted a formal energy efficiency and renewable energy target which is synergistic with climate change goals. The target is to lend or invest a minimum of US$1 billion in energy efficiency and renewable energy projects during the period 2006–2010. This figure compares to a total of €674 million achieved during the 5-year period 2001–2005 (EBRD, 2006).

Projects supported by the Asian Development Bank (AsDB) in the Asian region tend to focus on the expansion and upgrade of electrical transmission lines, reflecting the large and growing population and rapid economic growth, although support for energy reforms has also been a priority up until the most recent years. As in the case of the EBRD, the AsDB is attempting to promote energy efficiency projects as part of a portfolio of activities in selected countries. The AsDB has developed a new Clean Energy and Environment programme, which is made up of several initiatives. The first stage of the Energy Efficiency Initiative (EEI), which defined an action plan, was completed in June 2006. Operational details will be prepared in consultation with its developing member countries up until December 2007 and implemented between 2007 and 2010. The EEI will target US$1 billion annual lending for energy efficiency through a proposed Asia Pacific Fund for Energy Efficiency (World Bank, 2007).

TABLE 6 Regional bank support for energy 1997–2005 by category (US$ million)

European Bank for Reconstruction and Development									
	1997	1998	1999	2000	2001	2002	2003	2004	2005	Total
Power	133	133	133	326	326	326	326	326	326	2,355
Renewables						13			1	14
Energy efficiency	41	41	41	20	53	100	100	201	197	794
Oil and gas	183	183	183	241	241	241	241	241	241	1,995
Total	357	357	357	587	620	680	667	768	765	5,158

Asian Development Bank									
	1997	1998	1999	2000	2001	2002	2003	2004	2005	Total
Power	471	100	217	484	499	400	404	520	410	3,505
Renewables				58	6	305			37	406
Efficiency	40									40
Oil and gas	150					72		187	230	639
General energy	163	300	482	500	158	150	250			2,003
Total	824	400	699	1,042	663	927	654	707	677	6,593

Inter-American Development Bank									
	1997	1998	1999	2000	2001	2002	2003	2004	2005	Total
Power	307	606	461	757	826	25	194	31	202	3,409
Renewables	337	50	3	207				81	786	1,463
Energy efficiency	35	30		137	361		50	35	58	706
Oil and gas	450	326		70		132	135			1,113
General energy	2	250		1		27		5	10	295
Total	1,131	1,261	464	1,172	1,188	184	379	152	1,056	6,986

The Inter-American Bank supports projects throughout Latin America, and power generation to meet the needs of the poor has been the most dominant category for funding. Support for energy projects has generally declined over the period 1997–2005. However, in 2005, a single large hydro-electric dam in Venezuela was approved for funding, thereby skewing the amount of funds for renewables.

The Global Environment Facility (GEF) is a unique mechanism among the institutions supporting energy projects. It occupies a special position in the context of the UNFCCC as the operating entity of the financial mechanism of the Convention. It has committed $1.6 billion for all projects relating to climate, since its foundation as a pilot programme in 1991 (GEF, 2004). Regarding energy, the GEF's mission is to develop and transform markets for energy and mobility in developing countries so that over the long term, they will be able to grow and operate efficiently towards a less carbon-intensive path. However, GEF funding is limited, representing only 2% of funds from bilateral and multilateral sources for energy projects. While the level of support is small, the operational programmes of the GEF focus mainly on cost-effective energy efficiency and renewable energy investments, as well as on providing the incremental cost of promising climate-friendly technologies, e.g., solar thermal power plant, mobile and stationary fuel cell applications, grid-connected photovoltaic, and advanced biomass combustion (World Bank, 2006b; see also Table 7).

There are two other multilateral banks that also support energy projects in developing countries, namely the African Development Bank (AfDB) and the European Investment Bank (EIB). A review of the limited data for 2004/2005 from the AfDB suggests that the categories receiving the most support include health, education, water and sanitation, and emergency relief, although a few energy projects were funded in these years.[8] A general lack of data prevents the inclusion of the African Development Bank in this article, but the information available for 2004/2005 suggests that the addition of the AfDB would make only a marginal difference to the broad conclusions drawn in this article. The AfDB is promoting regional electricity markets in Africa via investments in transmission infrastructure to improve energy access. The AfDB is also revising its Energy Sector Policy, which is expected to place greater emphasis on the financing of low-carbon projects, including renewable energy and energy efficiency projects (World Bank, 2007).

TABLE 7 Global Environmental Facility support for energy between 1997 and 2005 by category (US$ million)

GEF	1997	1998	1999	2000	2001	2002	2003	2004	2005	Total	Percentage of total
Energy efficiency	44.5	42.8	45.9	13.3	53.6	45.4	42.6	45.6	39.1	372.8	35%
Gas power			0.7							0.7	
Hydro		4.9	1.5	0.7			0.4		0.5	8	1%
Gas Dist.	5.1			6.5			3.3			14.9	1%
Coal bed methane		6.2								6.2	1%
Wind				2.9	15.4		25.3	16.8	12.4	72.8	7%
Geothermal						5	26.7			31.7	3%
Power renew	56.3	55.3	21.6	39	60.7	33.8	19.9	15.6	71	373.2	35%
Solar	30.3	3.9	13.6	50.6	4.1	13.6	2.6	56.6	1.7	177	17%
Total	136.2	113.1	83.3	113	133.8	97.8	120.8	134.6	124.7	1,057.3	

The main mission of the EIB is to contribute towards the integration, balanced development, and economic and social cohesion of the member countries. It is governed by mandates from the European Union (EU). It began lending to Asia and Latin America in 1993, mainly for manufacturing, transport and telecommunication projects. For the period 2007–2013, the EIB is authorized to lend up to €3.8 billion for these regions. The €3.8 billion regional ceiling is broken down into indicative sub-ceilings of €2.8 billion for Latin America and €1.0 billion for Asia. It also operates in 79 African, Caribbean and Pacific countries.[9] In 2003–2008, the EIB is expected to channel €3.7 billion to these countries. The amounts allocated per country or per sector for both regions are not available. It has also announced plans to sell a 5-year euro 'climate awareness bond', whose returns are linked to the performance of a new index of companies with environmentally friendly policies. The proceeds will be used for renewable energy efficiency projects (EIB, 2007).

Several United Nations programmes also support energy projects in developing countries. For example, the United Nations Development Programme (UNDP) supported 546 energy-related projects between 1996 and 2005, with total financing of US$2.5 billion. This figure includes UNDP regular resources, resources from the Thematic Trust Fund, GEF grants and parallel funding, as well as other co-financing, such as government contributions. Improving equitable access to energy services by poor women and men to alleviate poverty and improve living conditions is an important goal that ranks higher than concern for climate change in many developing countries (Reddy, 2002). The UNDP's energy projects focus on three priority areas:

- strengthening national policy frameworks to support energy for poverty reduction and sustainable development
- promoting access to energy services in rural areas to support growth and equity
- financing for clean energy technologies for sustainable development.[10]

The UNDP plays an important role in promoting many small-scale projects to reach the poor, for example expanding access to modern cooking and heating fuel and decentralized electrical energy systems. Almost all UNDP funding comes from the GEF, bilateral sources and private financing. To avoid double-counting, these funds have not been included in our analyses.

6. Conclusions

Bilateral and multilateral support for energy projects totalled over US$64 billion during 1997–2005, with multilateral institutions accounting for nearly 70% of the support. It has remained in the range of 6–10% of all development assistance during this period, but has generally declined in real terms for the last 7 years. There has been a shift among the major categories receiving support. As can be seen in Figure 3, all bilateral and multilateral funds are averaged over two periods (1995–1997 and 2003–2005) to smooth the influence of individual years. Between those two periods, the power sector declined markedly, due largely to a decrease in support from the World Bank Group, IADB and bilateral programmes, as has support for coal projects. Energy efficiency has doubled on a percentage basis, while renewables have increased less dramatically. In many cases, these trends have probably been driven by factors other than climate change, but there apparently has been some recognition that lower GHG-emitting technologies need to be promoted and diffused among developing countries.

The various energy efficiency and renewable energy initiatives identified in this article tend to suggest that the MDBs are getting the message; that is, that the goals of mitigating

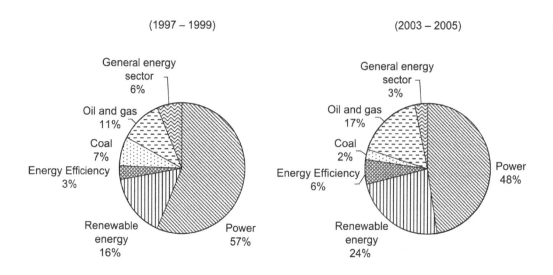

FIGURE 3 Bilateral and multilateral support for energy by category for selected periods

climate change, promoting sustainable development, and reducing poverty, can be complementary and integrated into operational programmes. Improving coordination among MDBs is now also a recognized need, and a few donors have taken steps to fill the resource gap.[11] However, given the need for a revolution to transform the global energy system, a much broader and sustained commitment will be needed by donors. The variability and decline in overall funding for lower GHG-emitting technologies over the 1997–2005 period suggests that programmes that address poverty, sustainable energy and climate change are fragile at best.

It should be noted that funding levels for projects do not tell the whole story. There is a continuing evolution of aid modalities under way as development financing for project-based activities is supplemented with macro-economic and sector-wide assistance. Increasingly, development assistance is being targeted at promoting policy reforms, institutional change, and capacity building, which are all needed to create enabling conditions for, and to reduce the investment risk of, private investors. Support for these activities is small relative to project investments,[12] but conceptually it may lead to more lasting and far-reaching changes than single projects in the energy sector of developing countries. How the environmental opportunities and consequences of these approaches will be addressed, and whether all such reforms will be 'climate-friendly', is not evident at this point (OECD, 2005).

In the coming decades, the demand for energy and financing in developing countries will be great. The International Energy Agency has projected a need for US$20 trillion, most of which will be needed by developing countries, to meet the demand for energy by 2030 (IEA, 2006). There is therefore a considerable gap between current public funding and projected financing requirements. While most of this gap may be filled by private capital, public funding, particularly grants, will be needed in order to reduce the risks associated with the introduction of new technologies and to encourage developing countries to implement the more environmentally friendly, but more costly, options. If large developing countries begin to fill this gap, and if their lending standards differ from those of the OECD countries, the ability and efforts of OECD countries and the MDBs to promote environmentally sustainable energy projects could be undermined.

The data also suggest that too much attention has been focused on the GEF in the context of the UNFCCC process. While this is understandable, given the unique relationship between the two, it seems apparent that greater attention should be directed to bilateral (OECD and non-OECD) and multilateral development assistance efforts, in order to encourage a further shift in the direction of renewables and energy efficiency. Japan and Germany, in particular, have a great opportunity to provide leadership by further mainstreaming energy efficiency and renewable projects in their development assistance portfolios, while still supporting the specific needs of developing countries. It might be said that 'as Japan and Germany go, so goes the direction of bilateral development assistance for energy'.

Several challenges will need to be met in the future. The first is to increase funding for the MDBs, to ensure that they do not become irrelevant and can remain viable institutions that promote a sustainable energy future (World Bank, 2007). While this article has shown that the level of MDB funding for energy is small relative to overall ODA and FDI, it is not irrelevant, as the MDBs often leverage project support with those of the private sector by a factor of five or more (EBRD, 2006). Filling the resource gap is largely the job of finance ministers, but ensuring that the ministers are 'educated, engaged and committed' will require a sustained effort. The meetings of the G8, UNFCCC and the annual meetings of the MDBs are forums wherein this dialogue can take place on a regular basis. The second challenge is to 'green' private-sector funds so as to ensure that investments made today do not pollute tomorrow. Governments can help through educational programmes, and the MDBs by catalysing investments in low-carbon technologies with private banks, but coalitions of stockholders, environmental non-governmental organizations and insurance companies who are concerned about climate change and financial risks will need to be mobilized, and in some cases empowered, to create this 'green energy' revolution. To be effective they will need good data on private sector investments, which are not easily accessible in most countries today.

Finally, as noted previously, different institutions use different categories and formats for tracking funding for energy projects. The lack of a common reporting format makes it difficult to determine whether and how multilateral institutions and bilateral programmes are shifting to respond to climate change and the challenge of building a more sustainable energy future. Tracking investments over the coming decades may become as important to the UNFCCC process as the monitoring of emission inventories, since investment data will enable short-term forecasts of changes in emissions to be made. An effort to standardize the collection and reporting of data on investments for energy projects appears warranted in order to make data more comparable and trends more reliable.

Acknowledgements

The authors would like to thank the following individuals for providing data and insightful comments: Jan Corfee-Morlot (OECD), Sujata Gupta (AsDB), Alan Miller (IFC), Christine Woerlen (GEF), Laura Berman (WB), Sam Frankhauser (EBRD), Gianpiero Nacci (EBRD) and Luis Gomez Echeverri (UNDP). The authors would also like to thank Andrzej Suchodolski and the OECD DAC statistics team for providing invaluable help in accessing the CRS data.

Notes

1. The Conference of the Parties to the UNFCCC, at its thirteenth session (Bali, Indonesia), established an *ad hoc* working group to address long-term cooperative actions beyond 2012, including the need to address enhanced financial resources (see UNFCCC Decision 1/CP.13).
2. See www.un.org/millenniumgoals/
3. See www.oecd.org/dac/stats/crs/guide
4. Iraq was excluded from the analysis of bilateral assistance for energy development in this article.
5. Personal communication from Eric Usher, United Nations Environment Programme, Paris.
6. See 'G8 calls for increased scrutiny of aid', *Financial Times*, 28 March 2007.
7. Multilateral institutions included in this study are: the World Bank Group (WBG), Asian Development Bank (AsDB), European Bank for Reconstruction and Development (EBRD), Inter-American Development Bank (IADB) and the Global Environment Facility (GEF).
8. See www.afdb.org/portal/page?_pageid=473,1&_dad=portal&_schema=PORTAL
9. See www.eib.europa.eu/
10. Personal communication with Luis Gomez-Echeverri, United Nations Development Programme, New York.
11. The UK has pledged US$1.6 billion for an environmental Transformation Fund and Japan has pledged US$2.1 billion in aid to the ADB to combat climate change and promote greener investment in the Asian region.
12. We estimate that, for the period covered by this article, bilateral funding for energy policy and administrative management was approximately US$2.5 billion.

References

Bayliss, K., McKinley, T., 2007, 'Providing basic utilities in sub-Saharan Africa: why has privatization failed?,' *Environment* 49(3), 24–32.

Easterly, W., 2006, *The White Man's Burden: Why the West's Efforts to Aid the Rest have Done So Much Ill and So Little Good*, Penguin Press, New York.

EBRD, 2006, *Energy Operations Policy Paper: Fuelling Sustainability and Growth*, BDS06-093, European Bank for Reconstruction and Development, London.

EIB, 2007, *Press Release*, Reuters News Service, London, 23 May 2007.

Ellis, J., Winkler, H., Corfee-Morlot, J., Gagnon-Lebrun, F., 2007, 'CDM: taking stock and looking forward', *Energy Policy* 35, 15–38.

G8, 2007, *Growth and Responsibility in the World Economy*, Summit Statement, 7 June 2007, Heiligendamm, Germany.

GEF, 2004, *Program Study on Climate Change*, Document GEF/ME/C.24/Inf.2, Washington, DC.

IEA, 2006, *World Energy Outlook 2006*, International Energy Agency, Paris.

IEA, 2007, *CO_2 Emissions from Fuel Combustion: Highlights 1971–2005*, International Energy Agency, Paris.

Kozloff, K., 1995, 'Rethinking development assistance from renewable electric power', *Renewable Energy* 6(3), 215–231.

Miller, A., 2008, 'Financing the integration of climate change mitigation into development', *Climate Policy* 8(2), 152–169.

Modi, V., McDade, S., Lallement, D., Saghir J., 2005, *Energy Services for the Millennium Development Goals*, International Bank for Reconstruction and Development, The World Bank and The United Nations Development Programme, Washington, DC.

OECD, 2005, *Development, Investment and the Environment: In Search of Synergies*, ENV/EPO C/GSP/2004/14, Organisation for Economic Cooperation and Development, Paris.

OECD, 2006, *Development Co-operation Report 2006*, Organisation for Economic Cooperation and Development, Paris.

OECD, 2007, *Common Reporting System User Guide: Statistical Methods and Terminology*, Organisation for Economic Cooperation and Development, Paris [available at www.oecd.org/dac/stats/crs/guide].

Reddy, A.K.N., 2002, 'Energy technologies and policies for rural development', in: *Energy for Sustainable Development*, Policy Agenda, UNDP, New York.

Tharakan, P.J., de Castro, J., Kröger, T., 2007, 'Energy sector assistance in developing countries: current trends and policy recommendations', *Energy Policy* 35(1), 734–738.

UNCTAD, 2006, *World Investment Report 2006: FDI from Developing and Transition Economies – Implications for Development*, United Nations Conference on Trade and Development, New York and Geneva.

World Bank, 1993, *The World Bank's Role in the Electric Power Sector*, World Bank, Washington, DC.

World Bank, 2003, *Private Participation in Infrastructure in Developing Countries: Trends, Impacts, and Policy Lessons*, Working Paper No. 5 (by C. Harris), World Bank, Washington, DC [available at http://rru.worldbank.org/Documents/PapersLinks/1481.pdf].

World Bank, 2004, *Operational Guidance for World Bank Staff: Public and Private Sector Roles in the Supply of Electricity Services*, World Bank, Washington, DC.

World Bank, 2006a, *Improving Lives: World Bank Progress on Renewable Energy and Energy Efficiency in Fiscal Year 2006*, World Bank, Washington, DC.

World Bank, 2006b, *An Investment Framework for Clean Energy and Development: A Progress Report*, Vice Presidency for Sustainable Development, Washington, DC.

World Bank, 2007, *Clean Energy for Development Investment Framework: The World Bank Group Action*, DC2007-0018, World Bank, Washington, DC.

Financing the integration of climate change mitigation into development

ALAN S. MILLER*

International Finance Corporation, 2121 Pennsylvania Ave NW, MS F3K-300 Washington, DC 20433, USA

The Bali Action Plan and many other authoritative recent climate reports point to expectations that additional financing will be central to future international agreements to address climate change. Several donor governments have announced commitments to contribute significant additional amounts of funding to support climate change financing in developing countries. However, the context for financing of climate change mitigation is evolving rapidly, with significant implications for climate policy. Two key changes are the dramatic improvement in access to capital in many of the most rapidly growing, large greenhouse-gas-emitting, developing nations and the increasing shift of wealth to oil-exporting countries and Asian central banks. Energy investment is fundamental to development and is capital-intensive, and access to finance is not equally available across countries and for different types of investments. Less carbon-intensive, clean energy investments frequently remain more difficult to finance, due to their smaller scale and innovative nature. Taking climate risk into account as an element of financing is potentially consistent with the investor's need to balance risks with expected returns, but the methodologies, geographical scale, and data required are not yet commensurate with the time periods and project scope typical of financing for developing countries. The policy challenge is in making the financing available commensurate with the scale and short time available for addressing climate change. Most of the likely targeted financing programmes will not be adequate for this purpose. Rather, policy makers need to focus on creating adequate signals that climate change will be an important and continuing factor in government policies for the foreseeable future in ways that will affect investor expectations of relative risk and reward. If this is done, financing will follow.

Keywords: developing countries; development; finance; investment; Global Environment Facility; mitigation; policies and measures; sustainable development; World Bank

Le plan d'action de Bali et autres rapports notoires récents sur le climat désignent l'attente d'un financement supplémentaire qui serait central aux futurs accords internationaux sur le changement climatique. Plusieurs gouvernements bailleurs ont annoncé leur engagement à contribuer des montants importants pour le soutien au financement du changement climatique dans les pays en développement. Cependant, le contexte de financement de l'atténuation du changement climatique évolue rapidement avec des conséquences importantes pour la politique climatique. Deux changements importants incluent d'une part l'amélioration considérable d'accès au capital dans de nombreuses grandes nations où l'augmentation des émissions de gaz à effet de serre est la plus rapide et, d'autre part, le transfert croissant des richesses vers les pays exportateurs de pétrole et les banques centrales asiatiques. L'investissement énergétique est fondamental au développement et est intensi en capitaux, et l'accès au financement n'est pas accessible à même mesure selon les pays et les différents types d'investissements. L'investissement dans les énergies propres ou plus sobres en carbone reste fréquemment plus difficile à financer à cause de leur plus petite échelle et leur nature innovante. La prise en compte du risque climatique en tant qu'élément de financement est potentiellement en accord avec le besoin des investisseurs d'équilibrer les risques avec les retours attendus, mais les méthodologies, l'échelle géographique, et les données requises ne sont pas encore à la mesure de la durée et de l'échelle des projets typiquement financés pour les pays en développement. Le défi politique est de rendre accessible un financement qui soit proportionnel à l'amplitude du changement climatique et la courte durée qu'il existe pour y

■ *Corresponding author. E-mail:* amiller2@ifc.org

CLIMATE POLICY 8 (2008) 152–169
doi:10.3763/cpol.2007.0432 © 2008 Earthscan ISSN: 1469-3062 (print), 1752-7457 (online) www.climatepolicy.com

lutter. Les programmes ciblés de financement les plus usuels ne seront pas appropriés à cette fin. Les décideurs devraient plutôt se concentrer sur la création de signaux adéquats visant le changement climatique en tant que facteur important et continu dans les politiques des gouvernements dans un futur prévisible, qui affecteront les attentes des investisseurs sur les risques et gains relatifs. Dans ce cas, le financement suivra.

Mots clés: atténuation; développement; développement durable; finance; investissement; la Banque Mondiale; le Fonds pour l'Environnement Mondial; pays en développement; politiques et mesures

1. Introduction

Access to finance is frequently cited as one of the key requirements for addressing climate change. Commitments to financing were central to the Bali Action Plan adopted at COP-13. The heart of the agreement, expressed in Paragraph 1(b), conditions 'nationally appropriate mitigation actions by developing country Parties' on the provision of 'technology, financing and capacity-building'. The importance of commitments to financial assistance, investment and technology transfer to developing countries is emphasized in the following paragraphs, which identify some of the expectations to be addressed during the negotiating process to go on until COP-15 in Copenhagen. Resources should be additional, adequate, predictable and sustainable; 'positive incentives' should be created for developing-country implementation of mitigation strategies; innovative means of funding for meeting the costs of adaptation by particularly vulnerable countries; public- and private-sector funding and investment should be mobilized (Para. 1(e)).

The Bali decisions reflected numerous reports and authoritative statements on financing during the year. The IPCC Working Group III report states that 'Funding sources for greenhouse gas (GHG) mitigation in developed and developing countries is a crucial issue in the international debate on tackling climate change' (Gupta and Tirpak, 2007). A report prepared by the UN Framework Convention on Climate Change on financial flows relevant to an international response to climate change quantified the additional investment that may be required in 2030 to return GHG emissions to current levels. The authors conclude that about US$200 billion of incremental financing will be needed for mitigation and adaptation globally – seemingly a large amount in absolute terms but equivalent to only about 0.5% of expected GDP and 1.1–1.7% of global investment in 2030 (UNFCCC, 2007). Numerous experts and organizations have made proposals for clean energy financing as an essential element of any future international climate change agreement (e.g. GLCA, 2007). Recent announcements by donor governments also indicate that sizable new commitments of funds for climate change mitigation are increasingly likely (DFID, 2007; ENB, 2007; World Bank, 2007a; Planet Ark, 2008).

While pronouncements of climate change financial needs proliferate, the context for international financing has evolved enormously in recent years. In particular, the developed countries and international financial institutions no longer have the influence and primacy they once did. The largest developing countries have substantial internal financial reserves, and high oil prices are causing a massive wealth transfer to oil-exporting companies and countries. There is a financial challenge, but it has much more to do with directing resources towards more climate-friendly options and less to do with simply making financing available. Investments and, more generally, financial flows are closely associated with development choices that will determine both the growth in GHG emissions and the vulnerability of societies to the impacts of climate change.

This article reviews the issues associated with making additional financing available for financing climate change mitigation in developing countries, in several parts: a brief review of the financing implications associated with baseline forecasts of GHG emission increases and new global financial realities, and then identifying the policy implications and opportunities for governments.

2. New financial and market realities

As the Bali Action Plan shows, financing – properly channelled – is widely seen to be a key requirement for reducing emissions. However, currently the availability of capital and its contribution to rapid economic growth are directly responsible for the rapid build-up in GHG emissions. The rise in GHG emissions and corresponding concerns about climate change reflect the rapid rate of economic growth in many developing countries. The rise in emissions has been closely associated with the rate of economic growth and, less obviously, the carbon intensity of that growth. Increasingly, much of that growth in economies and carbon emissions is coming from developing countries. In 2006, developing-country economies grew by 7%, or more than twice as fast as high-income countries, accounting for 38% of the increase in global output relative to a 22% share of global GDP (World Bank, 2007b). This trend is projected to continue, with the developing-country share of world output rising to almost one-third in 2030.

Economic growth in developing countries – particularly in China and India – has been closely associated with the increasing use of energy in general and electricity from coal in particular. According to projections by the International Energy Agency, in a business-as usual scenario, emissions from developing countries are projected to more than double between 2002 and 2030 (from 8.2 to 18.4 Gt CO_2) – much of this due to the combustion of coal and other fossil fuels for electricity (IEA, 2006, 2007). Growth in Chinese fossil fuel consumption has exceeded most forecasts, and recent analysis indicates that China may already have overtaken the USA as the largest emitter of GHG emissions, a decade ahead of some earlier predictions (Logan, 2006; Environmental News Service, 2007). The financing challenge for climate change is thus implicit within this new reality: channelling the increasing flow of investment dollars in more sustainable, climate-friendly directions without slowing or penalizing development goals.

3. The critical role of financing in energy choices

The availability of financing, whether from public or private sources, is critical for energy supply projects, due to their capital intensity. Coal mining and transportation, power plants, oil refineries, and transmission systems are among the most capital-intensive projects in any economy. Thus, expectations of continued economic growth are based on the assumed availability of very large sums for investment. The IEA estimates that, between 2005 and 2030, developing countries will need to invest $10 trillion in energy-related infrastructure ($3.7 trillion in China); more than half of total global requirements, much of this in power plants alone (IEA, 2006). On average, 1–1.5% of GDP is invested in energy worldwide, or $300–400 billion a year, with much higher levels in many developing countries (Goldemberg and Johansson, 2004). The cost and availability of capital is therefore key to making clean energy services available for development and, insofar as the climate regime can help direct more capital to such services, it can have a major positive impact (Gentry, 2000; Ogden, 2006).

From a global perspective, these percentages are consistent with historic norms and, while relatively large, are not infeasible. However, the challenge in raising these funds is changing with the increasing share of energy-related capital required by developing countries due to their higher growth rates. The total current investment in energy infrastructure in the OECD and developing countries is about equal. However, according to the International Energy Agency (IEA), in order to support projected economic growth to 2030, investment in energy infrastructure will have to increase by more than 50% in developing countries while remaining roughly constant in the OECD (IEA, 2006).

Channelling investment towards alternative, more climate-friendly, forms of energy requires addressing multiple problems, as discussed below. Renewable energy technologies are typically equally capital-intensive – a high proportion of costs are incurred up-front but with near zero operating (fuel) costs – but are usually smaller and less mature. Efficiency technologies are highly dispersed and embodied in consumer decisions at all levels of scale, from individual home appliances to small enterprises to large manufacturers. New technologies, such as carbon capture and storage, typically require some initial public support due to their high risks and the uncertainty of rewards to any individual firm.

4. Financing development: new and more distributed sources of wealth and investment

Net private capital flows to developing countries jumped dramatically to record levels in 2005, exceeding $500 billion, with roughly the same amount expected in 2006.

> The combination of several years of low interest rates has increased global liquidity substantially. Despite the increase in short-term interest rates, the persistence of low long-term interest rates, due in part to high savings rates among oil-exporting countries, has kept global liquidity abundant (World Bank, 2006a).

Bank lending and booming stock markets in emerging markets also reflect these positive financial developments. Many developing countries have taken advantage of these trends by issuing bonds with longer maturities, buying back debt to lower interest costs, and pre-funding future financing requirements. Repayments more than offset increases in foreign aid; net official flows of grants and loans was a *negative* $71.4 billion in 2005, led primarily by net repayments to the IMF of $41.1 billion (World Bank, 2006b).

Recent higher oil prices have been another source of wealth accumulation, leading to new sources of investment managed in oil-producing nations (Mufson, 2007). In 2006, oil-exporting countries became the largest source of global capital flows – almost $500 billion, a significant source of liquidity and lower interest rates (Farrell and Lund, 2007, 2008).

The growth in financial flows to developing countries has, however, been unevenly distributed and roughly corresponds with the largest and most rapidly growing sources of carbon emissions – in 2005, China, India and South Africa received almost two-thirds of portfolio equity flows (World Bank, 2006b). The attractiveness of the investment climate is partly a function of market size and location, but government policies are also increasingly recognized as important factors.

> They influence the security of property rights, approaches to regulation and taxation, the provision of infrastructure, the functioning of financial and labor markets, and broader governance features such as corruption. Improving government policies and behaviors that shape the investment climate drives growth and reduces poverty (World Bank, 2007a).

While policy uncertainty is the constraint most often cited in business surveys, the issues are country-specific. In Bangladesh, the 'number one' issue is the lack of reliable power, in Hungary high tax rates, and in Guatemala crime, theft and disorder.

From a climate-change perspective, a key point is that the countries with the most ready access to the capital markets include those responsible for the lion's share of growth in GHG emissions. Thus the availability of capital *per se* is not a primary constraint or barrier to clean energy investments. If capital is not available, it is due primarily to other factors such as inappropriate regulatory policies, perceived technical risks, or other factors leading to an inadequate expected return on investment. Insofar as the primary source of development financing is increasingly domestic in the largest GHG-emitting nations, a further implication is that *a focus on national policies to influence investment flows is essential*. National energy policies and regulations, as well as economic policies that encourage some types of investments (e.g. energy subsidies) and discourage others (e.g. import duties), are increasingly important influences on financing related to climate investments, while external influences, including the programmes of international financial institutions, are correspondingly in decline. The evaluation and support of such national programmes is therefore an important focus (see examples from China, India and Mexico discussed below).

Another consequence of improved access to capital in many developing countries has been the emergence of technically advanced, global leaders in clean energy technologies based in developing countries. The vocabulary of 'technology transfer', still prevalent in Convention processes, which assumes a largely one-directional flow from North to South, is thus increasingly out-of-date.[1] Developing countries are increasingly among the global leaders in renewable energy investment and additions to capacity. China is expected to invest more than $10 billion in renewable energy technologies in 2007, second only to Germany; Brazil is a global leader in ethanol; and China and India are rapidly establishing themselves as leading manufacturers of wind energy (Martinot, 2006; Martinot and Junfeng, 2007; World Bank, 2007b).

A poor investment climate is a deterrent to investment in many of the poorest developing countries, which includes many of those most vulnerable to climate change. Consequently, these countries continue to be the most dependent on externally provided assistance (ODA) and debt relief. Net disbursements of ODA increased dramatically to $106.5 billion in 2005; $27 billion above the 2004 level. However, much of this increase was attributable to debt relief and special-purpose grants, including the response to the tsunami and other disaster relief. In general, more aid is going to the poorest countries, particularly those in Africa, and more is being given in the form of grants (World Bank, 2006b). The implication for climate change is that aid trends have been moving away from influencing the largest sources of GHG emission growth in favour of greater emphasis on meeting the energy needs of the poor – a trend that may be at odds with requirements for future climate change mitigation agreements.

Another consequence of the increasing accumulation of wealth in developing countries has been a corresponding growth in financial transactions among developing countries. For example, South–South foreign direct investment was $47 billion or 36% of the total FDI to developing countries in 2003, versus $14 billion (16%) in 1995 (World Bank, 2006b). Developing countries are becoming greater sources of development aid, including debt forgiveness for Africa, concessional loans, and preferential export credits. By 2010, China's export promotion programme may be lending and guaranteeing more than $70 billion annually for infrastructure and other large-scale investments in developing countries (Rich, 2007).

The availability of alternative sources of investment outside the transparency required by international financial institutions is another new factor in development finance. In contrast with aid programmes administered by the industrialized countries, the Chinese programme is outside international agreements on environmental standards and reporting and, according to official statements, comes with 'no strings attached'. From a climate-change perspective, this represents another source of financing so far largely outside efforts to move investment in a more climate-friendly direction. The environmental and social consequences of China's external investment have been the subject of some criticism (Rich, 2007). The Chinese government has recently shown awareness of the need to make the banking sector a partner in screening its lending for environmental risk, although so far without noting the applicability of such policies to investments outside the country (IFC, 2007a).

As should already be apparent, the fact that financing is increasingly available in the largest markets for conventional investments does not mean that it is readily available to address climate-change needs. As noted earlier, financial terms are most favourable for what is known and proven, which tends to mean fossil fuels and conventional, as opposed to innovative, more energy-efficient technologies, and standard design and construction practices as opposed to those that may be more climate-safe (WBCSD, 2007). Financing programmes will also not be utilized if the costs are too high and the benefits too uncertain. There are also biases in the institutions and traditional criteria for lending that tend to relatively favour particular investment types, as discussed further below.

5. Access to capital for more climate-friendly investments

Capital flows follow expected commercial returns; unless policy intervenes, established perceptions of risk and reward will dictate investment choices. In the energy sector, this tends to mitigate against what is new and therefore less proven; investments made at a smaller scale (unless means are found to offset proportionately higher transaction costs); and fundamentally against anything that costs more.[2] The issues associated with climate-friendly and safe financing vary by country, technological opportunity and market circumstances. Numerous justifications have been offered to explain the need for dedicated climate change financing programmes, including evidence of inadequate commercial lending for energy efficiency improvements (particularly in developing countries), the high initial costs for early-stage application of promising new technologies, and the absence of demonstrated models for assessing climate risks and adopting response measures. These issues reflect some of the diversity of financing challenges.

The challenges vary for different technologies, investment scales, and different investors. As noted in a report of the World Business Council for Sustainable Development (WBCSD):

> Project based investments in emerging and lower carbon energy technologies are some of the more complex and risky forms of investment. They are normally highly capital intensive and play into a world where the average consumer is unwilling to pay a premium for their energy services (WBCSD, 2007).

A World Bank assessment similarly concludes:

> unless the policy framework changes and appropriate instruments are in place to facilitate investments in new technologies, developing countries are expected to follow a carbon-intensive development path similar to that of their developed country counterparts (World Bank ESSD, 2006).

Understanding how to channel financing more effectively to climate-friendly technologies requires a more detailed discussion of the diversity of climate solutions and the barriers they face.

5.1. Financing energy efficiency and renewable energy technologies

Investments to reduce energy demand can reduce net capital requirements but have their own challenges. They typically imply higher up-front capital costs and reduced operating costs relative to conventional equipment, but the higher initial cost can be much more than offset by the value of savings, particularly if credit is given for avoided investment in new supply. For example, an IEA alternative policy scenario for 2005–2030 reduces CO_2 emissions by 16% or 6.3 Gt, equivalent to the total current emissions of the USA and Canada. Total energy investment is lower than in the reference scenario but the allocation of investment changes significantly; spending on end-use equipment and buildings increases by $2.4 trillion, but more than $3 trillion less is spent on supply-side investment. 'On average, an additional dollar invested in more efficient electrical equipment, appliances and buildings avoids more than two dollars in investment in electrical supply' (IEA, 2006; Enkvist et al., 2007). Obvious problems arise when consumers are not well informed on the value of savings from higher initial costs or are not in a position to fully benefit from them (e.g. if the saving accrues to the utility or if the buyer is a landlord and the tenant pays energy costs).

Many less obvious economic and social benefits of energy efficiency improvements are typically not considered in evaluating investment choices, including increased energy security and labour productivity, lower pollution and maintenance costs, and indirect public and occupational safety (Goldstein, 2007). Despite these benefits, motivating cost-effective investments in energy efficiency continues to be surprisingly difficult. As a consequence, many authorities have concluded that regulatory measures, including minimum standards for buildings and appliances, may be required in order to achieve widespread adoption of cost-effective efficiency opportunities (Stern, 2006; Enkvist et al., 2007).

Renewable energy technologies have a very high proportion of capital costs, as once put into operation they require no fuel (excluding biomass systems) and minimal maintenance. (Biomass systems are a significant exception, as the identification and cost of feedstock is an important contributor to total cost.) Costs are also closely associated with changes in technology (reflected in manufacturing costs and product performance) and materials. In the long term, the former is expected to result in continuing cost declines, particularly for products such as solar cells that can be manufactured in small scales that typically result in declining costs with production experience ('learning curves'). In the short term, however, capital costs for wind and solar energy have in general been rising in recent years due to increasing material costs and growth in demand faster than can be met with existing manufacturing capacity (EIA, 2006).

Expectations of continuing high oil prices have brought substantial investment into clean energy alternatives. A study by the UN Environment Programme (UNEP) estimates that global investment in clean energy in 2006 reached $100 billion, of which about $30 billion was for corporate buyouts and the remainder for new investments (UNEP, 2007a). Most capital is still going to developed-country markets in response to subsidies and incentive policies such as mandatory purchase obligations for utilities, but developing-country investments are growing faster and now exceed $14 billion annually. The carbon market is another promising source of investment in clean energy, although it is still at an early stage.

5.2. Financing smaller-scale clean energy technologies and enterprises

Clean energy technologies come in many scales but, compared with conventional power plants, most are relatively small. A large wind machine today is typically about 3 megawatts (MW) versus about 400–600 MW for a full-sized coal burning power plant. Solar cells are typically produced in panels in factories that may manufacture the equivalent of 250 MW per year. Panels can be sold individually for households or grouped together to provide 1 MW or more. Efficiency technologies are a feature integrated throughout the economy and thus can be found at all scales, as small as improved lighting devices costing a few dollars, and as large as new devices for making steel, costing millions of dollars.

The dispersed, smaller scale of many efficiency and renewable energy technologies is advantageous for many reasons; opportunities can be found in almost every economy, and large-volume manufacturing creates the potential for economies of scale and learning from experience. However, financing smaller-scale enterprises and applications is a barrier in developing countries. The interest rates and borrowing terms available to these groups are typically less favourable, and few developing-country banks offer loans for efficiency upgrades which lack conventional collateral. This gap is particularly important for promoting energy efficiency throughout the economy, including such household products as refrigerators and air-conditioners, which are increasingly popular consumer goods in the most rapidly growing developing countries. Consumer decisions are also important for energy use in the building sector, a rapidly growing segment of developing countries due to urbanization and population growth. Energy use in this sector in developing countries is projected to grow at almost 3% per year until 2030 (EIA, 2006).

As discussed below, the International Finance Corporation (IFC) and other international financial institutions have had some success in dealing with this problem by providing local banks with a combination of technical assistance (TA) and partial risk guarantees. The TA provides training in understanding the risks and opportunities associated with energy efficiency lending, while the risk guarantees provide banks with some confidence in taking the risks associated with new markets.

Financing of small enterprises can be critical for business development. For example, numerous donor programmes have sought to nurture small clean energy companies providing energy services to rural households without access to electricity. These firms often lack access to the capital needed to become established and grow, and furthermore may need help with business planning. While costly and labour-intensive, the effort to help small firms survive may be essential seed capital for future development. Some efforts to address this need have adopted the framework of 'patient capital', a reference to the need for investors with a tolerance for investments on longer terms with lower return requirements, compensated by greater environmental, social and development impacts (EC, 2006).

Another variant of this problem is the need for regulatory frameworks and business models compatible with distributed generation technologies, modern small-scale means of generating power well suited to the needs of power-starved developing countries. The financing costs for these smaller-scale technologies can be very high relative to those for larger power plants; a problem that might be amenable to a combination of standardized regulatory policies for power purchases; master agreements or standard contracts for end-user finance; and risk-sharing through utility purchase and eventually securitization.

5.3. Financing new climate-friendly technologies

The most established and accepted case for government intervention in support of climate-friendly investments is with respect to the development and use of new technologies, primarily for electricity generation. Attracting investment to the early stages of new technology development is particularly difficult due to the higher risk, the likelihood of longer time periods before earning a return, and the greater uncertainty with respect to which firms will eventually succeed in a competitive market. Relative to other sectors of the economy, investment in early-stage energy technology has fared poorly in recent decades. Total public spending on research and development increased by almost 50% between 1988 and 2004, but spending on energy-related research and development declined nearly 20% over the same period. Private investment also declined. Key factors were the decline in oil prices, privatization leading to competition and increased emphasis on short-term returns, and regulatory uncertainty (Stern, 2006; WBCSD, 2007).

Recent increases in public energy expenditures have only partially offset this trend and the *Stern Report* recommends a doubling of investments to around $20 billion a year, as well as an increase in deployment incentives of two to five times from the current level of $34 billion (Stern, 2006). The need is primarily for a public subsidy to offset the risks of early-stage development as opposed to financing *per se*. In response to the recent run-up in oil prices and concerns about energy security, there has been a dramatic increase in risk capital available for some types of alternative fuels, particularly biofuels, although such funding is not as available in developing countries where land use and other conditions may actually be more suitable (Mathews, 2007).

There are few sources of dedicated financing for the commercialization of new energy technologies in developing countries. One of the few, and almost certainly the largest, is the Global Environment Facility (GEF), discussed more generally below. Over roughly a decade, the GEF has approved more than $350 million, mostly in the form of grants, in support of 25 new technology commercialization projects in developing countries (Miller, 2007). A wide range of technologies have been supported, but the largest recipients have been solar thermal power plants, fuel cell-powered buses, and several approaches to a more efficient use of biomass for power combustion. This effort has so far achieved very modest results, with many projects dropped or cancelled without completion of any operational facility. Recently the GEF has proposed that this strategy be assigned very low priority going forward.

In the context of the Montreal Protocol, there has been some noteworthy success with focused efforts to develop and transfer new technologies for replacing chemicals that threaten the ozone layer. In order to make certain that their suppliers did not use ozone-depleting chemicals regulated in the industrialized countries, large electronics companies developed alternatives and provided training and technical assistance to firms in developing countries. The result was technically and economically effective in a relatively short period of time. While some financial assistance was available through the Multilateral Ozone Fund, the key to success was, in many cases, the transfer of manufacturing knowledge in a commercial context and not the provision of financing (Andersen and Sarma, 2002; Andersen et al., 2007). The World Bank Group also recently stated that it is exploring options for accelerating the implementation of new technologies in its client countries – a significant shift from past practice and a further indication that a business-as-usual approach to climate change will not be sufficient (World Bank SDN, 2007b).

6. Financing energy services for poverty alleviation and its relationship to financing for climate-friendly investments

A further challenge to making more financing available for climate-related investments is to assure poorer countries that funds are not being redirected from the primary objective of overseas development aid (ODA), poverty alleviation. Resources provided to developing nations need to be 'new and additional' (Bali Action Plan, par. 1(e)(i)). This is a legitimate concern because the growth in GHG emissions is coming from a relatively small number of countries and is associated with power generation and manufacturing rather than the provision of basic energy services to the poor.

The two goals are distinct except insofar as climate change may make it more difficult to meet development goals; both will require substantial focusing of resources to meet international goals.[3] From the perspective of GHG emissions, what matters is how modern energy services are provided to the poor. Socolow (2006) has calculated that if the basic human needs for the estimated 1.6 billion people without access to electricity and the 2.6 billion people without clean cooking fuel were to be met overnight, the increased energy use required would produce less than a 3% increase in global CO_2 emissions. However, emissions could be much greater if the poor are provided with electricity supplied by inefficient coal plants using poorly managed transmission systems with high loss rates, and if electricity is used for inefficient lighting and other energy-wasteful purposes. On the other hand, emissions could also be much lower if using energy-efficient technologies and low-carbon energy sources.

One example of an effort to promote climate-friendly development in a form that addresses the energy needs of the poor is a World Bank programme called Lighting Africa, which aims to promote the use of low-power lighting devices for the rural poor. By combining light emitting diodes (LEDs) with solar power, high-quality lighting can be provided to rural households at lower cost than kerosene and conventional batteries, while avoiding any increased emission of greenhouse gases (see, generally, http://lightingafrica.org).

7. Climate-friendly financing: existing mechanisms and recent experience

There have been many efforts to channel investment in clean energy technologies to developing countries. These experiences offer some valuable lessons and include some significant successes, but also highlight the difficulties that frequently arise from putting too much emphasis on financing as a means of changing energy systems.

> The [World Bank Group's] ability to work across multiple sectors and to deal at both the policy and project level; its presence in the field; its ability to innovate; the leverage which its finance provides; and its convening power – all of these advantages need to be brought to bear on what is one of the largest and most complex problems the development community has faced (World Bank SDN, 2007a).

It is also difficult to find any precedents for efforts to deal at the scale and rate of change required to address climate change.

While private financial flows now substantially exceed official development assistance (ODA), the latter is still an important resource for poor countries unable to borrow on reasonable terms, new technologies, and for advisory services such as capacity-building for policy and regulatory reforms (World Bank SDN, 2007b). ODA specifically available for clean energy and climate change purposes has been relatively limited. The primary source of public information on trends in development assistance, the OECD Development Assistance Committee (DAC), lumps all energy- and transportation-related aid within the category 'economic infrastructure'. Disbursements under this heading – which includes support for fossil-fuel-related activities as well as clean energy activities – declined from $18.4 billion in 1984/1985 to $13.3 billion in 2004/2005 (OECD, 2006). Donor-identified energy funding was about 3% of total bilateral aid in 2005, and slightly less than 4% of World Bank finance.

The World Bank (WB) reports a steady increase in energy-related commitments, about $7 billion for the 3-year period FY03–05 versus more than $10 billion expected over the subsequent 3-year period, FY06–08 (World Bank SDN, 2007a). Clean-energy-related lending by the World Bank has also been increasing in recent years, as discussed below, and was almost $1.5 billion in FY07, or 40% of total energy commitments (World Bank, 2007a).

Targeted financing programmes are not a universal panacea and must be tailored to local markets and banking. The World Bank and other international financial institutions have established numerous such programmes only to find an absence of consumer demand because of other problems related to regulatory frameworks, market awareness and affordability (Taylor et al., 2008). The barriers to a good investment climate noted above, particularly those related to inadequate government policies (such as lack of protection for property rights and lengthy delays in establishing new businesses), lack of essential infrastructure, and project sponsors with weak credit ratings will undermine or block the efficacy of otherwise attractive financing programmes.

7.1. Institutional remedies: the influence of the World Bank and other IFIs on financing for climate change

The international financial institutions (IFIs) have had a modest, albeit growing, commitment to support access to clean energy services as an essential element of poverty alleviation: the attainment of the Millennium Development Goals for health, education, clean water, etc. depend on the availability of modern energy services. The IFIs have also been increasing their commitment to support energy efficiency and renewable energy in recent years, although starting from very low baseline levels. For example, at the Bonn Renewable Energy Conference in 2004, the World Bank Group (WBG) announced a commitment to increase its lending for defined clean energy projects by an average of 20% per year for 5 years. As part of this effort, the Bank issues an annual progress report and, based on the first two years' results, has substantially exceeded its targets, increasing lending on 'new renewables' and energy efficiency from $459 million in FY2005 to $821 million in FY2007. A joint report by the WB and other IFIs found that this trend was generally true in all of them: 'All the MDBs [multilateral development banks] are giving priority to energy efficiency', bringing small-scale renewable energy technologies to client countries 'is a key priority', and all the MDBs 'have embarked on efforts to catalyse low-carbon investments through new financial instruments which can mobilize additional funding, promote innovation, and help fund the incremental costs of these projects' (ADB et al., 2007). Critics of the WBG and other IFIs argue that these institutions should eliminate all support for fossil-fuel-related investments in favour of clean energy projects (Bank Information Center, 2006). This argument has been considered and rejected as inconsistent with the Bank's primary focus on development, but most probably will be reconsidered in the context of climate change (EIR, 2003; Bank Information Center, 2007).

The ability and influence of the Bank to act effectively as a promoter of clean energy has also been a continuing question. The Bank has historically had mixed results with projects that provide substantial subsidies for higher-cost technologies, and arguably also has limited experience and comparative advantage with respect to commercializing new technologies (IFC, 2007b; Miller, 2007). Insofar as the Bank and other IFIs are primarily lending institutions, their influence is contingent on the willingness of borrowers to take on debt for specific purposes. As other sources of capital have become more available, the Bank's ability to impose conditions and dictate priorities has also been in decline. Where clean energy projects make economic sense and policy environments are favourable, alternative sources of financing are often available on equivalent or even better terms. As discussed above, the rise in oil prices and increasing availability of capital globally mean that the IFIs are in a less dominant position as financiers, except when policy advice and concessional resources are required.

Targeted clean energy financing programmes have had some notable success within the WBG with the application of targeted technical assistance and partial risk guarantees to engage local banks in lending for clean energy investments (primarily efficiency upgrades). These projects require some concessional resources but have very high leverage; once banks become comfortable with the different lending criteria needed to evaluate investments justified by energy saving, the projects become self sustaining and even self-replicating as other banks duplicate product offerings. In the case of the International Finance Corporation (IFC), projects are now in effect in eight countries including two of the largest and least energy-efficient, Russia and China. With $54 million in support from the GEF and other donors supporting clean energy investments by more than 20 financial institutions, banks have lent more than $120 million for projects with a much greater value (World Bank, IFC and MIGA, 2007). The IFC is now proposing to scale-up such activities to support $500 million worth of lending annually, without the need for donor funds. Such projects can only be implemented where financial markets are adequately developed and receptive; conditions which, fortunately, are being met in a growing number of countries.

Another role for the European Bank for Reconstruction and Development (EBRD) and IFC, the two most private-sector-oriented of the IFIs, is to demonstrate more aggressive means of identifying opportunities for clean energy upgrades associated with their mainstream investments (EBRD, 2007; World Bank, IFC and MIGA, 2007). Both institutions describe ongoing efforts to 'push the envelope' through review of their portfolios, financing audits (EBRD), requiring clients to evaluate GHG emissions (IFC), and establishing benchmarks for different types of investments (EBRD). These measures benefit from donor support but may be replicable by interested private banks through cooperative information-sharing efforts (e.g. the Equator Principles).

An important need arguably inadequately addressed by existing international arrangements is to share lessons and experience across countries and institutions. The IEA remains linked to the OECD but is gradually expanding its efforts with respect to clean energy technologies, and is also seeking to engage more effectively with large developing countries. The Bonn Renewable Energy Conference in 2004 resulted in REN21, an ongoing secretariat for information exchange on trends in the global renewable energy market. Some energy experts propose the creation of an international clean energy agency to assume responsibility for information exchange and technology promotion in this field, although this idea has yet to receive much governmental support (Geller, 2003).

Most probably there is little government appetite for the creation of new international institutions. However, as already hinted above, there is some indication of a willingness among the IFIs to take on expanded mandates in the funding of low-carbon energy programmes in partnership with their largest clients. An exploration of this approach became possible with the agreement of the G8 on a climate action plan at Gleneagles in July 2005 (G8, 2005). In response, the World Bank Group, in cooperation with other leading IFIs (particularly EBRD and ADB), have spent the past year preparing approaches for significantly expanding the scale of their support for clean energy finance in large developing countries – particularly the 'Plus 5' countries: China, India, Brazil, Mexico and South Africa. The World Bank released two reports on a Clean Energy Investment Framework in 2006, a short 'Action Plan' in March 2007, and a progress report in September 2007 (World Bank ESSD, 2006; World Bank SD, 2006; World Bank SDN, 2007a, 2007b).

7.2. Financing via the Global Environment Facility (GEF)

The Global Environment Facility (GEF), a financial mechanism of the UNFCCC governed by an independent Council of 32 donor and recipient countries, has been the most important source of dedicated financing for climate change mitigation projects. As of 2004, the GEF had committed more than $1.6 billion for over 500 projects and activities in more than 80 countries, with a total investment value now four to six times greater than at its founding as a pilot programme in 1991 and subsequent restructuring as an independent entity in 1994 (Hennicke et al., 2007). Projects have included financing for the removal of barriers to cost-effective energy efficiency and renewable energy investments, substantial subsidies for several promising climate-friendly technologies (e.g. solar thermal power plants, mobile and stationary fuel cell applications, grid-connected PV, advanced biomass combustion), and measures to promote low-carbon transportation alternatives (e.g. bikeways and bus rapid transit).

7.3. Financing via the carbon market

The GEF was initially a unique source of financing for climate change mitigation projects but, in recent years, carbon trading has become a much larger resource. With the onset of the first commitment period rapidly approaching in 2008, the volume and (inconsistently) the prices paid for carbon offsets have been steadily rising. In 2005, the aggregated value of global carbon markets exceeded $10 billion, with much greater than expected values in the first half of 2006. About half of traded volumes, or about $5 billion, was in developing countries (World Bank and IETA, 2006). Carbon trading cannot be directly compared with the GEF, as the two have very different roles and reach very different types of investments. In contrast with the GEF, which is publicly administered and adopts its programme priorities based primarily on the expected long-term market on GHG emissions, carbon trading is primarily intended to engage the power of the market to find the lowest possible costs of carbon abatement (although numerous specialized funds and 'premium' buyers provide some demand for blended products that achieve a wider range of developmental characteristics).

In the short run, the greatest carbon offset value has been for investments in reducing methane and other GHGs with very high warming effects relative to CO_2. More than half the traded volumes in 2005 were for the destruction of hydrofluorocarbons (HFCs); because of their very high GHG value and low destruction cost, reductions can be had for a cost equivalent to $1/tCO_2$ or less, and accomplished relatively quickly. Once such projects are included in the CDM pipeline, the likelihood of success is very high – more than 90%, compared with 64% for wind projects according to UNEP analysis (UNEP, 2007a). Going forward, the availability of reductions from HFCs is finite and, in the most recently available pipeline data (1 April 2007), account for about a quarter of projected 2012 CERs (Certified Emission Reductions).

In contrast, energy efficiency and renewable energy projects are typically relatively small and consequently have correspondingly high transaction costs. Renewable energy projects also tend to have much higher abatement costs. Together, these clean energy projects amounted to only about 10% of volumes in 2005, although this share appears to be rising based on the status of the CDM/JI pipeline as of 1 April 2007 (UNEP, 2007a). In the short term, the concern is the marginal development benefit associated with HFC destruction. In one major project managed by the World Bank in China, the government has agreed to put a substantial share of the proceeds into a trust fund for projects with defined sustainable development benefits.

The HFC projects illustrate the tension inherent in balancing the desire for low-cost carbon abatement in the interests of achieving the overriding objectives of the climate convention, with requirements for a wider range of local development benefits. Both objectives are of obvious importance, although if the imposition of developmental benefits is imposed in an overly restrictive way, the decline in trading could mean few benefits of any kind. This challenge has attracted growing interest from 'think tanks' and individual experts including the World Resources Institute and IISD, resulting in some interesting proposals (e.g. the WRI proposal for Sustainable Development Policies and Measures and the Development Dividend project of the IISD).

7.4. Channelling resources via national policies

The rapid rise in financial resources within the largest and most rapidly growing developing countries suggests that an important priority for influencing financial flows is to identify policies to channel local resources in a more climate-friendly and safe direction. The potential for such strategies has been promoted in numerous recent studies such as the *World Energy Assessment*, beginning with reducing market-distorting subsidies for fossil fuels, which approach $100 billion per year in non-OECD countries (Goldemberg and Johansson, 2004). Bilateral aid agencies and international financial institutions have increasingly focused on such measures to create sustainable frameworks for clean energy development.

In China, a Renewable Energy Promotion law, developed and implemented with the benefit of more than $200 million from the World Bank and Global Environment Facility, took effect on 1 January 2006. The Chinese government adopted the law after an assessment of international models and experience, based on a feed-in tariff approach used in Germany and Spain, in which the purchase of specifically identified renewable energy technologies is mandated at a fixed price. The implementation experience to date has produced mixed results, as the regulations provided a fixed price for biomass but relied on competitive bidding for wind farm development. The winning prices proved to be so low that the developers selected had difficulty in obtaining financing and construction was delayed (Cherni and Kentish, 2007; Wang, 2007).

Another World Bank clean energy programme with GEF support is under development for India, in this case focused on coal-fired power plant rehabilitation. Fossil-fired power plants in India are among the least efficient in the world, about 13% below the world average. If power plants in India, China, and other inefficient countries could be brought up to the standards of those in the Nordic countries and Japan, this would reduce CO_2 emissions by over 800 Mt (Graus et al., 2007). The government of India has initiated a programme to rehabilitate its existing coal-fired stations. The World Bank is supporting this effort with a project to demonstrate energy-efficient rehabilitation as a model for operational practices nationwide (GEF, 2006).

In Mexico, several GEF projects support various elements for the successful development of a wind industry. A UNDP project has been established to enable the creation of a wind turbine research facility, train technicians, and promote joint ventures with wind turbine manufacturers. UNEP is assessing solar and wind resources to provide the basic information essential for siting wind projects. Finally, the World Bank is working with the government to develop and implement electricity regulatory policies favourable to the purchase of wind-generated power, including a competitive purchase system and performance-based incentive payments through a 'green fund', with GEF support (Mata, 2006; REN21, 2006).

These policies are indicative of a growing trend for adoption of renewable energy policies in developing countries. Martinot (2006) identifies such policies, reflecting diverse degrees of commitment and diverse approaches, in Brazil, Chile, Columbia, Egypt, India, Madagascar, Malaysia, Mexico, Morocco, Pakistan, the Philippines, South Africa, Thailand, Tunisia, Turkey and Uganda. From a financial perspective, these policies sometimes provide a critical source of revenue (e.g. via feed-in tariffs and mandatory purchase requirements), but more generally provide project developers with legitimacy and a higher level of public recognition helpful in capital markets. The fact that such policies are designed and implemented by national and local authorities also improves the likelihood that climate change, energy security, and general environmental concerns will be considered alongside other development goals.

8. Implications for policy makers

References to the need for new and additional financing in the Bali Action Plan and recent promises by several donor governments need to be understood in the context of radical changes in the realities of international finance. Financial power is dispersing as oil-rich countries and Asian central banks are becoming increasingly important players, and potential sources of investment are becoming more diffuse and, in some cases, less transparent. However, these resources are much more volatile, are unevenly distributed, and from a climate-change perspective tend to be more accessible for larger, more established, and more conventional energy sources as opposed to energy efficiency, renewable energy, and other more climate-friendly alternatives. The basic ground rules for commercial investment have not changed; money is drawn to the highest potential return adjusted for risk. Climate-friendly investments are disadvantaged by higher risk, smaller transaction size, and regulatory uncertainty; all of which makes them less attractive relative to more conventional alternatives. Higher oil prices have begun to change this picture and, if maintained over time, will be a powerful inducement to continue the rise in private investment in clean energy.

Financing issues also vary by market and technology. Support for research on early-stage carbon capture and storage is a very different challenge than financing a wind energy project, or a household solar water heater. Local market conditions and the policy environment also always matter; the willingness to invest in a wind project depends not only on the wind regime, but also on regulatory policies that establish the value and certainty of the price to be paid for the electricity generated. A generally good investment climate such as in the USA has only a mixed record in supporting wind energy because the primary form of federal support has been insufficiently predictable – a tax credit approved for relatively short periods that requires regular reauthorization.

The carbon market and GEF-funded projects are two significant, but inadequate, sources of funding for the incremental costs of climate-friendly and safe investments. Policies to channel locally based resources to these goals are beginning to be significant and may have to bear the largest share of the burden in developing countries. As national and local authorities are in the best position to integrate climate change with development goals, this trend may prove to be a highly positive consequence of the new financial realities.

Recent trends with respect to investment in climate-friendly technologies have been promising. However, the challenge for climate policy is the need to move quickly to promote changes on a much larger scale than ever before. This can be done most effectively if policy makers engage with the financial sector to identify the necessary assurances that investments in climate-friendly technologies will – on a competitive basis – be rewarded in the market place. Once the risk of climate change is properly reflected in the investment calculus, financing will follow.

Acknowledgements

The views expressed are the author's own and do not necessarily reflect those of the IFC.

Notes

1. Discussions at Bali revealed many examples of both the old rhetoric of technology as something owned by the North to be 'transferred' to the South and some insightful discussions of the importance of national policies in creating conditions for investment in technology, as well as examples of technology leadership in developing countries. See, in particular, the High-Level Roundtable Discussion on International Technology Cooperation, a plenary event at COP-13 and part of the Convention video archive (available at www.un.org/webcast/unfccc/2007/index.asp?go=071213).
2. Comparative evaluation of costs of technologies with different characteristics is not a simple matter. For example, investments in gas turbines require assumptions about future gas prices, while investments in wind energy require

localized wind data and an analysis of the system value of an intermittent resource. Moreover, companies and financiers use different decision criteria when making investments, depending on local circumstances and priorities, e.g. net present value, internal rate of return, and payback period. The investment perspective of an individual consumer weighing an additional up-front cost for a more efficient refrigerator will be substantially different from the decision approach employed by a utility seeking to improve its system reliability and expand capacity (WBCSD, 2007).

3. The United Nations Millennium Development Goals (MDGs), adopted by international agreement in 2000, define development targets for reducing world poverty by 2015, including halving the share of the global population living on less than $1 a day (see, generally, www.un.org/millenniumgoals). While there is no energy-focused MDG, numerous studies and reports have focused on the importance of providing modern energy services as a precondition to achieving goals for water, health, sanitation and hunger reduction (Flavin and Aeck, 2005).

References

ADB (Asia Development Bank), Africa Development Bank, European Bank for Reconstruction and Development, European Investment Bank, Inter-American Development Bank, World Bank Group, 2007, *The Multilateral Development Banks and the Climate Change Agenda: A Joint Report* [available at http://go.worldbank.org/V2B1OCEKK0].

Andersen, S., Sarma, K., 2002, *Protecting the Ozone Layer: The United Nations History*, Earthscan, London.

Andersen, S., Sarma, K., Taddonio, K., 2007, *Technology Transfer for the Ozone Layer*, Earthscan, London.

Bank Information Center, 2006, *How the World Bank's Energy Framework Sells the Climate and People Short* [available at www.seen.org/PDFs/Energy_Framework_CSO.pdf].

Bank Information Center, 2007, *Comments on the World Bank Group's Extractive Industries Review Implementation Report* [available at www.bicusa.org/en/Article.3127.aspx].

Cherni, J., Kentish, J., 2007, 'Renewable energy policy and electricity market reforms in China', *Energy Policy* 35(7), 3616–3629.

DFID (UK Department for International Development), 2007, *DFID and the G8/Climate Change* [available at www.dfid.gov.uk/g8/climate.asp].

EBRD (European Bank for Reconstruction and Development), 2007, *Sustainability Report 2006: Promoting Sound Sustainable Development*, EBRD, London.

EC (European Commission), 2006, *European Commission Proposes 100 Million Euro Global Risk Capital Fund for Developing Countries to Boost Energy Efficiency and Renewables*, Johannesburg Renewable Energy Coalition [available at http://ec.europa.eu/environment/jrec/energy_fund_en.htm].

EIA (Energy Information Administration), 2006, *International Energy Outlook 2006*, United States Department of Energy, Washington, DC [available at www.eia.doe.gov/oiaf/ieo/index/html].

EIR (Extractive Industries Review) 2003, *Striking a Better Balance; the World Bank Group and Extractive Industries. The Final Report of the Extractive Industries Review*, Extractive Industries Review, Washington, DC.

ENB (Earth Negotiations Bulletin), 2007, *Earth Negotiations Bulletin* 12(353), 14 December 2007.

Enkvist, P., Naucler, T., Rosander, J., 2007, 'A cost curve for greenhouse gas reduction', *McKinsey Quarterly* 1, 35–45.

Environmental News Service, 2007, *China Now Number One in Carbon Emissions; USA Number Two* [available at www.ens-newswire.com/ens/jun2007/2007-06-19-04.asp].

Farrell, D., Lund, S., 2007, 'The world's new financial power brokers', *McKinsey Quarterly* December 2007.

Farrell, D., Lund, S., 2008, 'The new role of oil wealth in the world economy', *McKinsey Quarterly* January 2008.

Flavin, C., Aeck, M., 2005, *Energy for Development: The Potential Role of Renewable Energy in Meeting the Millennium Development Goals*, Worldwatch Institute, Washington, DC.

G8, 2005, *G8 Gleneagles 2005* [available at www.g8.gov.uk/servlet/Front?pagename=OpenMarket/Xcelerate/ShowPage&c=Page&cid=1091235520309].

GEF (Global Environment Facility), 2006, *Status Report on the Climate Change Funds*, GEF Council Paper GEF/C.28/4/Rev.1, May 2006.

Geller, H., 2003, *Energy Revolution: Policies for a Sustainable Future*, Island Press, Washington, DC.

Gentry, B., 2000, 'Private capital flows and climate change: maximizing private investment in developing countries under the Kyoto Protocol,' in: L. Gomez-Echeverri (ed.), *Climate Change and Development*, Yale School of Forestry and Environmental Studies, New Haven, CT, 187–199.

GLCA (Global Leadership for Climate Action), 2007, *Framework for a Post-2012 Agreement on Climate Change* [available at www.unfoundation.org/files/pdf/2007/GLCA_Framework2007.pdf].

Goldemberg, J., Johansson, T. (eds), 2004, *World Energy Assessment: Overview 2004 Update*, United Nations Development Programme, New York.

Goldstein, D.B., 2007, *Saving Energy, Growing Jobs*, Bay Tree Publishing, Point Richmond, CA.

Graus, W., Voogt, M., Worrell, E., 2007, 'International comparison of energy efficiency of fossil power generation', *Energy Policy* 35(7), 3936–3951.

Gupta, S., Tirpak, D., 2007, 'Policies, instruments, and co-operative arrangements', in: *IPCC Fourth Assessment Report: Mitigation. Report of Working Group III*, Cambridge University Press, Cambridge, UK.

Hennicke, P., Borbonus, S., Woerlen, C., 2007, 'The GEF's interventions towards climate change mitigation and sustainable development', *Energy for Sustainable Development* 11(1), 13–25.

IEA (International Energy Agency), 2006, *World Energy Outlook 2006*, IEA, Paris.

IEA (International Energy Agency), 2007, *World Energy Outlook 2007: China and India Insights*, IEA, Paris.

IFC (International Finance Corporation), 2007a, *Chinese EPA to Base Green Financing Guidelines on IFC Environmental, Social Standards*, Press Release, 30 November 2007 [available at ifcnet.ifc.org/intranet/news_events.nsf/Content/NewsflashPlus_112907ChinaEPA].

IFC (International Finance Corporation), 2007b, *Selling Solar: Lessons from a Decade of IFC and World Bank Experience*, International Finance Corporation, Washington, DC.

Logan, J., 2006, *Surging Chinese Carbon Dioxide Emissions*, EarthTrends, 20 November 2006 [available at earthtrends.wri.org/updates/node/110].

Martinot, E., 2006, *Renewables Global Status Report 2006 Update*, REN21 Secretariat, Paris, and Worldwatch Institute, Washington, DC [available at www.ren21.net/globalstatusreport/download/RE_GSR_2006_Update.pdf].

Martinot, E., Junfeng, L., 2007, *Powering China's Development: the Role of Renewable Energy*, Worldwatch, Washington, DC.

Mata, J., 2006, *Renewable Energy in Mexico*, Presentation at the International Grid Connected Renewable Energy Policy Forum, 1 February 2006, Mexico City [available at www.gridre.org].

Mathews, J., 2007, 'Biofuels: what a biopact between North and South could achieve', *Energy Policy* 35, 2550–3570.

Miller, A., 2007, 'The Global Environment Facility program to commercialize new energy technologies', *Energy for Sustainable Development* 11(1), 5–12.

Mufson, S., 2007, 'Oil price rise causes global shift in wealth', *Washington Post*, 10 November 2007, p. A1.

OECD (Organisation for Economic Co-operation and Development), 2006, *Development Database on Aid from DAC Members* [available at www.oecd.org/document/33/0,2340,en_2649_34447_36661793_1_1_1_1,00.html].

Ogden, J., 2006, 'High hopes for hydrogen', *Scientific American* 295(3), 94–101.

Planet Ark, 2008, *UN Climate Head Welcomes Marshall Plan Climate Fund*, 17 January 2008 [available at www.planetark.org/dailynewsstory.cfm/newsid/46461/story.htm].

REN21, 2006, *Mexico Renewable Energy Initiative* [available at www.ren21.net/iap/commitment2.asp?id=95].

Rich, B., 2007, 'Blank checks for unsustainability', *Environmental Forum* 24(2), 30–34.

Socolow, R., 2006, *Stabilization Wedges: Mitigation Tools for the Next Half-Century*, Keynote address at the World Bank Energy Week, 6 March 2006 [available at www.worldbank.org/energyweek].

Stern, N., 2006, *The Economics of Climate Change: The Stern Review*, Cambridge University Press, Cambridge, UK.

Taylor, R., Govindarajalu, C., Levin, J., Meyer, A., Ward, W., 2008, *Financing Energy Efficiency: Lessons from Brazil, China, India and Beyond*, World Bank, Washington, DC.

UNEP (United Nations Environment Programme), 2007a, *CDM Pipeline Overview* [available at http://cd4cdm.org/].

UNEP (United Nations Environment Programme), 2007b, *Global Trends in Sustainable Energy Investment 2007*, UNEP and New Energy Finance [available at www.unep.org/pdf/SEFI_report-GlobalTrendsInSustainableEnergyInverstment07.pdf].

UNFCCC (United Nations Framework Convention on Climate Change), 2007, *Investment and Financial Flows to Address Climate Change*, UNFCCC, Bonn, Germany.

Wang, X., 2007, 'Legal and policy frameworks for renewable energy to mitigate climate change', *Sustainable Development Law & Policy* 7(2), 17–20, 77–78.

WBCSD (World Business Council for Sustainable Development), 2007, *Investing in a Low-Carbon Energy Future in the Developing World*, WBCSD, Geneva, Switzerland.

World Bank, 2006a, *Global Economic Prospects 2007: Managing the Next Wave of Globalization*, World Bank, Washington, DC.

World Bank, 2006b, *Global Development Finance: The Development Potential of Surging Capital Flows*, Vol. I, World Bank, Washington, DC.

World Bank, 2007a, *Forest Carbon Partnership Facility Launched at Bali Climate Meeting*, 11 December 2007, Press Release [available at http://web.worldbank.org/WBSITE/EXTERNAL/EXTABOUTUS/ORGANIZATION/EXTPRESIDENT2007/0, contentMDK:21582088~menuPK:64822319~pagePK:64821878~piPK:64821912~theSitePK:3916065,00.html].

World Bank, 2007b, *Atlas of Global Development*, Collins, Glasgow, UK.

World Bank ESSD (Environment and Socially Sustainable Vice Presidency and Infrastructure Vice Presidency), 2006, *Clean Energy and Development: Towards an Investment Framework* [available at http://siteresources.worldbank.org/DEVCOMMINT/Documentation/20890696/DC2006-0002(E)-CleanEnergy.pdf].

World Bank, IFC (International Finance Corporation), MIGA) Multilateral Investment Guarantee Agency, 2007, *Catalyzing Private Investment for a Low-Carbon Economy: World Bank Group Progress on Renewable Energy and Energy Efficiency in Fiscal 2007*, World Bank, Washington, DC.

World Bank SD (Vice Presidency for Sustainable Development), 2006, *An Investment Framework for Clean Energy and Development: A Progress Report* [available at http://siteresources.worldbank.org/DEVCOMMINT/Documentation/21289621/DC2007-0002(E)-CleanEnergy.pdf].

World Bank SDN (Sustainable Development Network), 2007a, *Clean Energy for Development Investment Framework: The World Bank Group Action Plan*, 6 March 2007 [available at http://siteresources.worldbank.org/DEVCOMMINT/Documentation/21289621/DC2007-0002(E)-CleanEnergy.pdf].

World Bank SDN (Sustainable Development Network), 2007b, *Clean Energy for Development Investment Framework: Progress Report of the World Bank Group Action Plan*, 28 September 2007 [available at http://siteresources.worldbank.org/DEVCOMMINT/Documentation/21510693/DC2007-0018(E)CleanEnergy.pdf].

World Bank, IETA (International Emissions Trading Association), 2006, *State and Trends of the Carbon Market 2006*, World Bank, Washington, DC.

climate policy

■ synthesis article

Adaptation and the poor: development, resilience and transition

ANNE JERNECK[1], LENNART OLSSON[2]*

[1] Department of Economic History, Lund University, Sweden
[2] LUCSUS – Lund University Centre for Sustainability Studies, Lund University, Sweden

Risk minimization is no longer a sufficient survival strategy for poor people in livelihood systems increasingly exposed to frequent extreme events. This calls for comprehensive adaptation to climate change. Within the climate change regime, adaptation is as central as mitigation but needs to be much more explicitly addressed at local, national and global levels. There is also a need for policy renewal in other international regimes that are central to adaptation, such as environment, human rights, development and trade. Accordingly, this article addresses poverty-relevant adaptation through the medium of three discourses: development, resilience, and transition theory. *Development*, as a post-war project of theories, strategies and policies, spells out the links between rich and poor countries and offers modernization trajectories but few solutions for adaptation and sustainability transitions. *Resilience*, as an analytical framework emerging in ecology in the 1970s in reaction to ideas of equilibrium, depicts incremental changes and capacity to preserve systems within given frames but does not recognize that social change mainly implies transitions to renewed forms of production, consumption and distribution with new combinations of organization, institutions and technology. *Transition theory* focuses on profound multilevel changes in complex (sub)systems, thereby offering a powerful framework for theorizing empirical findings and promoting adaptation as a transition to sustainability.

Keywords: adaptation; climate change; development; insurance; poverty alleviation; resilience; transition theory

Minimiser les risques n'est plus une stratégie de survie suffisante pour les personnes pauvres dans des systèmes de subsistance de plus en plus exposés a des événements extrêmes fréquents. Cela nécessite une adaptation au changement climatique intégrale. Dans le régime du changement climatique l'adaptation est tout aussi centrale que l'atténuation mais a besoin d'être abordée de manière plus explicite aux niveaux local, national et mondial. Il y a aussi un besoin de renouvellement des politiques dans d'autres régimes internationaux qui sont centrales à l'adaptation, y compris l'environnement, les droits de l'homme, le développement et le commerce. Par conséquent cet article aborde l'adaptation des pauvres à travers trois types de discours: le développement, la résilience, la théorie des transitions. Le développement, en tant que projet de théories, stratégies et politiques de l'après-guerre, révèle les liens entre les pays riches et les pays pauvres et propose des trajectoires de modernisation, mais ne propose que peu de solutions de transitions en adaptation et durabilité. La résilience, en tant que cadre analytique écologique qui a émergé dans les années 70 en réponse aux idées sur l'équilibre, décrit les changements par étapes et la capacité de préservation des systèmes à l'intérieur de cadres particuliers, mais ne reconnaît pas que le changement social implique surtout une transition vers des formes renouvellées de production, de consommation et de distribution selon de nouveaux groupements organisationnels, institutionnels et technologiques. La théorie des transitions se concentre sur le changement multi-niveaux profond dans des (sous)systèmes complexes offrant de ce fait un cadre puissant pour établir les données concrètes dans un cadre théorique et promouvoir l'adaptation en tant que transition vers la durabilité.

Mots clés: adaptation; assurance; changement climatique; développement; lutte contre la pauvreté; résilience; théorie des transitions

■ *Corresponding author[1]*. *Email*: Lennart.Olsson@lucsus.lu.se

CLIMATE POLICY 8 (2008) 170–182

doi:10.3763/cpol.2007.0434 © 2008 Earthscan ISSN: 1469-3062 (print), 1752-7457 (online) www.climatepolicy.com

1. Introduction

The climate change regime, with the United Nations Framework Convention on Climate Change (UNFCCC) and the Kyoto Protocol (KP) as its main components, is primarily concerned with mitigation of climate change, i.e. reductions in greenhouse gas (GHG) emissions. We argue that adaptation is as central to the Convention as mitigation and that the regime allows for this, but the UNFCCC needs to be elaborated in terms of adaptation. Without reducing the urgency of mitigation, the potentials of adaptation must be addressed more specifically and strongly in research and action. This is especially so in the context of the poorest of the poor who, for the reasons discussed below, suffer the most, not only from the general weight of poverty but also from climate vulnerability (IPCC, 2007b).

This article suggests how adaptation can be addressed at different levels and within various international regimes. For that purpose, adaptation is discussed through the lenses of three major discourses: development, resilience and transition theory. We define adaptation as the adjustment of ecological and socio-economic systems to current or projected climate changes (Verheyen, 2002). Following the IPCC (IPCC, 2007b) we define vulnerability to climate change as the degree to which natural and social systems are susceptible to, and unable to cope with, adverse impacts. We define discourse as a system of thoughts composed of ideas, beliefs, attitudes, actions and practices (Lessa, 2006).

The need for adaptation is urgent in the context of developing countries, where adaptation must be coupled with efforts to improve rural and urban livelihoods, especially for the poorest and most vulnerable (UNHABITAT, 2003). Development, as theory, strategy and practice, advocates and promotes profound change to eradicate poverty. But despite its policy-oriented and problem-solving capacity (Meier, 1995), development fails to deliver economic and social inclusion, especially in sub-Saharan Africa, where levels of poverty and inequality are still significant and even increasing within many countries (World Bank, 2006). Consequently, transition processes that offer social change in terms of sustainable livelihoods (Ellis, 2000), equality and freedom (Sen, 1999) are urgently needed.

The goal of the UNFCCC, according to Article 2, is to stabilize GHG in the atmosphere at levels that prevent *dangerous* anthropogenic interference with the climate system. But the interpretation of 'dangerous' is relative and contextual rather than absolute. What is dangerous in an actual situation is, in the end, often determined by a society's capacity to cope with and to adapt to climate change. To add to the complexity, danger can be interpreted externally by objective measurements such as actual loss of physical property, or internally by perceived danger and subjectively experienced fear (Dessai et al., 2004). And if a society's adaptive capacity is low, even minor climate changes might entail danger. This allows us to conclude that adaptation is as central to the climate change regime as mitigation.

However, as regards binding commitments in the current climate regime, the language on adaptation is vaguer and more ambiguous than on mitigation. In the UNFCCC and the KP, the texts on adaptation focus solely on planning rather than action. The UNFCCC says 'prepare for' (4.1.e) rather than implement, and 'take climate change considerations ... to the extent feasible' (4.1.f) rather than giving them highest priority. The KP says 'strive to' (2.3) rather than implement policies and measures. Hence, we argue that, compared to mitigation, for which there are legally binding commitments and compliance mechanisms, the legal base of adaptation is very weak. Yet, the adaptation agenda is advancing, with the Nairobi Work Programme lasting five years from COP-12 in 2006 and aiming at improved understandings of climate change impacts, vulnerability and adaptation. Nevertheless, there is more focus on improved data and assessment methods than on international commitments.

The vagueness in language and weakness in policy are partly explained by politics in the negotiations of the Convention and partly by the priority given to mitigation over adaptation as a solution to the problem of climate change. When the UNFCCC was negotiated, it was anticipated that climate change effects would have severe social repercussions only in a distant future, thus providing a motive for giving less attention to adaptation as a tool for coping with climate change. Another reason for not giving equal priority to adaptation was the fear that it would distract attention and action from mitigation. Much evidence now indicates that it is time to correct these misunderstandings (IPCC, 2007a, 2007b; UNEP, 2007).

2. Reasons for adaptation

In 2007, the IPCC established that, due to low adaptive capacity and potentially severe climate change impacts, developing countries are more vulnerable to climate change impacts (IPCC, 2007b). This, in combination with certain other factors, makes adaptation particularly important, especially for the poorest of the poor, most of whom depend on agriculture, fisheries or forest-related activities, mainly at subsistence level. Most agricultural systems are very vulnerable to extreme climate events, such as drought, storms and floods (World Bank, 2007). Also, owing to the variability of hydrological regimes, even irrigated agriculture is highly susceptible to climate variability (IPCC, 2007b). Large rural and agricultural populations, many of which are poor, are located in semi-arid areas in Africa, Asia and Latin America or in low-lying coastal and riverine areas, especially in Asia. Since many of the world's poorest people live in sub-Saharan Africa, in places with limited access to food markets (World Bank, 2006), there is further stress on already vulnerable livelihoods in cases of food emergency (Mwabu and Thorbecke, 2004). Hence, we argue that, in particular, the following four factors make adaptation increasingly important.

2.1. Accelerating climate change

The rate of build-up of atmospheric CO_2 was unprecedented in the last decade, thereby increasing the risk of rapid and dangerous climate change. Climate scientists agree that, even in the hypothetical case of immediate stabilization of CO_2 levels, the temperature increase is expected to continue for a century, making substantial climate change unavoidable. (IPCC, 2007b).

2.2. Increasing vulnerability to climate variability impacts

Irrespective of climate change, vulnerability to climate impacts may increase due to rising populations in climate-sensitive areas such as parts of Bangladesh, China, Egypt and Pakistan (IPCC, 2007b), as recently seen in Bangladesh in late 2007.

2.3. Increasing vulnerability due to multiple stressors

In some settings, certain conditions increase the vulnerability to climate impacts, such as (i) low agricultural productivity partly caused by poor or decreasing access to inputs; (ii) malfunctioning markets and distribution systems due to poor or deteriorating infrastructure (World Bank, 2006); and (iii) shortage of labour because of rural–urban migration (Tiffen, 2003; Olsson et al., 2005). In addition, (iv) deterioration of natural and modified ecosystems caused by land-use change may increase the risk and severity of climate impacts, while (v) imports of subsidized food may out-compete local production and exacerbate domestic agricultural conditions (Kates, 2000; O'Brien and Leichenko, 2000; World Bank, 2007).

2.4. Deteriorating social conditions and health status

High and increasing burdens of diseases such as HIV/AIDS, malaria and TB contribute to making climate impacts more damaging. Labour shortages may cause shrinking food production and collapsing social services that could increase risks of food crises as a result of even minor climate impacts (de Waal and Whiteside, 2003).

3. Development

Development defies simple definitions due to its long post-war history of ideology, theory and practice rooted in 'the Enlightenment' and the ideas of the early nineteenth century. Methodologically, development implies both goals and means (Cowen and Shenton, 1996). If goals are expressed in long-term aims and means in short-term policies, then the aim of expanding people's choices could be achieved through policies of increased participation. However, context-bound conditions and conflicting interests are overlooked in such general definitions (Rist, 1999). Modernization and industrialization are other goals and means of development, but experiences of pollution and resource depletion (Angel and Rock, 2005) imply that 'modernity no longer seems so attractive in view of ecological problems' (Pieterse, 2001). In light of these and other contested views of development, the relevance of the discourse may be questioned (Cornwall, 2007).

Development is highly institutionalized at universities; in international conventions; via the influential Bretton Woods system, and through official development assistance (ODA). Although development continuously mainstreams new issues into its domain, the common denominator, in idea and practice, is poverty alleviation – aiming at poverty eradication (Burnell, 2002). But instead of describing poverty theoretically as 'getting by', the daily practice to make ends meet, and 'getting out', the long-term strategy of social mobility (Lister, 2004), development visions are framed in simplified images or quantitative terms, such as *reducing the number* of people living *under the poverty line* (Millennium Development Goals); *lifting people out of poverty* (Fan and Hazell, 2001); or encouraging people to *make it to the first step of the development ladder* (Sachs, 2005). We argue that an ambition to build sustainable livelihoods (Ellis, 2000), thereby addressing vulnerability and adaptation needs, serves the poorest in a more constructive way.

Development theory neglects the dynamics of the physical environment in which (socio-economic) development is supposed to take place (Cowen and Shenton, 1996; Pieterse, 2001). Even when development theory highlights the fact that poverty and environment are intertwined, it often stops there, or resorts to sweeping statements on the need for an efficient use of resources. It may even state that the topic of development and environment is highly controversial (Meier, 1995). With the assumption, thrown up by global climate change, of profound global, regional and local repercussions on the natural resources and assets on which livelihoods of the poor are based (IPCC, 2007b), it becomes a problem when the development discourse externalizes negative impacts of resource exploitation and pollution. While the scientific community agrees that climate change will alter the conditions for production and consumption substantially, the development discourse lacks a systemic analysis of the Earth system and its social implications.

Development visions may lack an explicit focus on risks posed by increasing climate change impacts, but construction projects often include them. In the planning and construction of long-lasting infrastructure, such as bridges, dams and roads, investors must consider climate variability and potential climate change relevant for the expected life span of the investment; a good example is the guidelines developed by the World Bank for screening their investments in climate-sensitive sectors (van Aalst, 2006). Many development ambitions and efforts, such as national and regional development strategies, could (in our view) learn from such thinking.

Mainstreaming, as a process, may not solve burning social, political and environmental issues. The continued loss of biodiversity (Mace et al., 2005) and the lingering absence of gender equality (Moser, 2005) are conspicuous examples. Mainstreaming may create conflicting goals, loss of political edge, and methodological problems resulting from an overloading of the discourse. As examples, sustainable development is more complex than the 'greening' of development projects, while gender inequalities are more complex than the often simplified 'gendering' of development projects (Kabeer, 2005).

In contrast, sustainable development (SD), as a paradigm and transition process, strives to deal with both temporal and nature–society complexities. As we see it, SD offers at least three advantages over the development discourse. First, SD theorizes the Earth system *per se* as well as short- and long-term dynamics and relations to society; secondly, as a consequence of severe and partly unavoidable future impacts of climate change, SD involves future generations and societies; and, thirdly, SD appeals to all countries to embark on a sustainability transition, whereas development appeals only to developing countries. These core aspects of SD are under-theorized by development theory, absent from development practice, but compatible with transition theory.

4. Resilience

The idea of resilience of social-ecological systems (SES) is a strong and, in some circles, predominant way of addressing adaptation. But there is considerable confusion about the meaning of resilience, both theoretically (Gallopin, 2006) and in practice (Klein et al., 2003; Armitage and Johnson, 2006). To trace its origins, the concept of resilience was successfully introduced in ecology in the early 1970s as a response to the, then predominant, idea of ecosystems striving towards equilibrium:

> Resilience determines the persistence of relationships within a system and is a measure of the ability of these systems to absorb change of state variable, driving variables, and parameters, and still persist (Holling, 1973).

More recently the concept of resilience has found its way into social sciences:

> The ability of human communities to withstand external shocks or perturbations to their infrastructure, such as environmental variability or social, economic or political upheaval, and to recover from such perturbations (Adger, 2000).

In the context of climate change, resilience has become a common concept related to vulnerability and adaptation. Vulnerability is sometimes described as the flipside of resilience, implying that the loss of resilience results in vulnerability to changes that previously could be absorbed (Folke et al., 2002). This is illustrated by the three dimensions of resilience adopted by the Resilience Alliance (Carpenter et al., 2001):

- The amount of disturbance a system can absorb and still remain within the same state or domain of attraction
- The degree to which the system is capable of self-organization
- The degree to which the system can build and increase the capacity for learning and adaptation.

A fundamental problem with resilience, as we see it, is the implicit normative assumption of preservation of the system and thus resistance to change (Gallopin, 2006). In many cases where ecological systems are closely linked with social systems, such as agriculture and aquaculture, there is a strong desire to prevent major changes to the ecological system (such as degradation of the soil or coastal vegetation). But for the ecological system to remain within its domain of attraction, the social system needs to change radically or even sever its links with the ecological system. Hence, there is a built-in contradiction in the concept of resilience when it is applied to complex systems where subsystems with conflicting goals are linked.

From a resilience perspective, a logical policy response to adaptation needs is that insurance can provide a means of strengthening the adaptive capacity, i.e. society's resilience (Linnerooth-Bayer et al., 2005; Gurenko, 2006a, 2006b). But, from the point of view of the poorest of the poor, there are two crucial limitations to insurance. First, it implies that you *have* assets to insure and, second, that you *have the financial means to buy* the insurance. We have identified three types of livelihoods where insurance might even be counterproductive because insurance would delay a long-term solution to the problem by encouraging people to continue with a livelihood for which there is no sustainable basis.

- Livelihoods where the resource base is at risk of being permanently and severely damaged owing to anticipated climate change. Examples include dryland agriculture in areas where increased frequency and intensity of droughts are anticipated; coastal regions in danger of flooding due to sea-level rise; and irrigated agriculture in areas in danger of profound change of hydrological regimes.
- Livelihoods where the resource base is gradually eroded by other processes, such as fishing livelihoods in areas of over-fishing and/or severe pollution; and livelihoods based on water extracted from diminishing water reserves.
- Livelihoods where social and/or economic conditions gradually erode the long-term basis through replacement of technology, shifts in world market preferences, etc.

Many regions where vulnerability to climate change is high, such as southern Africa, the Sahel and the Greater Horn of Africa, suffer from more or less chronic food insecurity. Conventional insurance schemes for crops have been tested in many countries but have failed (Hess and Syroka, 2005). Weather-based insurance, where the claims are based on meteorological data rather than reported losses, is another kind of insurance that is currently being tested in several countries, such as Bangladesh, India, Nepal, Pakistan and Malawi (Linnerooth-Bayer and Mechler, 2006; Mechler et al., 2006). Some of the problems of conventional crop insurance can be avoided, but success in this requires well-functioning markets and timely meteorological information – two factors notoriously lacking in areas dominated by smallholders and subsistence farmers. Another potential hurdle for insurance to reach the poorest of the poor is the many localized climatic impacts that may not be extreme in a climatic sense but which may cause a collapse of households on the margin (Hutchinson, 1998). We argue that if such events become more frequent they may cause much damage that goes unrecorded because it is too localized or the magnitude is below the threshold for reporting.

5. Transition

A different view on adaptation emerges from transition theory rooted in social theory and technology systems studies (Rotmans et al., 2001; Foxon, 2007). Transitions are transformation processes in which societies, or subsystems thereof, change profoundly in terms of structures, institutions and relations between actors. After a transition, the society, or a subsystem, operates according to new assumptions and rules (Rotmans et al., 2001), thus indicating a range of new practices.

The Green Revolution (GR) can serve to illustrate transition theory. The GR is often described as a technological change involving new crop varieties and agrochemicals. But the GR was in fact part of a much more fundamental change in national and international politics, markets and institutions (Djurfeldt and Jirström, 2005); thus it was a transition in which new technologies based on scientific research were introduced and supported by a new and comprehensive institutional package, which in turn gave rise to several other adaptation processes (Burton et al., 1993).

Technology and its relationship with institutions is a central theme in transition theory. Viewed through the lens of transition theory, adaptation problems with livelihoods at risk from climate change will be understood as part of a complex system with multiple chains of causality. It may also be characterized by institutional as well as technological lock-ins (Foxon, 2007). And, importantly, the allocation of power plays an important role in an analysis spanning multiple levels, such as niches, regimes and landscapes (Rip and Kemp, 1998).

These three levels represent a useful heuristic for understanding technological and social change (Geels, 2002) rather than an ontological description. The *niche level* refers to individual actors (or groups of actors), technologies or practices. On this level, the symptoms of the problem are identified – in this case the risk of damage from climate change impacts on the livelihood. The *regime level* refers to the web of institutions governing the predominant practices at the niche level – in this case it could represent regional markets, local credit systems and government services. The *landscape level* refers to slowly changing social, physical and natural structures, such as physical infrastructure, international political institutions, macro-economic conditions, and the natural environment – in this case transportation constraints, agricultural trade policies and subsidies, structural adjustment programmes, and global climate change.

The regime level is removed from the visible symptoms of the problem and often characterized by resistance to changes, due to internal interactions, alliances and linkages (Foxon, 2007). The landscape level may promote incremental change. In this case it could be price adjustments or insurance schemes, while the niche level may need radical changes for the sake of sustainable livelihoods, such as a complete shift from crop production to livestock production or from rural to urban location. Using credits rather than insurance represents a logical policy implication of analysing adaptation as a transition. While insurance may conserve the current livelihood, credits may instead promote change.

Adaptation can occur at any level, from plant, field or farm, to national or international policy; adaptation is therefore a multifaceted decision-making process (Smit and Skinner, 2002). In the context of transitions, this would mean interdependent multiple levels, from niche to regime and landscape. A good example would be a change from crop production to livestock, involving a change in agricultural practices at the niche level, but also regime-level changes in markets and infrastructure, as well as changes in international trade at the landscape level.

The political and social responses after the Dust Bowl events in the 1930s in the Midwest of the USA represent a concrete example of a major transition relevant for adaptation to climate change. The late 1920s saw good crop yields and high prices for wheat, leading to a rapid expansion of the cropped area. Everybody was badly hurt, though, when drought hit the Great Plains in 1930, resulting in mass migration. By 1940, 2.5 million people had left. The multiplicity of responses to this crisis was a successful transition in which niches, regimes and the landscape level interacted to promote and maintain the transition to a sustainable agricultural region through soil conservation. As shown in Table 1, interventions occurred at different levels and in all domains: economic, social, political, legal, infrastructure and scientific (see Hansen and Libecap, 2004).

TABLE 1 Categorization of various responses to the Dust Bowl problem in the US Midwest organized chronologically and according to the levels proposed by Geels (2002) (information compiled from Worster, 1979)

	Niche (micro)	Regime (meso)	Landscape (macro)
1933		Farm Credit Act: set up a system for local banks to provide credits to farmers. Federal Surplus Relief Corporation (FSRC): set up to distribute emergency relief.	Emergency Banking Act: restore faith in the banking system. Emergency Farm Mortgage Act: prevent farm closure by helping farmers who cannot pay their mortgages. Stabilization policy: stabilize prices of agricultural products.
1934	Soil Conservation Service (SCS): establish 79 demonstration areas to encourage farmers to adopt soil conservation measures.	Farm Bankruptcy Act: restrict banks' ability to dispossess farmers. Grazing Act: make federal land available for grazing.	Soil Conservation Services: develop and implement new soil conservation programmes.
1935		Drought Relief Service: buy livestock at reasonable prices to be distributed by FSRC.	Works Progress Administration (part of New Deal): offer employment for 8.5 million people. Resettlement Administration: buy land to be set aside from agriculture.
1936			
1937	Tree planting programmes.	Formation of Soil Conservation Districts: fund and force farmers to practice soil conservation measures.	

The example shows that this transition was enabled through a set of substantial multilevel political changes (local, regional, national) in several domains (science, economy, law). This profound social transformation can be seen as a successful process of adaptation to climate variability, and thus a transition to sustainability.

6. Addressing adaptation at the international regime level

In the interests of the poorest of the poor, a range of international regimes addressing environment, human rights, development and trade can be linked. Concerning the environment, adaptation to climate change needs to be related to other international environmental regimes such as the United Nations Convention on Biodiversity (UNCBD) and the United Nations Convention to Combat Desertification (UNCCD). Accordingly, the three Conventions, UNFCCC, UNCBD and UNCCD, are mutually encouraged to coordinate their activities (Arts 7.2 and 8.2 in UNFCCC, Arts 5 and 24 in UNCBD, and Arts 8.1 and 23 in UNCCD). But in order to identify synergies and potential conflicts it is necessary to go beyond vague formulations on coordination.

Climate change is expected to affect the geographical distribution of biodiversity substantially (IPCC, 2007b). Moreover, biodiversity is a crucial source of income and security for poor people (Millennium Ecosystem Assessment, 2005). It is therefore urgent to strengthen the protection of biodiversity resources and to provide opportunities for local communities to harness such resources sustainably. However, the current situation is characterized by misunderstanding, mistrust and regulatory confusion for both providers and users of genetic materials (Wynberg and Laird, 2007). The inclusion of Reductions of Emissions from Deforestation and Degradation (REDD) as a mechanism in the climate regime is a concrete proposal with implications for UNFCCC and UNCBD (Zahabu et al., 2007). But, while theoretically attractive, there are methodological and ethical considerations that need to be further developed.

Climate change can potentially be linked to desertification through the important synergy of biological sequestration of carbon. Several studies demonstrate a substantial potential to reduce atmospheric CO_2 through improved land management in drylands. Such activities would provide an important synergy between mitigation and adaptation (Sanchez, 2000; Olsson and Ardö, 2002; FAO, 2004). Even if the aim of carbon sequestration through land management is to achieve win–win situations, there is an asymmetry in the relationship between the two wins. While the KP requires meticulous verification of the amount of carbon stored, there is no such verification to guarantee that the benefits are transferred to the right beneficiaries. This is an area where policy should be strengthened to serve the adaptation needs better.

6.1. Rectificatory justice

The international legal basis for adaptation needs to be strengthened, especially in relation to the regimes of development and human rights. Such amendments can be based on the ethical principles of rectificatory and redistributive justice. Rectificatory, or corrective, justice deals with injustice from the past (Bell, 2004). Accordingly, it can be argued that countries with high historical GHG emissions should decrease their contemporary and future emissions substantially. The logic is that countries which were low emitters historically should be compensated today, for example through adaptation.

6.2. Redistributive justice

Even though the rich in poor countries contribute substantially to GHG emissions, climate change as we know it today is primarily a problem caused by rich countries with high GHG emissions. Ironically, poor countries are more vulnerable to the impacts of climate change and should therefore be compensated through adaptation.

Migration is an important and long-standing response to disasters, whether human-induced or natural (Hugo, 1996). International migration is highly regulated by international Conventions. The Geneva Convention defines the criteria for being accepted as a refugee and achieving asylum in another country. Among the eligible reasons for acquiring refugee status, the current definition covers 'external aggression, occupation, foreign domination or events seriously disturbing public order in either part or the whole of his country of origin or nationality' (Keely, 1981). We argue that, in the case of extreme climate change impacts, where localities or whole regions become completely uninhabitable, as a result of, for example, sea-level rise or desiccation, the above definition could be amended to incorporate people affected by climate change. For policy makers it would be advantageous to create such a legal framework before severe climate change impacts generate large flows of refugees. Apart from providing a last resort for affected people, legal improvements would be a powerful signal to the international community to take climate change seriously.

In the development debate there is a long-standing discussion of whether to advocate 'trade over aid' or 'aid over trade'. And, since the emergence of the Bretton Woods system in the 1940s, there is also a debate on free trade. Despite there being agreement that agricultural production will be severely hit by climate change and that agriculture is the most conflicted area of international trade negotiations, it is often argued by influential international organizations such as the World Bank that developing countries, especially in Africa, should focus more on, and increase, exports of agricultural goods (World Bank, 2007). This is, of course, a real dilemma experienced at all levels, from local farms via national to international settings and with implications for all global regimes. We see that the contemporary debate on free, fair and ethical trade is relevant here (Potter et al., 2004). However, it must be expanded to include the need to adapt to climate change according to some principle of fair burden-sharing.

The recent surge in the use of agricultural products as biofuels in the USA and EU has driven food prices to record highs (Runge and Senauer, 2007). In this context it must be noted that a majority of the poorest of the poor are food-insecure subsistence farmers or slum dwellers who cannot afford these rising prices. It is an irony that the most vulnerable to climate change impacts may suffer from such an act of mitigation. This example shows how important it is to include not only adaptation to climate change in international negotiations, but also to include adaptation needs that result from responses to climate change.

7. Concluding remarks

Our key message is that there is an urgent need to strengthen adaptation in the international climate change regime, particularly in the context of poor people subject to increasing vulnerability. We argue that adaptation needs to be facilitated, promoted and achieved in the local context where vulnerability to climate change is perceived and experienced, especially among the poorest populations. But the international community also needs to realize that adaptation must be addressed at all levels from the local to the global. The question remains how best to achieve this.

Since the very outset, development has been a normative international project aiming at the eradication of poverty mainly through modernization and industrialization. In that sense it is truly social and takes various scales into consideration, ranging from the international to the regional, national and local. However, the development discourse suffers from two crucial conditions that constitute an obstacle to tackling the challenge of adaptation to climate change:

- The development discourse does not examine the problems inherent in the dynamics between society and nature and is therefore blind to the way in which this crucial relationship changes profoundly in the wake of climate change.
- Development focuses primarily on obstacles to change in developing countries rather than on the relationship between rich and poor and the role of rich countries.

Development as a paradigm is rooted in the dichotomy between developed and underdeveloped countries, and is thus in essence a polarized paradigm with developed countries seen as the model for modernization and social change. This type of perspective has less relevance in times of global change when the problems rooted in the type of production, consumption and distribution in industrialized countries must also be examined explicitly in relation to developing countries.

Resilience is a very useful concept when describing the need for adaptation in systems in which there is no inherent conflict between linked social and ecological subsystems. Incremental changes to the management of such systems may be effective, such as insurance schemes. However, in cases characterized by conflicts between subsystems, incremental changes will not work and indeed may even exacerbate the problems. Moreover, the ideas of resilience underline recovery more than fundamental change. Another problem with the conceptual framework of resilience is that it refers to systems where levels and domains are not addressed, owing either to invisibility or to exclusion from the system. In the context of adaptation, this invisibility becomes a real obstacle in those situations where there is need for fundamental change. In situations of conflicting goals, resilience will not be helpful because profound change rather than incremental changes may be required if adaptation is to be effective.

Transition theory offers a radically different view on adaptation which is particularly appealing when considering linked social and ecological systems characterized by goal and power conflicts.

Acknowledgement

This paper has been made possible through the two EU Sixth Framework Programme projects, MATISSE and ADAM.

Note

1. Both authors contributed equally to this paper.

References

Adger, W.N., 2000, 'Social and ecological resilience: are they related?' *Progress in Human Geography* 24, 347–364.

Angel, M.T., D.P. Rock, 2005, *Industrial Transformation in the Developing World*, Oxford University Press, Oxford, UK.

Armitage, D., Johnson, D., 2006, 'Can resilience be reconciled with globalization and the increasingly complex conditions of resource degradation in Asian coastal regions?' *Ecology and Society* 11, 1–19.

Bell, D.R., 2004, 'Environmental refugees: What rights? Which duties?' *Res Publica* 10, 135–152.

Burnell, P., 2002, 'Foreign aid in a changing world', in: V. Desai, R.B. Potter (eds), *The Companion to Development Studies*, Arnold, London, 473–477.

Burton, I., Kates, R.W., White, G.F., 1993, *The Environment as Hazard*, Guilford Press, New York.

Carpenter, S., Walker, B., Anderies, J.M., Abel, N., 2001, 'From metaphor to measurement: resilience of what to what?' *Ecosystems* 4, 765–781.

Cornwall, A., 2007, 'Buzzwords and fuzzwords: deconstructing the development discourse', *Development in Practice* 17, 471–484.

Cowen, M.P., Shenton, R.W., 1996, *Doctrines of Development*, Routledge, London.

de Waal, A., Whiteside, A., 2003, 'New variant famine: AIDS and food crisis in southern Africa', *Lancet* 362, 1234–1237.

Dessai, S., Adger, N.W., Hulme, M., Turnpenny, J., Köhler, J., Warren, R., 2004, 'Defining and experiencing dangerous climate change', *Climatic Change* 64, 11–25.

Djurfeldt, G., Jirström, M., 2005, 'The puzzle of the policy shift: the early Green Revolution in India, Indonesia and the Philippines', in: G. Djurfeldt, H. Holmen, M. Jirström, R. Larsson (eds), *The African food Crisis: Lessons from the Asian Green Revolution*, CABI Publishing, Wallingford, UK.

Ellis, F., 2000, *Rural Livelihoods and Diversity in Developing Countries*, Oxford University Press, Oxford, UK.

Fan, S., Hazell, P., 2001, 'Returns to public investments in the less-favored areas of India and China', *American Journal of Agricultural Economics* 83, 1217–1222.

FAO, 2004, *Carbon Sequestration in Dryland Soils*, Food and Agricultural Organization, Rome.

Folke, C., Carpenter, S., Elmqvist, T., Gunderson, L., Holling, C.S., Walker, B., 2002, *Resilience and Sustainable Development: Building Adaptive Capacity in a World of Transformations*, ICSU, Paris.

Foxon, T.J., 2007, 'Technological lock-in and the role of innovation', in: G. Atkinson, Dietz, S., Neumayer, E. (eds), *Handbook of Sustainable Development*, Edward Elgar, Cheltenham, UK.

Gallopin, G.C., 2006, 'Linkages between vulnerability, resilience, and adaptive capacity', *Global Environmental Change* 16, 293–303.

Geels, F.W., 2002, 'Technological transitions as evolutionary reconfiguration processes: a multi-level perspective and a case-study', *Research Policy* 31, 1257–1274.

Gurenko, E.N., 2006a, 'Conclusions and recommendations', *Climate Policy* 6, 683–684.

Gurenko, E.N., 2006b, 'Introduction and executive summary', *Climate Policy* 6, 600–606.

Hansen, Z.K., Libecap, G.D., 2004, 'Small farms, externalities, and the Dust Bowl of the 1930s', *Journal of Political Economy* 112, 665–694.

Hess, U., Syroka, J., 2005, *Weather-based Insurance in Southern Africa: The Case of Malawi*, World Bank, Washington, DC.

Holling, C.S., 1973, 'Resilience and stability of ecological systems', *Annual Review of Ecology and Systematics* 4, 1–24.

Hugo, G., 1996, 'Environmental concerns and international migration', *International Migration Review* 30(1), 105–131.

Hutchinson, C.F., 1998, 'Social science and remote sensing in famine early warning', in: D. Liverman, E. Moran, R. Rindfuss, P. Stern (eds), *People and Pixels: Linking Remote Sensing and Social Science*, National Academy Press, Washington, DC, 189–196.

IPCC, 2007a, *Climate Change 2007: The Physical Science Basis*, Cambridge University Press, Cambridge, UK.

IPCC, 2007b, *Climate Change 2007: Impacts, Adaptation and Vulnerability*, Cambridge University Press, Cambridge, UK.

Kabeer, N., 2005, 'Gender equality and women's empowerment', *Gender and Development* 13, 13–24.

Kates, R.W., 2000, 'Cautionary tales: adaptation and the global poor', *Climatic Change* 45, 5–17.

Keely, C.B., 1981, *Global Refugee Policy: The Case for a Development-oriented Strategy*, Public Issues Paper of the Population Council; PI-05, Population Council, New York.

Klein, R.J.T., Nicholls, R.J., Thomalla, F., 2003, 'Resilience to natural hazards: how useful is this concept?' *Environmental Hazards* 5, 35–45.

Lessa, I., 2006, 'Discursive struggles within social welfare: restaging teen motherhood', *British Journal of Social Work* 36, 283–298.

Linnerooth-Bayer, J., Mechler, R., 2006, 'Insurance for assisting adaptation to climate change in developing countries: a proposed strategy', *Climate Policy* 6, 621–636.

Linnerooth-Bayer, J., Mechler, R., Pflug, G., 2005, 'Refocusing disaster aid', *Science* 309, 1044–1046.

Lister, R., 2004, *Poverty*, Polity Press, Cambridge, UK.

Mace, G., Masundire, H., et al., 2005, 'Biodiversity', in: R.T. Watson, A.H. Zakri (eds), *Ecosystems and Human Well-being: Current State and Trends*, Vol. 1, Island Press, Washington, DC.

Mechler, R., Linnerooth-Bayer, J., Peppiatt, D., 2006, *Microinsurance for Natural Disaster Risks in Developing Countries: Benefits, Limitations and Viability*, A ProVention/IIASA Study, IIASA, Laxenburg, Austria.

Meier, G.M., 1995, *Leading Issues in Economic Development*, Oxford University Press, Oxford, UK.

Millennium Ecosystem Assessment, 2005, *Ecosystems and Human Well-being: Synthesis.*, Island Press, Washington DC.

Moser, C., 2005, 'Has gender mainstreaming failed?' *International Feminist Journal of Politics* 7, 576–590.

Mwabu, G., Thorbecke, E., 2004, 'Rural development, growth and poverty in Africa', *Journal of African Economies* 13, ABRC Supplement, i16–i65.

O'Brien, K.L., Leichenko, R.M., 2000, 'Double exposure: assessing the impacts of climate change within the context of economic globalization', *Global Environmental Change* 10, 221–232.

Olsson, L., Ardö, J., 2002, 'Soil carbon sequestration in degraded semiarid agro-ecosystems: perils and potentials', *Ambio* 31, 471–477.

Olsson, L., Eklundh, L., Ardö, J., 2005, 'A recent greening of the Sahel: trends, patterns and potential causes', *Journal of Arid Environments* 63, 556–566.

Pieterse, J.N., 2001, *Development Theory, Deconstructions/Reconstructions*, Sage Publications, London.

Potter, R., Binns, T., Elliott, J., Smith, D.W., 2004, *Geographies of Development*, Pearson Educational, Harlow, UK.

Rip, A., Kemp, R., 1998, 'Technological change', in: S. Rayner, Malone, E.L. (eds), *Human Choices and Climate Change*, Battelle Press, Columbus, OH.

Rist, G., 1999, *The History of Development: From Western Origins to Global Faith*, Zed Books, London.

Rotmans, J., Kemp, R., van Asselt, M., 2001, 'More evolution than revolution: transition management in public policy', *Foresight* 3, 15–31.

Runge, C.F., Senauer, B., 2007, 'How biofuels could starve the poor', *Foreign Affairs* 86(3).

Sachs, J.D., 2005, *The End of Poverty: How We Can Make It Happen in Our Lifetime*, Penguin, London.

Sanchez, P.A., 2000, 'Linking climate change research with food security and poverty reduction in the tropics', *Agriculture, Ecosystems and Environment* 82, 371–383.

Sen, A., 1999, *Development as Freedom*, Oxford University Press, Oxford, UK.

Smit, B., Skinner, M.W., 2002, 'Adaptation options in agriculture to climate change: a typology', *Mitigation and Adaptation Strategies for Global Change 7*, 85–114.

Tiffen, M., 2003, 'Transition in sub-Saharan Africa: agriculture, urbanisation and income growth', *World Development* 31, 1343–1366.

UNEP, 2007, *Global Environmental Outlook: 4*, United Nations Environment Programme, Nairobi, Kenya.

UNHABITAT, 2003, *The Challenge of Slums*, UN Human Settlements Programme, Nairobi, Kenya.

van Aalst, M., 2006, *Managing Climate Risk: Integrating Adaptation into World Bank Group Operations*, World Bank Group, Global Environment Facility Programme, Washington, DC.

Verheyen, R., 2002, 'Adaptation to the impacts of anthropogenic climate change: the international legal framework', *Review of European Community and International Environmental Law* 11, 129–143.

World Bank, 2006, *World Development Report 2006: Equity and Development*, Oxford University Press, New York.

World Bank, 2007, *World Development Report 2008: Agriculture for Development*, World Bank, Washington, DC.

Worster, D., 1979, *Dust Bowl: The Southern Plains in the 1930s*, Oxford University Press, New York.

Wynberg, S., Laird, S., 2007, 'Bioprospecting: tracking the policy debate', *Environment* 49, 20–32.

Zahabu, E., Skutsch, M.M., Sosovele, H., Malimbwi, R.E., 2007, 'Reduced emissions from deforestation and degradation', *African Journal of Ecology* 45, 451–453.

■ synthesis article

Adapting development cooperation to adapt to climate change[1]

SHARDUL AGRAWALA[1]*, MAARTEN VAN AALST[2]

[1] OECD Environment Directorate, 2 rue André Pascal, 75016 Paris, France
[2] Red Cross/Red Crescent Climate Centre, PO Box 28120, 2502 KC The Hague, The Netherlands

Climate change can affect the efficiency with which development resources are invested and the eventual achievement of many development objectives. Drawing upon illustrative case studies in six developing countries: Bangladesh, Egypt, Tanzania, Uruguay, Nepal and Fiji, this article examines the synergies and trade-offs involved in integrating adaptation to climate change in development cooperation activities. Key barriers facing such integration are identified. An agenda is proposed for enhancing development efforts by mainstreaming climate risk management, organized around improving the usability of climate information, developing and testing climate risk screening tools, employing appropriate entry points for climate information, focusing more on implementation, and improving coordination and sharing of good practices.

Keywords: adaptation; climate change vulnerability; climate risk management; development; development assistance; poverty reduction; risk; sustainable development; synergy

Le changement climatique peut affecter l'efficacité par laquelle les ressources pour le développement sont investies et l'éventuel accomplissement de nombreux objectifs de développement. Sur la base d'études de cas illustratives dans six pays en developpement: le Bangladesh, l'Egypte, la Tanzanie, l'Uruguay, le Népal et Fiji, cet article examine les synergies et concessions mutuelles impliquées dans l'intégraion de l'adaptation au changement climatique aux activités de coopération pour le développement. Les obstacles fondamentaux à une telle intégration sont identifiés. Un agenda est proposé, visant à augmenter les efforts au développement en intégrant la gestion du risque climatique, par l'amélioration de la facilité d'emploi de l'information climatique, le développement et la mise à l'essai des filtres à risque climatique, l'utilisation de points d'accès adaptés pour l'information climatique, une concentration plus axée sur la mise en oeuvre, et l'amélioration de la coordination et du partage des bonnes pratiques.

Mots clés: adaptation; assistance au développement; développement; développement durable; gestion du risque climatique; réduction de la pauvreté; risque; synergie; vulnérabilité au changement climatique

1. Introduction

Climate change poses a serious challenge to social and economic development. Developing countries are particularly vulnerable because their economies are generally more dependent on climate-sensitive natural resources, and because they are less able to cope with the impacts of climate change. In principle, a range of activities oriented towards reducing poverty, improving nutrition, and promoting sustainable livelihood opportunities would also help reduce vulnerability to many climate-change impacts. A healthier, better-educated population with improved access to resources is likely to be in a better position to cope with climate change.

■ *Corresponding author. E-mail*: shardul.agrawala@oecd.org

CLIMATE POLICY **8 (2008) 183–193**
doi:10.3763/cpol.2007.0435 © 2008 Earthscan ISSN: 1469-3062 (print), 1752-7457 (online) www.climatepolicy.com

In many cases, however, the risks posed by climate change can affect the efficiency with which development resources are invested and the eventual achievement of many development objectives (e.g. AfDB et al., 2003). Hence the need to integrate (or 'mainstream') adaptation to climate change within a range of development activities. This is particularly true for decisions today that may have a footprint over the medium to long term, when many climate-change impacts will manifest themselves. One reason is that it can be more cost-effective to implement adaptation measures early, particularly for long-lived infrastructure. Another reason is that current development activities may irreversibly affect future options for adaptation to the impacts of climate change. Examples include the destruction of coastal mangroves and the building of human settlements in areas that are likely to be particularly exposed to climate change. In such instances, even near-term policies may need to consider the long-term implications of climate change.

As activities by government and development cooperation agencies often have long-term horizons, they are especially relevant. Private investment, particularly foreign direct investment (FDI), has also become important for developing countries, particularly those in the upper-middle income category (Figure 1). However, for the least developed countries, as well as those in the low- and middle-income categories, official flows – grants and loans – are much more significant, and therefore a higher priority to integrating consideration of climate risks. It is these development cooperation activities which are the focus of this article, which draws upon insights drawn from in-depth case studies in six illustrative developing countries: Bangladesh, Egypt, Tanzania, Uruguay, Nepal and Fiji.[2]

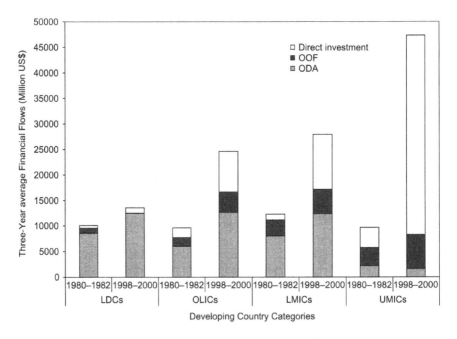

FIGURE 1 Official and private financial flows to developing countries*

*Classification according to the OECD Development Assistance Committee (DAC) categories: Least Developed Countries (LDCs); Other Low Income Countries (OLICs); Lower Middle Income Countries (LMICs); Upper Middle Income Countries (UMICs). ODA stands for official development assistance, OOF for other official flows (non-concessional and/or for non-developmental purposes).

2. How much aid goes to climate-sensitive activities?

Donor agencies are increasingly interested in incorporating climate change concerns in their core development activities. The World Bank, GTZ and Norad, to cite some prominent examples, have reported on the extent to which climate risks are factored into their ongoing development assistance activities (Burton and van Aalst, 1999, 2004; Klein, 2001; Eriksen and Næss, 2003). A comprehensive evaluation of the extent to which development activities are affected by climate change would require detailed assessments of all relevant projects and consideration of site-specific climate-change impacts, both of which are beyond the scope of this analysis. Instead, this article seeks to determine what proportion of total aid portfolios may be in sectors potentially affected by climate risk, where climate change concerns may thus need to be taken into account. This is accomplished through an analysis of the data from the OECD/World Bank Creditor Reporting System (CRS) database of official flows[3] for the six developing countries (Bangladesh, Egypt, Tanzania, Uruguay, Nepal and Fiji) that were examined for this study.

To even out the variation in aid flows from year to year, the analysis uses a 3-year sample of aid commitments, for 1998–2000. The assessment of the proportion of aid flows that might be affected by climate change is accomplished through an analysis of aid commitments to specific activity areas, such as initiatives to promote agriculture in areas that might become more, or less, viable under climate change, to infrastructure investments that could be at risk from impacts such as permafrost melt, glacier retreat and sea-level rise. Also included are projects that affect the vulnerability of other natural or human systems to climate change. For instance, new roads might be weatherproof from an engineering standpoint, but might trigger human settlement in areas at high risk of particular impacts of climate change, such as coastal zones vulnerable to sea-level rise. Such considerations might therefore also need to be taken into account in project design and implementation. By contrast, development activities related to education, gender equality, and governance would be much less directly affected by climate change, and therefore aid flows directed at such activities are not considered to be affected by climate change.

The results presented in Figure 2 show that a significant proportion of this aid is directed at activities potentially affected by climate risks, including climate change. Estimates range from 50–65% of total national official flows, in Nepal, to 12–26% in Tanzania. In monetary terms, this represents half a billion US dollars of official aid flows in Bangladesh and Egypt, and about US$200 million in Tanzania and Nepal. In Fiji, while the absolute amount may be low, it constitutes roughly one-third of all aid flows. Uruguay is the exception, because it receives very little ODA; as it is an upper-middle-income developing country, most of its official flows are loans, primarily in activities not directly exposed to climate risk. These findings are consistent with similar analyses of a subset of the World Bank's project portfolio (World Bank, 2006).

While there is a risk of oversimplification in any such classification, the analysis underscores the fact that that consideration of climate risk (including climate change) could be central to the achievement of general development goals as well as the success of individual investments and projects. The amount of official aid flows in activities potentially affected by climate risks is considerably higher than funding committed to financing climate change adaptation *per se* (through the global climate change funding mechanisms under the United Nations Convention on Climate Change and earmarked bilateral donor financing for adaptation). Thus, efforts to promote adaptation should focus not just on financing within the international climate change regime, but particularly on mainstreaming adaptation within core development activities. Another implication of the analysis relates to the question of the optimal use of limited global climate

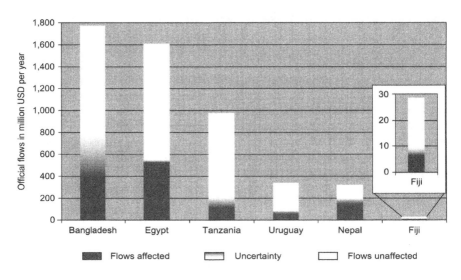

FIGURE 2 Annual official flows and share of activities potentially affected by climate change

change adaptation funds: one possibility might be to use them to trigger mainstreaming of adaptation, particularly in the context of regular development investments.

3. Do development activities take climate change adaptation into account?

The significance of climate change for core development activities, as illustrated above, highlights the need to assess the extent to which such concerns are being addressed in current development strategies and plans. National plans, donor country assistance strategies and project documents were examined for the six case study countries: Bangladesh, Egypt, Fiji, Nepal, Tanzania and Uruguay, to determine how much attention is currently being paid to climate risk, in general, and to climate change, in particular. For each case study country, the review covered the most important planning documents, assistance strategies for the principal donors to that country, and projects in sectors vulnerable to climate change.[4] The assessment of the above-mentioned documents and activities for the six case study countries reveals a fairly nuanced picture in terms of the degree of attention to climate change concerns.

On the one hand, considerable progress has been made over the past decade or so with regard to activities specific to climate change, particularly including greenhouse gas emission inventories and policy options for greenhouse gas mitigation, but also impact and adaptation assessments. Institutional mechanisms to address climate change have been established, and certain countries (such as Tanzania) have developed climate change action plans. Donors have provided financial and technical support for many of these activities. In some cases – as in Bangladesh and Fiji – donors have also worked with the national government to better articulate the links between responses to climate change and priorities for development. However, many of these initiatives are at the level of assessments and plans, and discernible progress in terms of policy action has been limited.

On the other hand, many core development activities that relate to areas that could be affected by climate change, from national development plans and long-term perspectives to country assistance strategies and poverty reduction strategy papers (PRSPs), generally pay little, if any, explicit attention to climate change. Some weather and climate considerations are routinely taken into account in a wide range of development activities, from crop selection to the design of highways and energy generation facilities. However, not all climate risks are being incorporated in decision making, even with regard to natural weather extremes. Moreover, practices that take into account historical climate are not necessarily suitable under climate change. Many planning decisions focus on shorter time-scales and tend to neglect the longer-term perspective. These findings are consistent with those of similar reviews for specific agencies, such as those of Burton and van Aalst (1999) for the World Bank, Klein (2001) for GTZ, and Eriksen and Naess (2003) for NORAD (for further details and comparisons of these analyses, see also Klein et al., 2007).

Of the six countries examined in this article, three – Tanzania, Nepal, and Bangladesh – have prepared PRSPs. Tanzania's PRSP recognizes that weather and climate hazards have a serious impact on development and on the poor, although the risks posed by climate change are not mentioned explicitly. However, a number of priorities highlighted in the PRSP, such as early warning systems, irrigation, improvements to food supply systems, and development of drought-resistant crops, would be synergistic with adaptation to climate change. Nepal, meanwhile, does not examine climate-related risks to poverty reduction and development, or the risks posed by climate change, in its tenth development plan, which is also the country's PRSP. These omissions are particularly significant because Nepal has already experienced significant climate-change impacts, including temperature increases in the high Himalayas, glacier retreat, and the expansion of glacial lakes, which have implications for development. A World Bank/IMF assessment of Nepal's PRSP (IDA/IMF, 2002) also does not mention the implications of current or future climate risks on Nepal's development prospects. Bangladesh's interim-PRSP recognizes the links between poverty and natural hazards, and mentions the likelihood that such hazards are likely to increase under climate change. Overall, however, climate change is given very limited consideration in the context of planning vulnerability reduction measures.

As in the case of PRSPs, donor country assistance strategies and projects seldom pay explicit attention to the risks posed by climate change, although some of the priorities reflected in such documents are synergistic with adaptation. One project that is perhaps most directly linked to climate change adaptation is the Tsho Rolpa risk reduction project in Nepal. The Tsho Rolpa is a high-altitude lake formed by the melting and retreat of a glacier as a result of rising temperatures. By 1998 it was the largest and the most dangerous glacial lake in Nepal, about 3.5 km long, 0.5 km wide, and containing about 90–100 million cubic metres of water. The expansion of the lake had considerably increased the risk of a catastrophic breach, with serious consequences for infrastructure and settlements over 100 km downstream, and threatening about 10,000 lives. Several international donors and the Government of Nepal therefore jointly initiated a project in 1998 to reduce the risk of a glacial lake outburst through a combination of measures, including partial drainage of the lake and the establishment of early warning systems downstream. While the phrase 'climate change' does not occur in the project documents, the project has clearly accomplished anticipatory adaptation to climate change by considerably reducing the risk of catastrophic flooding.

Examples of development cooperation projects such as the Tsho Rolpa, which are aimed at anticipatory adaptation to climate change, are rather rare. Somewhat more common are policies and projects addressing current vulnerabilities which may also be synergistic with adaptation to climate change. For example projects aimed at drainage rehabilitation and restoration of coastal embankments in Bangladesh, which will also be synergistic with adaptation to the risk of more severe flooding under climate change. In Egypt, meanwhile, projects aimed at facilitating cooperation among the Nile riparian countries or at better demand-side management of water use would also be synergistic with responses that might be needed to address the impacts of climate change, such as increased evaporation losses as a result of rising temperatures as well as reduced precipitation in the Nile headwaters. At the same time, however, there are a number of examples of development activities which either overlook or might even exacerbate the risks posed by climate change. For example, policies to encourage tourism and build infrastructure in vulnerable coastal areas, or plans to encourage ecotourism in the fragile Sundarbans, may pose added risks to already fragile systems that are also projected to be critically affected by climate change. An analogous problem exists in Tanzania, whose Kilimanjaro ecosystem is vulnerable to forest fires as a result of warmer and drier conditions; development policies may therefore need to take such risks into account so as not to aggravate existing vulnerabilities.

Development cooperation agencies are increasingly recognizing climate change as a serious challenge to their core activities through high-level declarations (e.g. EC, 2004; OECD, 2006), awareness-raising activities (e.g. van Aalst et al., 2007); as well as policy frameworks and guidelines (e.g. Asian Development Bank, 2005; DANIDA, 2006; World Bank, 2006; USAID, 2007). Such initiatives, however, are often at the level of high-level declarations or pilot activities initiated by the climate specialists in these agencies (Gigli and Agrawala, 2007). Agency-wide adoption of such objectives and their translation into operational practices is still at an early stage.

4. What are the main barriers to mainstreaming adaptation?

Lack of awareness of climate change within the development community and limitations on resources for implementation are the most frequently cited reasons for difficulties in mainstreaming adaptation to climate change within development activity. These explanations may hold true in many situations, but there is also a more complex web of reasons underlying them, which are discussed in the following paragraphs.

4.1. Barriers within governments and donor agencies

Climate change is often viewed primarily as a top-down, multilateral negotiations issue. Expertise on this subject is often the domain of environment departments in governments and donor agencies, and such departments have limited leverage over 'line departments', such as those dealing with finance, transport and agriculture, whose policies and frameworks might need to be modified for effective integration of climate risks. Sectoral managers and country representatives may also face 'mainstreaming overload', with issues such as gender, governance and environment also vying for integration in development activities. Moreover, as many development projects are funded over 3–5 years, they may not seem to be the best vehicle for long-term climate risk reduction. Adaptation to climate change *ex ante* may also have more difficulty attracting resources than more visible *ex post* activities such as emergency response and post-disaster recovery. International donors also increasingly seek to respond to the needs and priorities expressed by recipient countries themselves, preferably through PRSPs and sectoral strategies. It might therefore be difficult for international donors to push adaptation to climate change if such concerns do not feature prominently among the national priorities of the host country. Some observers also suggest that documents such as PRSPs are already overburdened by too large a number of specific separate policy issues, often driven by donor preferences, and that adding more issues such as climate change would undermine their credibility and effectiveness.

4.2. Insufficient relevance of available climate information to development-related decisions

Development activities are sensitive to a broad range of climate variables, only some of which can be reliably projected by climate models. Temperature, for example, is typically easier to project than rainfall, which in turn might be easier to project than variables such as wind intensity. The integration of climate risks may therefore be difficult where the climate sensitivity of development-related decisions is to variables that cannot be reliably projected. Many development activities are especially sensitive to changes in climate extremes rather than simply to trends in average climate conditions. Agriculture and stability of food supplies, for example, are especially affected by rising risks of extended hot and dry spells, rather than just by gradual changes in average temperature and rainfall (e.g. Schmidhuber and Tubiello, 2007). Deviations or changes in extremes, however, are often more difficult to predict through climate models than mean trends, and have received relatively little attention in impact modelling. There is also a mismatch between the time and space scales of climate change projections and the information needs of development planners. For example, the primary sensitivity of development activities to climate is at a local scale (such as that of a watershed or a city), for which credible climate change projections are often lacking. In many cases, however, there is scope for 'no-regrets' modifications of investments that better address current variability and extremes, thereby reducing the risk of impacts of a changing climate, but relying less on precise future projections, and generating immediate benefits. Such an integrated approach, managing rising risks primarily by enhancing risk management in the face of current variability and extremes, proposed for instance by Bettencourt et al. (2006), in effect addresses the 'adaptation deficit' (Burton, 2004) in the current climate, mirrored in the lack of attention to current variability and extremes in many of the documents that were reviewed (and, equally, in various other reviews of development and natural hazards, e.g. IEG, 2006).

4.3. Trade-offs with other priorities

While, in many cases, adaptation is synergistic with other development needs, in certain cases, there are direct trade-offs between development priorities and the actions required to deal with climate change. Governments and donors confronting immediate challenges, such as poverty and inadequate infrastructure, have few incentives to divert resources to investments that are seen as not paying off until climate-change impacts are full-blown. Putting a real value on natural resources and deciding when not to develop coastal areas or hillsides may be seen as hampering development. At the project level, mainstreaming of adaptation may be perceived as complicating operating procedures or raising costs. In addition, short-term economic benefits that often accrue to only a few in the community can crowd out longer-term considerations such as climate change. Shrimp farming, mangrove conversion, and infrastructure development, for example, provide employment and boost incomes, but they may also reduce the future ability to adapt to the impact of climate change and increase the vulnerability of critical coastal ecosystems.

5. How can adaptation be better integrated in development?

Several opportunities exist for the more effective integration of climate change adaptation within development activities. These include making climate change information more useful and easier to use, focusing more on implementing climate change and development strategies, and increasing coordination between development and climate change policies.

5.1. Making climate information more accessible, relevant and usable

Development practitioners and climate change specialists should join forces to make climate information more *accessible*, relevant and usable. Development practitioners need access to credible, context-specific climate information as a basis for decisions. This includes information on the cost and effectiveness of integrating adaptation measures within development planning. Perhaps even more fundamental is information on the likely impact of climate change and variability on particular development activities. While it would be naïve to call for a significant reduction in scientific uncertainty in climate model projections, more can be done to bridge the gap between producers of scientific information and development practitioners, assisting them to interpret the information, including the uncertainties, in the context of their operational responsibilities. Analysis of the costs and distributional aspects of adaptation could also assist sectoral decision makers in determining the degree to which they should integrate such responses within their core activities.

5.2. Developing and applying climate risk screening tools

The development community should develop tools and approaches to assess the potential exposure of a broad range of development activities to climate risks and to prioritize responses. One element that is needed are screening tools at the project level, which can warn project developers that their project may face potential climate risks early in the project development cycle (e.g. Burton and van Aalst, 2004). Risks to be assessed include direct physical risks, risks to project outcomes, or risks of triggering maladaptation. Should the screening tool raise a red flag, further project development would include a more substantial climate risk assessment and options analysis. Field-testing such screening tools and applying them in a wide range of project settings could greatly advance the integration of climate risks in development activities. In particular, more in-depth follow-up work on high-risk projects would also trigger further action beyond the specific investment, such as changes in government policies or engagement of local stakeholders in climate risk management efforts, and would help create capacity to interpret and apply climate risk information.

5.3. Using appropriate 'entry points' for climate information

Within donor agencies and governments alike, a number of entry points can be utilized to introduce climate change adaptation into development activities, such as land-use planning, disaster management strategies and infrastructure design. Attention should be given not only to investment plans but also to policies and legislation (including enforcement). While environmental impact assessments could be another entry point, guidelines for such assessments would need to be broadened to include climate-change impacts. Current guidelines consider only the impact of a project or activity on the environment, not the impact of the environment on the project. Climate risk management also requires attention in planning and budget allocations. Such processes are best managed by a sufficiently influential central coordinating department, such as the Ministry of Finance, the Office of the President, and Central Planning Units in key line agencies.

5.4. Shifting emphasis to implementation rather than developing new plans

In many instances, rather than requiring radically new responses, adaptation to climate change only reinforces the need to implement measures that already are, or should be, environmental or development priorities. Examples include water or energy conservation, forest protection and afforestation, flood control, building coastal embankments, dredging to improve river flow, and protection of mangroves. Often such measures have already been called for in national and sectoral planning documents but have not been successfully implemented. Reiterating these measures in elaborate climate change plans is unlikely to have much real effect unless barriers to effective implementation of the existing sectoral and development plans are confronted. Putting the spotlight on implementation, therefore, could put the focus on greater accountability in action on the ground.

5.5. Encouraging meaningful coordination and the sharing of good practices

Mainstreaming of adaptation to climate change is occurring already in a limited fashion as part of the regular risk management activities of national and sectoral planners. In addition, mechanisms related to the international climate change regime, especially the adaptation-related reporting and financing under the UNFCCC, also provide a trigger for action on adaptation, which could be used to jumpstart strengthening of climate risk management in national development planning. Efforts initiated from the latter perspective clearly need to be closely coordinated with the former, so that the two are mutually reinforcing. This requires special attention in the design of institutional mechanisms for coordination and exchange of good practice, particularly within countries (where the actors dealing with the UNFCCC may not be aware of climate risk management efforts in line agencies) but also between sectoral units in donor agencies (where adaptation may be perceived as an issue to be handled by the agency's environment unit).

5.6. Involving non-governmental partners

Another area that requires the special attention of donor agencies and governments alike is engagement of the private sector and local communities in mainstreaming climate risk management. Such non-governmental actors account for the lion's share of economic and development activities, and adaptation by such actors can either be supported or frustrated by government policies. Targeted awareness-raising and provision of appropriate information can help involve such actors in the development and climate dialogues that should be happening among various actors in the country (including donor agencies).

5.7. Transboundary and regional coordination

Another priority that has not received sufficient attention is transboundary and regional coordination. Most climate change action and adaptation plans are at the national level, although many of the impacts of climate change cut across national boundaries. Meaningful integration of a range of climate risks, from flood control to dry season flows to glacial lake hazards, would require greater coordination on data collection, monitoring and policies at the regional level. Finally, operational guidance on comprehensive climate risk management in development is needed to facilitate policy coherence, allow for joint building of experience, and promote the sharing of tools and experiences within and among governments and development cooperation agencies.

6. Conclusions

The analyses presented in this article show that there is ample opportunity to enhance development efforts by better integration of climate risk management. However, the climate change adaptation and development communities are not monolithic blocks that can be linked by a simple handshake. Rather, mainstreaming of climate risk management requires a meshing at multiple levels between the diverse range of actors and institutions. While considerable progress has been made in recent years in this direction, there is still a need for much greater coordination.

One element that would facilitate this process is clear guidance on comprehensive climate risk management in development assistance. Such guidance should not be telling professionals how to do the work they have always done, but rather provide entry points and checklists that might facilitate policy coherence among various agencies that are now all starting to integrate climate risk management into their investments, and promote the sharing of tools and experiences across and between governments and development agencies. In the coming years, the key test for such guidance will then be whether it truly fosters learning-by-doing by practitioners in climate-sensitive development activities. A large number of such hands-on applications will then contribute both to the local operational capacity to access and apply relevant climate risk information and, based on rigorous monitoring and evaluation, to the global body of knowledge on how such interactions should be shaped and standardized.

Notes

1. This paper draws upon sections of Agrawala, S. (ed.), 2005, *Bridge over Troubled Waters: Linking Climate Change and Development*, Organisation for Economic Cooperation and Development (OECD), Paris, © OECD 2005. The views expressed in this paper are the authors' own and not necessarily those of the OECD or its member countries.
2. The case studies are discussed in further detail in Agrawala (2005).
3. Including official development assistance (ODA) and other official flows (OOF).
4. The documents examined include: national development plans, poverty reduction strategy papers (PRSPs), sectoral development strategies, national strategies for sustainable development, national communications under the United Nations Framework Convention on Climate Change (UNFCCC) and the United Nations Convention to Combat Desertification (UNCBD), country assistance strategies, country strategy papers, sectoral development strategies, project design documents, project evaluations, and environmental impact assessments.

References

ADB (Asian Development Bank), 2005, *Climate Proofing: A Risk-Based Approach to Adaptation*, Pacific Studies Series, ADB, Manila, The Philippines.

AfDB (African Development Bank), ADB (Asian Development Bank), DFID (UK Department for International Development), et al., 2003, *Poverty and Climate Change: Reducing the Vulnerability of the Poor through Adaptation*, World Bank, Washington, DC.

Agrawala, S. (ed.), 2005, *Bridge Over Troubled Waters: Linking Climate Change and Development*, Organisation for Economic Cooperation and Development (OECD), Paris.

Bettencourt, S., Croad, R., Freeman, P., Hay, J., Jones, R., King, P., Lal, P., Mearns, A., Miller, G., Pswarayi-Riddihough, I., Simpson, A., Teuatabo, N., Trotz, U., van Aalst, M., 2006, *Not If, but When: Adapting to Natural Hazards in the Pacific Islands Region*, Policy Note, World Bank, Washington, DC.

Burton, I., 2004, 'The adaptation deficit', in: A. Fenech, D. MacIver, H. Auld, R. Bing Rong, Y. Yin (eds), *Building the Adaptive Capacity*, Environment Canada, Toronto, 25–33.

Burton, I., van Aalst, M., 1999, *Come Hell or High Water: Integrating Climate Change Vulnerability and Adaptation into Bank Work*, World Bank Environment Department Paper 72, World Bank, Washington, DC.

Burton, I., van Aalst, M., 2004, *Look before You Leap: A Risk Management Approach for Integrating Climate Change Adaptation into World Bank Operations*, World Bank Environment Department Paper 100, World Bank, Washington, DC.

DANIDA, 2006, *Danish Climate and Development Action Programme: A Tool Kit for Climate Proofing Danish Development Cooperation*, DANIDA, Copenhagen, Denmark.

EC, 2004, *Climate Change in the Context of Development Cooperation (Including EU Action Plan on Climate Change and Development)*, Communication from the European Commission, Brussels, Belgium.

Eriksen, S., Næss, L.O., 2003, *Pro-Poor Climate Adaptation: Norwegian Development Cooperation and Climate Change Adaptation: An Assessment of Issues, Strategies and Potential Entry Points*, Report 2003:02, CICERO, Oslo, Norway.

Gigli, S., Agrawala, S., 2007, *Stocktaking of Progress on Integrating Adaptation to Climate Change Into development Cooperation Activities*, Com/ENV/EPOC/DCD/DAC(2007)1, OECD, Paris.

IDA/IMF (International Development Association/International Monetary Fund), 2002, Nepal Joint Staff Assessment of the Poverty Reduction Strategy Paper, World Bank, Washington, DC.

Klein, R.T.J., 2001, *Adaptation to Climate Change in German Development Assistance: An Inventory of Activities and Opportunities, with a Special Focus on Africa*, Deutsche Gesellschaft für Technische Zusammenarbeit (GTZ), Eschborn, Germany.

Klein, R.J.T., Eriksen, S.E.H., Næss, L.O., Hammill, A., Tanner, T.M., Robledo, C., O'Brien, K.L., 2007, *Portfolio Screening to Support the Mainstreaming of Adaptation to Climate Change into Development Assistance*, Tyndall Working Paper 102, Tyndall Centre for Climate Change Research, Norwich, UK.

OECD (Organisation for Economic Cooperation and Development), 2006, *Declaration on Integrating Climate Change Adaptation into Development Cooperation*, OECD, Paris.

Schmidhuber, J., Tubiello, F.N., 2007, 'Global food security under climate change', *Proceedings of the National Academy of Sciences* 104, 19703–19708, doi:10.1073/pnas.0701976104.

USAID, 2007, *Adapting to Climate Variability and Change: A Guidance Manual for Development Planning*, USAID, Washington, DC.

van Aalst, M., Hirsch, D., Tellam, I., 2007, *Poverty Reduction at Risk: Managing the Impacts of Climate Change on Poverty Alleviation Activities*, prepared for the Netherlands Ministry of Foreign Affairs/DGIS, Netherlands Climate Assistance Program, Leusden, The Netherlands.

World Bank, 2006, *Clean Energy and Development: Towards an Investment Framework*, prepared for Meeting of the World Bank–International Monetary Fund Development Committee, April 23, World Bank, Washington, DC.

World Bank, IEG (Independent Evaluation Group), 2006, *Hazards of Nature, Risks to Development: An IEG Evaluation of World Bank Assistance for Natural Disasters*, World Bank, Washington, DC.

■ synthesis article

Climate adaptation from a poverty perspective

GEOFF O'BRIEN[1]*, PHIL O'KEEFE[1,2], HUBERT MEENA[3], JOANNE ROSE[1,2], LEANNE WILSON[2]

[1] Northumbria University, Division of Geography and Environmental Management, Ellison Building, Northumbria University, Newcastle Upon Tyne NE1 8ST, UK

[2] ETC (UK), 117 Norfolk Street, North Shields, Tyne and Wear, NE30 1NQ, UK

[3] The Centre for Energy, Environment Science and Technology (CEEST Foundation), PO Box 5511, Dar es Salaam, Tanzania

Adaptation to already discernible climate changes, particularly an increase in extreme events, is an urgent task for all nations. This article argues that adaptation is an urgent priority, especially for the developing world, to build a resilient society. For poor nations, poverty alleviation is the main policy driver, although changes in livelihood strategies are driven by a range of factors. Using a case study, direct and indirect adaptation is examined with reference to the specific livelihoods of the Chagga people on Kilimanjaro, Tanzania. Evidence suggests that coping strategies to maintain livelihood systems can work against long-term adaptation to climate change, unless there is linkage to poverty alleviation. Linking climate change adaptation to project development through notions of additionality does not carry sufficient leverage to simultaneously address poverty alleviation and climate change. It is suggested that, rather than micro-economic project management, a broader macro-economic frame be established. A rights-based approach is argued as a vital driver for informing financial, institutional, political and technological policies and instruments.

Keywords: adaptation; climate change; coping mechanisms; developing countries; livelihoods; poverty alleviation; resilience; rights-based approach; vulnerability

L'adaptation aux changements climatiques déjà discernables, en particulier l'augmentation des évènements extrêmes, est une tâche urgente pour toutes les nations. Cet article soutient que l'adaptation est une priorité urgente, particulièrement dans le but de permettre au monde en développement de construire une société résiliente. Pour les nations pauvres, la réduction de la pauvreté est le principal moteur des politiques, bien que l'evolution des stratégies de subsistance soit influencés par plusieurs facteurs. Sur la base d'une étude de cas, l'adaptation directe et indirecte sont examinées en faisant référence aux modes de subsistance particuliers des Chagga du Kilimandjaro en Tanzanie. L'évidence suggère que les stratégies de lutte au maintien des systèmes de subsistance peuvent aller à l'encontre de l'adaptation à long terme au changement climatique, à moins qu'il y ait un lien avec la lutte contre de la pauvreté. Intégrer l'adaptation au changement climatique au développement de projet à travers les notions d'additionalité n'a pas une portée suffisante pour attaquer simultanément la réduction de la pauvreté et le changement climatique. La mise en place d'un cadre macro-économique plus large serait préférable à une gestion de projet micro-économique. Il est argumenté qu'une approche fondée sur les droits est un moteur essentiel pour informer les politiques et instruments financiers, institutionnels, politiques et technologiques.

Mots clés: adaptation; approche fondée sur les droits; changement climatique; mécanismes d'adaptation; pays en développement; réduction de la pauvreté; résilience; subsistance; vulnérabilité

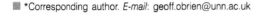

■ *Corresponding author. E-mail*: geoff.obrien@unn.ac.uk

CLIMATE POLICY 8 (2008) 194–201

doi:10.3763/cpol.2007.0430 © 2008 Earthscan ISSN: 1469-3062 (print), 1752-7457 (online) www.climatepolicy.com

1. Introduction

Climate change and variability is a multi-dimensioned hazard that can threaten life and livelihoods and impoverish people. Although weather-related disasters, such as hurricane Katrina, often appear as infrequent, but high-profile, events, the reality is that they account for some 90%, or $1.4 trillion, of recorded disaster-related economic losses. However, some 60% of losses derive from more mundane events such as temperature extremes and moderate droughts (McCarthy et al., 2001; Murnane, 2004; Mills, 2005). The Intergovernmental Panel on Climate Change (IPCC) predicts that climate-driven adverse impacts will increase. Many of these impacts will not be as catastrophic as hurricane Katrina, but are more subtle events that will gradually undermine livelihoods, particularly for poorer communities that are already on the edge of their coping capacity. With more frequent extreme events predicted in the near future, along with subtle and complex longer-term shifts in climate patterns, the challenge for public policy is effective risk reduction to both sudden extreme events and slow-onset disasters (IPCC, 2007).

This article explores the nature of vulnerability to climate change by focusing on issues of livelihood resilience. Using a detailed example from Tanzania, it explores how coping mechanisms develop in livelihood systems under stress, coming to the conclusion that a coping mechanism to maintain existing livelihood systems can work against long-term adaptation to climate change. Further discussion of the range of indirect adaptation possibilities as 'wicked problems' leads to the conclusion that project-based approaches to adaptation are insufficient. A broader programmatic approach based on poverty alleviation within and between countries is a necessary basis for future climate agreements.

2. Poverty, vulnerability and climate change

The science of climate change has largely focused on average changes in temperature and precipitation and the projected impact of sea-level rise. For most poor people living in developing countries, however, it is the increased variability associated with climate change that has more immediate impact and direct relevance (Kelly and Adger, 2000). Drought, flood and storm surge already dominate natural hazard impacts and will increasingly do so. Despite wide acknowledgement that adaptation without significant and sustained mitigation is not sufficient to avert climate impacts, the ability to adapt to climate change and variability is now an essential prerequisite for both sustainable development and poverty reduction (Kelly and Adger, 2000; Burton et al., 2002; Schipper, 2006; IPCC, 2007; UNDP, 2007).

Today, over 2 billion people are struggling to survive on an income of less than $1 a day. Even if the Millennium Development Goals are achieved on time – critically moving 1 billion people out of absolute poverty – demographic increases mean that by 2015 there will be the same number of people, if not more, in absolute poverty. Low income is only one component, however, of the multiple and interactive deprivations of human capabilities that sustain poverty (Sen, 1999; Baer et al., 2007). Millions of people around the world lack instrumental and substantive freedoms, including economic opportunities, political freedoms, social facilities, transparency guarantees, and protective security; this lack of freedom extends to the lack of the basic freedom to survive (Sen, 1999). Millions of people suffer unnecessary hardships, illness, misery and death – they are vulnerable.

Multiple vulnerabilities and risks form chronic and cumulative burdens for people living in poverty, particularly in situations where customary coping strategies are already at – or beyond – the brink of collapse, or alternatively work against longer-term adaptation initiatives.

The key concept here is the *erosion of resilience* (Bebbington, 1999; Kelly and Adger, 2000). Resilience is defined as the social capacity to resist and recover from shocks (O'Brien, et al., 2006). Disease epidemics, armed conflict and rapid urbanization are examples of how shocks and trends can disrupt and devastate livelihoods (Wisner et al., 2003). Climate variability – including varying seasonality – is a central component of vulnerability. Enhancing resilience through adaptation to climate variability, as well as other shocks and trends, demonstrates emerging good practice in development assistance targeted towards building sustainable livelihoods (DFID, 2004).

In the context of poverty, the adaptations that people are increasingly obliged to make in relation to increasing climate change impacts (such as heightened variability) are not easily discernable from the wider range of livelihood adjustments made in response to a variety of simultaneous and greater pressures; for example, globalization, political instability, urbanization and HIV/AIDS.

The basis of most foreign aid funds supported by donors who have signed the Kyoto agreement is that additional project costs due to climate hazard impact can be supported within development assistance (IISD, 2007). There are several difficulties with this; the first being that direct adaptation to climate change is difficult to separate from other livelihood adaptations. The second is that it proves to be extremely costly to accurately gauge additional project costs associated with adaptation (UNDP, 2007). Finally, the consideration of additionality implies a project-based approach to development, whereas most donors have abandoned this and moved towards sector-wide and core financial support to Treasury in programme modes, where these are largely focused on poverty alleviation.

3. Climate adaptation: the Tanzanian example

In the summer of 2007, a 1,000-household survey combined with qualitative analysis explored the relationships between livelihood vulnerability and climate adaptation. Fieldwork centred on the impact of climate change in the Kilimanjaro region. The survey instruments were originally used in a similar study in Rufiji, and refined in pilot surveys in Kilimanjaro (Stephenson, 2007). Both projects were directed by Hubert Meena, the Director of the Centre for Energy, Environment, Science and Technology (CEEST), a national think-tank that has contributed substantially to Tanzania's scientific submissions to the United Nations Framework Convention on Climate Change (UNFCCC).

The two systemic influences on East African climate, especially the precipitation that determines agricultural production, are the Inter-Tropical Convergence Zone, the high-pressure system that dominates, and the Southern Atlantic El Niño Oscillation (Paavola, 2004). There are indications that the former has moved, bringing greater aridity to both West and East Africa on a long-term basis, and that there is a 10–12-year cyclicity to the latter which coincides, over the last 50 years, with the occurrence of *njaa* ('hunger') in the region (Shariff, 2007).

Marked variability, not so much in temperature as in precipitation, is a well-documented phenomenon in Tanzania. In the Kilimanjaro region, annual precipitation varies by altitude, aspect and exposure. The precipitation is bimodal, falling in the short rains of October to December and the long rains of March to May. Total annual precipitation depends on the success of the short rains, and the onset, intensity and length of the long rains. In the study area, this can vary from 1,000–1,500 mm in the highlands to 700–900 mm in the lowlands. There is clear evidence, over the last 40 years, that temperatures have risen and precipitation has declined. More importantly, as the precipitation has declined, it has been accompanied by an increase in variability both across years and seasons (CEEST, 2007).

The Chagga, the people who live on the slopes of Kilimanjaro, have over the last century evolved a complex system of agroforestry gardens located at altitudes of 1,000–1,800 m above sea level. Trees 10–30 m tall shade bananas, which in turn shade coffee bushes. Ground cover includes herbs, beans and a variety of root crops, including yams (Soini, 2005; Hemp, 2006). On lower slopes where rainfall is less, some distance from their gardens, they plant maize and beans or, in very dry places, finger millet and cowpeas. It is, however, the gardens that are the centre of their livelihood system. The Chagga obtain food and a range of natural resources, especially wood, on which their family economies depend. These agroforestry systems are under threat from a range of drivers.

First, the population has increased from around 600,000 in the 1960s to around 2,000,000 today (Government of Tanzania, 2002). Second, this population increase has been accompanied by a significant diet change from bananas to maize as the key carbohydrate. Third, there is no longer any open savanna left on the lower slopes onto which they can expand their maize farms, and they are restricted on moving up the slopes by a combination of local government decisions that seek to preserve open space between the gardens and the higher montaine forest in order to help define the National Park – a major tourist attraction. Fourth, coffee production, the major cash crop from the gardens, has declined rapidly over the last 20 years, with output almost halving, reflecting a similar fall in real prices available from the world market. Finally, the gardens themselves are watered by a communal irrigation system that is now competing with the growth of commercial irrigated farming, including cut flowers for Europe (CEEST, 2007). Collectively, these pressures mean that the vital ecological services that the Chagga gardens provide in the Kilimanjaro catchment area are under threat.

The Chagga have always been a resourceful people. In the aftermath of the Second World War, they established a coffee cooperative that, among other things, paid for secondary schooling and university for their children. Following Independence in 1961, many moved into government and parastatal jobs, and this tradition has continued in local, regional and national labour markets (Coulson, 1982). Nearly all Chagga households have off-farm income from either formal employment or business activities. Other Tanzanians regard them as a relatively wealthy group because of their natural resource endowment and entrepreneurial activities. But there is real poverty and recurrent food insecurity.

Food insecurity is strongly gendered (Shariff, 2007). Women have lost control of the resources that were traditionally their income, particularly food crops. Timber products, coffee, honey and livestock were male income products but, with a collapse in the value of these products, not least from deforestation, men have moved into the women's realm. More importantly, especially for widowed or divorced women, loss of land entitlement and the poor protection offered by land law means that their entitlements are limited. Despite the proliferation of women's groups and their involvement in non-governmental organizations (NGOs), their future, if they do not receive remittances from their children, is bleak (Shariff, 2007).

Agricultural extensification is constrained by a lack of land availability on the slopes of Kilimanjaro (Hemp, 2006). Conventional agricultural intensification, by mechanized monocropping, is impossible because of the steepness of the slopes and the three-dimensional multicropping garden system. Intensification of the agroforestry system by recognizing its environmental service role in maintaining water quality, perhaps eventually financed through the Clean Development Mechanism, coupled with coffee rehabilitation that includes both production and processing to maximize local benefits, offers some hope. In terms of climate adaptation, returning to a banana diet would help, as maize suffers much more under drought conditions on the lower slopes and cannot be grown successfully on the higher slopes. Even if it were possible, this is unlikely to occur spontaneously among the Chagga people or any other groups in eastern and southern Africa.

For the Chagga themselves, increased variability in precipitation, which causes droughts – leading to food insecurity, is not the greatest threat to their livelihoods. Insecure employment markets, fluctuating foreign exchange rates and declining global coffee prices are experienced and expressed as a great threat to livelihoods. Their immediate coping mechanism is to cut the larger trees for sale, to sustain their local livelihood. This response may well jeopardize their longer-term adaptation requirements, not least because it lowers the atmospheric water content on Kilimanjaro leading, in turn, to less snow accumulation and run-off (Kaser et al., 2004). The fieldwork concluded that there is no simple or single causal factor in the pressures faced by the Chagga people. Beyond declining markets, there is a real threat to the Kilimanjaro catchment system since, without water, there will be no Chagga gardens.

As the case study demonstrates, people often experience simultaneous pressures, and climate change may not be perceived as the greatest of these. A clear conclusion that emerges from detailed fieldwork in Tanzania is that adaptation to global market signals is perceived as more immediately pressing than adaptation to climate change.

4. Indirect adaptation

Adaptation – and the broader climate change problematique – can be described as a 'wicked problem', where the answers are incomplete, contradictory and set against changing requirements; other examples include globalization, political instability, urbanization and HIV/AIDS. Climate adaptation is a problem where large groups of individuals have to change their mindsets and behaviour. One consequence of this is that many of the adaptations must be seen as indirect (Rittel and Webber, 1973). In a further exploration of the nature of 'wicked problems', Richey (2007) lists ten characteristics:

1. There is no definite formulation of the problem.
2. There is no exit strategy from the problem.
3. Answers are not true or false, but better or worse.
4. There is no immediate solution and no ultimate test of a solution.
5. Any intervention in a wicked problem counts significantly because there is no opportunity to learn by trial and error.
6. Wicked problems do not have a well-defined set of potential solutions.
7. Every wicked problem is unique.
8. Every wicked problem is a symptom of another wicked problem.
9. The logic of explanation of a wicked problem determines the solution.
10. Planners must be liable for the actions they generate in responding to a wicked problem.

Necessarily, in response to 'wicked problems', it is often 'indirect' adaptations that occur as a by-product of some other livelihood support or coping mechanism that increase resilience to climate hazards in the short term for poor people. Examples of 'indirect' adaptation include diversified cropping strategies; increasing food security through higher income or more secure access to productive land; and improving access to safe and reliable water and sanitation, energy, education and employment.

Some of the characteristics of indirect adaptations are listed below.

■ Indirect adaptations are not a specific response to the impacts or risk of climate change. Without food or water, for example, a person is unlikely to prioritize climate risk or benefit fully from any other forms of intervention until basic needs are met.

◼ Indirect adaptations may or may not increase the resilience of those experiencing chronic and absolute poverty to the additional pressures induced by increasing climatic hazard.
◼ Indirect adaptations are effective in the short term as – theoretically – they more accurately reflect the immediate needs of poor people and communities.
◼ Indirect adaptations can enhance the effectiveness of some forms of planned climate adaptation strategies, such as community-based disaster preparedness.

Looking at the range of indirect adaptations, it is obvious that they are a programmatic rather than a project-based response. Indirect adaptation to climate risk is a necessary, but not a sufficient, condition in moving beyond poverty. Many forms of adaptation are necessary but not sufficient in moving towards sustainable development while averting climate risk and disaster. It is clear that it is no longer plausible to proceed as if the global poverty crisis exists in isolation of climate change (Baer et al., 2007) and it is also vital to ensure that short-term adaptations do not preclude longer-term sustainable livelihoods.

5. A programmatic response from a poverty alleviation perspective

The economics of dealing with climate change – both adaptation and mitigation – must be addressed at the level of macro-economics (Stern, 2007; UNDP, 2007). The recognition that climate change requires a macro-economic or programmatic approach means that linking climate change to the global poverty alleviation programme is a useful way forward. The IPCC estimated the macro-economic costs for mitigation to stabilize the global climate ranges up to 5.5% of global GDP (IPCC, 2007).[1] The *Stern Report* estimated that if no action is taken to address climate change, then damages could cost between 5% and 20% of global GDP, while estimating that the cost of action to stabilize the climate and adapt to existing climate change would only cost around 1% of global GDP (Stern, 2007).

In the past, one radical climate change position has been 'Contraction and Convergence', which proposed an emission allowance on a per capita basis (Aubrey, 2001). However, to date, Contraction and Convergence is based on per capita emissions on a national scale that essentially prevents any consideration of the often significant wealth disparities within national borders.

Global poverty alleviation must be the starting point of any global climate change agreement. This is not only because the world's poorest people are most vulnerable to the additional impacts of climate change and variability, not only because they are least responsible for climate change, but also because they are the least able to adapt. Ultimately, averting dangerous climate change, stabilization of atmospheric GHG concentrations – at whatever level – requires that annual emissions be brought down to more than 80% below current levels while simultaneously protecting the development aspirations of those least responsible for climate change (Baer et al., 2007).

The Greenhouse Development Rights Framework builds upon, and is a potential route through, the stymied UNFCCC negotiations on 'common but differentiated responsibilities' (Baer et al., 2007). It is based on the 'Polluter Pays' principle that is already well established in most OECD (Organisation of Economic Cooperation and Development) countries since the 1970s. The Framework proposes an annual global 'middle-class income' development threshold of $9,000 (Purchasing Power Parity value) below which people bear no responsibility for curbing their (carbon) consumption. It is assumed that, below this income, people are 'surviving' rather than 'consuming' and are therefore exempt from per capita calculations that quantify national mitigation and adaptation obligations.

By exempting the poorest people, this allows meaningful consideration of the 'common but differentiated' national obligations that are faced by all countries, while preventing the obfuscation of the stark disparities in wealth present within both poor and rich nations.

Consumers above the global middle-class income level of $9,000 would bear the responsibility to pay the incremental costs of adaptation and clean technology 'leapfrogging'.

The $9,000 value has been proposed in order to draw a transparent and equitable income level beyond which is defined a collective and individual responsibility for implementing a 'global emergency programme' to avert catastrophic climate change. This global income level guarantees that those least responsible, and least able to adapt to climate change, are not locked into a poverty future. It also provides a platform for developing countries to join the negotiations without the risk that by so doing they will potentially retard their economic development prospects for the future.

The Greenhouse Development Rights Framework estimates that it would cost between 1% and 3% of global GDP to avert catastrophic climate change in an equitable fashion. Based on the proposed 'Capacity and Responsibility Indicator', in terms of national responsibilities for the global burden of costs, the USA would bear around one-third, the EU would bear around one-quarter, China would bear less than one-fifteenth, and India less than one three-hundredth. The indicator is important because it considers national obligations towards funding a global climate change initiative based upon the size of population enjoying a lifestyle above and beyond the global middle-class threshold.

The Framework also argues that in order to reduce emissions and decarbonize energy futures in developing countries, there needs to be financial, technological, political and institutional support given by the industrialized world (Baer et al., 2007). Technology 'leapfrogging' is an essential component of attaining global emissions reductions of over 80% and stabilizing the climate below a 2°C increase. In order to contribute towards poverty reduction and sustainable livelihoods, this technology 'leapfrogging' will need to address the lack of access and control over new and old technologies by the poorest people (O'Brien et al., 2007). It is also imperative that consumers above the global middle-class level financially support adaptation and emissions mitigation in the developing world, while the richer industrialized nations simultaneously reduce their structural reliance on fossil fuels (Baer et al., 2007; Smith, 2007).

6. Conclusions

This article used a case study to explore the links between climate change and poverty alleviation, arguing that it is the poverty alleviation challenge that is the priority, particularly in developing countries. Using the case study, we explored how direct and indirect adaptation is driven by issues beyond solely climate change. Trying to link climate change adaptation to project development through notions of additionality of cost because of climate impact does not carry sufficient leverage to simultaneously address poverty alleviation and climate change. It is suggested that, rather than micro-economic project management, a broader macro-economic frame be established, politically working on from the *Stern Report* towards the Greenhouse Development Rights Framework to address both mitigation and adaptation on a global scale.

Note

1. These models do not currently take account of non-technical options such as lifestyle changes.

References

Aubrey, M., 2001, *Contraction and Convergence: The Global Solution to Climate Change*, Green Books, Schumacher Briefings No 5.

Baer, P., Athanasiou, T., Kartha, S., 2007, *The Right to Development in a Climate Constrained World: The Greenhouse Development Rights Framework*, Ecoequity, Christian Aid, Heinrich Boll Foundation and Stockholm Environment Institute, Boston, MA.

Bebbington, A., 1999, 'Capitals and capabilities: a framework for analysing peasant viability, rural livelihoods, and poverty', *World Development* 27(12), 2021–2044.

Burton, I, Huq, S., Lim, B., Pilifosova, O., Schipper, E.L., 2002, 'From impacts assessment to adaptation priorities: the shaping of adaptation policy', *Climate Policy* 2, 149–159.

CEEST, 2007, *Proceedings of the CEEST Working Seminar on Climate Change Adaptation*, 16–18 July 2007, Moshi, Tanzania.

Coulson, A., 1982, *Tanzania: A Political Economy*, Clarendon Press, Oxford, UK.

DFID, 2004, *Key Sheet 5: Responding to the Risks of Climate Change: Are Different Approaches to Poverty Eradication Necessary?* [available at www.dfid.gov.uk/pubs/files/climatechange/5risks.pdf].

Government of Tanzania, 2002, *2002 Population Census*, Government of Tanzania, Dar es Salaam, figures accessed from Moshi District Statistics Bureau, 22/6/07.

Hemp, A., 2006, 'The banana forests of Kilimanjaro: biodiversity and conservation of the Chagga homegardens', *Biodiversity and Conservation* 15(4), 1193–1217.

IISD, 2007, *Sharing Climate Adaptation Tools: Improving Decision Making for Adaptation*, Geneva Workshop, 11–12 April 2007 [available at www.iisd.org/pdf/2007/sharing_climate_adaptation_tools.pdf].

IPCC, 2007, *Climate Change 2007: Impacts, Adaptation and Vulnerability. Contribution of Working Group II to the Intergovernmental Panel on Climate Change Fourth Assessment Report*, Cambridge University Press, Cambridge, UK.

Kaser, G., Hardy, D.R., Mölg, T.M., Bradley, R.S., Hyera, T.M., 2004, 'Modern glacier retreat on Kilimanjaro as evidence of climate change: observations and facts', *International Journal of Climatology* 24, 329–339.

Kelly, P.M., Adger, W.N., 2000, 'Theory and practice in assessing vulnerability to climate change and facilitating adaptation', *Climatic Change* 47, 325–352.

O'Brien, G., O'Keefe, P., Rose, J., Wisner, B., 2006, 'Climate change and disaster management', *Disasters* 30(1), 64–80.

O'Brien, G., O'Keefe, P., Rose, J., 2007, 'Energy, poverty and governance', *International Journal of Environmental Studies* 64(5), 607–618.

McCarthy, J.J., Canziani, O.F., Leary, N.A., Dokken, D.J., White, K.S. (eds.), 2001, *Climate Change 2001: Impacts, Adaptation and Vulnerability*. Cambridge University Press, Cambridge, UK.

Mills, E., 2005, 'Insurance in a climate of change', *Science* 309, 1041.

Murnane, R.J., 2004, 'Climate research and reinsurance', *Bulletin of the American Meteorological Society* 85(5), 697–707.

Paavola, J., 2004, *Livelihoods, Vulnerability and Adaptation to Climate Change in the Morogoro Region, Tanzania*, CSERGE Working Paper EDM 04-12 [available at www.uea.ac.uk/env/cserge/pub/wp/edm/edm_2004_12.pdf].

Richey, T., 2007, *Wicked Problems: Structuring Social Messes with Morphological Analysis*, Swedish Morphological Society [available at www.swemorph.com/pdf/wp.pdf].

Rittel, H.W.J., Webber, M.M., 1973, 'Dilemmas in a general theory of planning', *Policy Sciences* 4, 155–169.

Sen, A., 1999, *Development as Freedom*, Oxford University Press, Oxford, UK.

Schipper, E.L.F., 2006, 'Conceptual history of adaptation in the UNFCCC process', *Review of European Community & International Environmental Law* 15(1), 82–92.

Shariff, S.Z., 2007, Food insecurity in Kilimanjaro region. MSc dissertation, University of Northumbria, UK.

Smith, K., 2007, *The Carbon Neutral Myth: Offset Indulgences for your Climate Sins*, Transnational Institute, Amsterdam.

Soini, E., 2005, 'Changing livelihoods on the slopes of Mt. Kilimanjaro, Tanzania: challenges and opportunities in the Chagga homegarden system', *Agroforestry Systems* 64, 157–167.

Stephenson, M., 2007, Climate variability and livelihood vulnerability in Tanzania. MSc dissertation, University of Northumbria, UK.

Stern, N., 2007, *The Economics of Climate Change: The Stern Review*, Cambridge University Press, Cambridge, UK.

UNDP, 2007, *Human Development Report 2007/2008. Fighting Climate Change: Human Solidarity in a Divided World* [available at http://hdr.undp.org/en/reports/global/hdr2007-2008/].

Wisner, B., Blaikie, P., Cannon, T., Davies, I., 2003, *At Risk: Natural Hazards, People's Vulnerability and Disasters*, 2nd edn, Routledge, London.

■ synthesis article

Sustainable development and climate change: lessons from country studies

KIRSTEN HALSNÆS[1]*, P.R. SHUKLA[2], AMIT GARG[2]

[1] UNEP Risø Centre, Risø National Laboratory, Technical University of Denmark (DTU), Frederiksborgvej 399, PO 49, DK-4000 Roskilde, Denmark
[2] Indian Institute of Management, Ahmedabad Vastrapur, India

Sustainable development has been suggested as a framework for integrating development and climate change policies in developing countries. Mainstreaming climate change into sustainable development policies would allow these countries to achieve their development goals while addressing climate change. A number of research programmes have investigated how potential synergies could be achieved at national level and what kind of trade-offs between the various aspects of sustainable development have to be faced. An overview of these studies is provided, focusing on national case studies. The energy and transportation sectors are covered in many studies, but some attention is also given to the infrastructure sector and water supply. Most existing development policies will not lead to a sustainable development pattern, since they insufficiently address climate change. However, good opportunities exist for integrated policies to achieve development goals while engaging with climate change. The energy and transportation sector studies identified many alternative national low-cost policies with much lower GHG emissions than the business-as-usual policy. Opportunities are identified for alternative national development policies for infrastructure and water supply that provide resilience against climate variability and climate change.

Keywords: adaptation; climate change; development pathways; energy scenarios; international cooperation; international studies; sustainable development; vulnerability

Le développement durable a été proposé comme cadre pour intégrer les politiques sur le développement et le changement climatique dans les pays en développement. L'intégration du changement climatique aux politiques de développement durable permettrait à ces pays d'accomplir leurs objectifs de développement tout en abordant le changement climatique. Un nombre de programmes de recherche ont étudié la manière de réaliser les synergies potentielles au niveau national et les concessions entre les différents aspects du développement durable qui doivent être abordés. Les secteurs de l'énergie et du transport sont couverts dans maintes études, et un certain degré d'attention est aussi porté au secteur de l'infrastructure et de l'approvisionnement en eau. La plupart des politiques de développement ne mèneront pas à un modèle de développement durable, vu qu'elles n'abordent pas de manière suffisante la question du changement climatique. Cependant, de bonnes opportunités existent pour intégrer les politiques en vue d'accomplir les objectifs de développement tout en s'engageant dans le changement climatique. Les études dans les secteurs de l'énergie ont identifié de nombreuses politiques nationales alternatives de faible coût à faibles émissions de GES comparé aux politiques habituelles. Des opportunités ont été identifiées pour des politiques nationales alternatives en infrastructure et approvisionnement en eau pourvoyant un ressort contre la variabilité climatique et le changement climatique.

Mots clés: adaptation; changement climatique; coopération internationale; développement durable; études internationales; scénarios énergetiques; voies de développement; vulnérabilité

■ *Corresponding author. E-mail*: kirsten.halsnaes@risoe.dk

CLIMATE POLICY 8 (2008) 202–219

doi:10.3763/cpol.2007.0475 © 2008 Earthscan ISSN: 1469-3062 (print), 1752-7457 (online) www.climatepolicy.com

1. Introduction

Developing countries face great challenges in meeting key development objectives, which in many cases are under stress from enhanced climate variability and future change. The policies of these countries give a high priority to poverty development and increased energy supply, implying increasing greenhouse gas (GHG) emissions, which can compromise international efforts to stabilize atmospheric GHG concentrations. The challenge is to explore how synergies can be established between development objectives and climate change adaptation and mitigation, where wide participation in international climate policy cooperation is facilitated.

In many developing countries, policies that are sensible from a climate-change perspective can emerge as side-benefits of sound development programmes, but they do not arrive automatically. In the energy sector, some policies such as price reforms, sector restructuring, and the introduction of energy efficiency measures and renewable energy technologies can lead to decreasing GHG emissions without being implemented with a direct reference to climate change. However, the current investments in energy supply in many developing countries are still dominated by large shares of fossil-fuel-based energy that, without specific GHG emission reduction objectives, do not automatically align with international climate change policy goals.

This article reports the results from international study programmes that have considered the potential synergies and trade-offs between national development goals and climate change. An overview is given of the methodological lessons and empirical results from the studies, and it is concluded that further incentives might be needed in order to support large GHG emission reductions in developing countries.

National policies in developing countries often include goals for eradicating extreme poverty and hunger, ensuring primary education for all, encouraging female empowerment, enhancing life expectancy, access to energy for all, and environmental sustainability. The relationships between these goals and climate change have been considered by the international study programmes that are reviewed in this article. The links between these policy goals have, in a number of the studies, been addressed by selecting a few focal indicators of various economic, social and environmental dimensions of sustainable development (SD) that can be used as measurement points.

Accordingly, a methodological approach for studies of GHG emission reductions in the energy sector can be structured around an evaluation of specific scenarios and policies in relation to a number of focal indicators that reflect key SD dimensions. One way to organize such an analysis is to formulate a general objective function for policy evaluation that includes arguments in terms of indices for energy supply, energy access for different income groups, investments in renewable energy, and local and global environmental impacts. In this way, the policy assessment addresses to what extent local development needs and global climate-change policy perspectives can be met simultaneously. Some empirical results based on this approach are given subsequently.

The research programmes that are discussed in this article are the Development and Climate Programme (Halsnæs and Garg, 2006a; Kok and Verhagen, 2007), the Growing in the Greenhouse Project (Bradley and Baumert, 2005), and the OECD Development and Climate Project (OECD, 2005). A brief overview of the scope of these programmes is given in Table 1.

Table 1 shows that SD and climate change studies have particularly focused on large countries such as Brazil, China, India and South Africa. Furthermore, given the full range of countries, it is striking how many Asian case studies have been performed, while relatively few least developed

TABLE 1 Overview of research programmes on national SD policies and climate change

Programme/Project	Scope	Case studies	Institutions involved
Development and Climate Programme		Bangladesh, Brazil, China, India, Senegal, South Africa	Bangladesh Centre for Advanced Studies, Bangladesh; Climate Centre, Federal University of Rio de Janeiro, Brazil; Energy Research Institute, China (energy component); Chinese Academy of Agricultural Sciences, China (land-use component); Indian Institute of Management/Ahmedabad, India; ENDA, Dakar, Senegal; Energy Research Centre, University of Cape Town, South Africa; UNEP Risø, Denmark (energy component); Netherlands Environmental Assessment Agency MNP), The Netherlands (land-use component); Wageningen University and Research Centre, The Netherlands (land-use component)
Energy component (Halsnæs and Garg, 2006a; Halsnæs et al., 2006, Halsnæs and Garg, 2006b; Garg, 2006; La Rovere et al., 2006, Winkler et al., 2006	Energy sector development and GHG emissions infrastructure and vulnerability		
Land-use component (Verhagen, 2007)	Vulnerability reduction and adaptation options in land-use sectors		
Growing in the Greenhouse Project (Bradley and Baumert, 2005)	SD policies and measures for reducing GHG emissions	Brazil, China, India, South Africa	World Resources Institute, USA
OECD Development and Climate Project (OECD, 2005)	Vulnerability and adaptation	Egypt, Fiji, Bangladesh, Nepal, Tanzania, Uruguay	OECD Environment and Development Directorates

countries (LDCs) have participated. This implies that the studies can predominantly be used to draw conclusions about the integration of emerging economies in international climate policies.

The energy sector has been covered extensively in the studies, but some work has also been done on climate change vulnerability in relation to agriculture, water and infrastructure, and some results from the infrastructure and water sector will be presented (OECD, 2005; Shukla, 2007).

It can be concluded that the available studies have not covered the full array of integrated development and climate change policies, but they represent a first attempt to identify areas, where there seems to be the potential for integrated sustainable development (SD) and climate policies. Some examples of the results are given below.

2. Energy and climate change

Sustainable development, energy and GHG emissions have been focal areas in the Development and Climate Programme and the Growing in the Greenhouse Project. The first project has focused on energy scenarios and development–climate links in a national context, while the latter has examined case studies for transportation, electricity, and carbon capture and storage in different countries.

The Development and Climate Programme, using national energy models, has yielded data for the relationships between economic growth, energy consumption and GHG emissions for Brazil, China, India and South Africa. This provides opportunities for systematically assessing what is required in order to align development pathways of these large countries with lower GHG emissions and international climate change policy ambitions. First, the baseline scenario results from the Development and Climate national case studies are presented. This is followed by a presentation of alternative policy scenarios that explore how lower GHG emissions can be combined with achieving development goals through SD policies.

2.1. Baseline scenario analysis

The trend in energy intensity of the gross domestic product (GDP) and related CO_2 emissions from the energy sector are presented for the period 1970–2030 for Brazil, China, India and South Africa (Figure 1). The data are based on IEA statistics for the period until 1999 (IEA, 2000b) and on national scenario projections from 2000 to 2030, which have been developed as part of the studies. No specific climate policies are assumed to be implemented. The IEA scenarios (WEO, 2006) have taken lower economic growth projections for China and India, while the reference scenarios considered in the present article projects more robust economic growth. These have implications on their energy and emission trajectories.

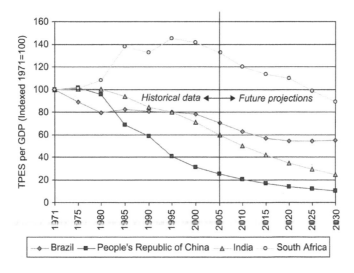

FIGURE 1 Energy intensity (TPES/GDP) for the period 1970–2030 in Brazil, China, India and South Africa, indexed; the GDP data are based on market exchange rates (IEA, 2000a, 2000b; Kejun et al., 2007; La Rovere et al., 2007; Shukla et al., 2007; Winkler et al., 2006).

Figure 1 shows that the energy intensity (total primary energy supply (TPES)/GDP) is decreasing over the whole period for China, India and Brazil. The picture is rather different for South Africa, where the TPES/GDP increases by about 40% from 1970 to 1995, followed by a decline. This initial rise was due to rising dependence on coal, including for oil conversion, and development of South Africa as an electricity (coal-based) abundant State. For China and India, energy intensity is expected to decrease sharply from 1970 to 2030 (more than 80% in the case of China, and about 70% in the case of India).

The trend in carbon intensity of energy use (CO_2/TPES) is very different from the energy intensity, as can be seen from Figure 2. For India, carbon intensity is projected to triple by 2030 compared with 1970, for Brazil to double, and for China to increase by about 50%. The increases are predominantly a consequence of the growing role of commercial fossil energy in the total primary energy supply of these countries as a consequence of shifting away from non-commercial traditional biofuels. In the case of Brazil, the limited capacity of hydropower leads to an increase in fossil-fuel-based power plants. The trend for carbon intensity of commercial fossil energy is, however, declining for most of the countries after the late 1990s. China is an exception, with a small increase in carbon intensity after 2000 due to increased coal use.

Figure 3 shows the resulting carbon intensity of the economy (CO_2/GDP) for the various countries. For one country (China), the energy intensity decrease is large enough to offset the increase in carbon intensity of energy, so the carbon intensity of the economy is decreasing. However, Brazil, India and South Africa initially experience an increasing carbon intensity of the economy, followed by an expected decrease in the period from 2000 to 2030.

It can be concluded from Figures 1, 2 and 3 that, in the period to 2030, where a very large GDP growth is anticipated in most of the countries, a large decrease in energy intensity can be expected. However, the carbon intensity of the economies tends to stay more or less constant or will only decrease after some period of time, which implies an absolute increase in carbon emissions per capita. Thus the baseline trends, reflecting current development choices, do not lead to significant

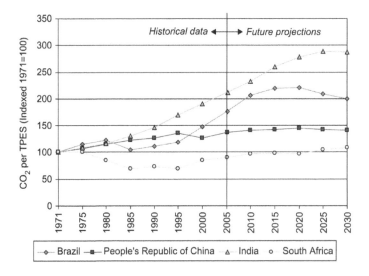

FIGURE 2 Carbon intensity of energy use (CO_2/TPES) for the period 1970–2030 in Brazil, China, India and South Africa (IEA, 2000a, 2000b; Kejun et al., 2007; La Rovere et al., 2007; Shukla et al., 2007; Winkler et al., 2007).

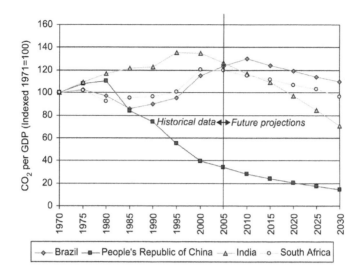

FIGURE 3 CO_2 intensity of GDP (CO_2/GDP) for the period 1970–2030 in Brazil, China, India and South Africa; the GDP data are based on market exchange rates (IEA, 2000a; IEA, 2000b; Kejun et al., 2007; La Rovere et al., 2007; Shukla et al., 2007; Winkler et al., 2007).

reductions in the carbon intensity of energy use, and this points to the policy conclusion that GHG emission reductions require particular policy instruments. This argument is further supported by Figure 4, which demonstrates the strong correlation between electricity consumption and economic output that has been seen in the period 1990–2030 for Brazil, China, India and South Africa.

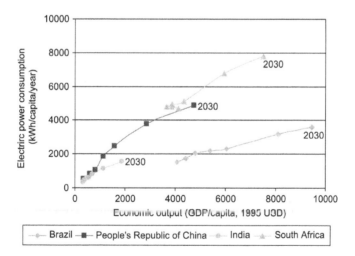

FIGURE 4 Relationship between GDP per capita and electricity consumption per capita: electricity consumption and economic growth projections for 1990–2030 for Brazil, China, India and South Africa (the seven points on the line indicate the years 1990, 1995, 2000, 2005, 2010, 2020 and 2030).

It is also important to recognize that energy consumption has a key social function: increased access to energy is important in poverty alleviation, welfare improvements, and employment creation policies. Therefore, global requirements for GHG emission reductions should not limit energy access in developing countries. Figure 5 shows present and future energy access based on the Brazilian, Chinese, Indian and South African baseline scenarios.

Figure 5 indicates that almost 100% of Chinese households had electricity access in 2000, while the percentage was only 55% in India and 63% for South Africa for the same year. By 2030, it is expected that more than 95% of the households in these countries will have electricity access, and this will require extensive expansion of the power supply and a large risk for increasing GHG emissions in these countries, which have very rich coal resources as the cheapest option.

When national electricity consumption data were studied in more detail, it was found that there are striking differences in per capita electricity consumption in rural and urban areas across the countries. Electricity access in India in 2000 was 45% and 82% for rural and urban households, respectively, and 45% and 75%, respectively, in South Africa (Halsnæs and Garg, 2006b).

Energy access also differs significantly across income groups. Table 2 shows the household expenditures on energy consumption for different income groups in India and China. Energy expenditures as percentage of income decreases with increasing income, and the share of the household budget spend in India and China for urban households varies between more than 10%, for the lowest-income group, down to around 5% for the highest-income households.

The development and climate studies are attempts to make an integrated assessment of various economic, social, and environmental SD dimensions based on indicators, and a brief overview of these results are given in Figure 6. The specific SD indicators shown here are economic growth, energy intensity, intensity of local pollution and GHG emissions, energy efficiency, investments in new power plants, renewable energy share and energy access. These indicators, taken together, provide an illustration of to what degree economic and social development objectives can be met in the countries without compromising the local and global environment.

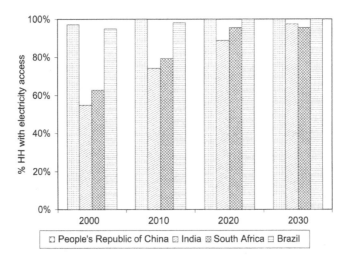

FIGURE 5 Households with electricity access: baseline scenarios for 2000–2030 for China, India, South Africa and Brazil

TABLE 2 Household expenditure on energy for Indian households in 2000 and Chinese households in 2004

HH income category	India rural, 2000		India urban, 2000		China urban, 2004	
	Absolute expenditure (US$, 2000 prices)	Share of total HH expenditure (%)	Absolute expenditure (US$, 2000 prices)	Share of total HH expenditure (%)	Absolute expenditure (US$, 2000 prices)	Share of total HH expenditure (%)
Poorest 0–5%	0.46	10.2	0.65	10.9	3.00	10.3
0–10%	0.51	10.1	0.80	10.7	3.33	9.8
10–20%	0.62	9.0	1.04	10.5	4.10	8.7
20–40%	0.73	8.7	1.46	10.1	4.79	7.9
40–60%	0.97	8.9	1.73	9.6	5.57	7.2
60–80%	1.15	8.6	2.13	8.9	6.55	6.6
80–90%	1.44	8.1	2.67	7.8	7.67	6.0
Top 90–100%	1.79	7.2	4.01	5.7	10.10	5.0

Note: Fuel and light expenditure for India (NSSO, 2001); water, oil and electricity expenditure for China (China Statistics Yearbook, 2005).

The figures are structured as multidimensional web diagrams showing the development over time from 2000 to 2030 in the index values of SD indicators for Brazil (Figure 6a), China (Figure 6b), India (Figure 6c) and South Africa (Figure 6d). The index values are defined in such a way that the nominal trend of the index reflects the fact that all these variables should increase over time in order to be considered as supporting SD.

The Brazilian baseline development trends from 2000 to 2030, shown in Figure 6a, are characterized by a large increase in power sector investments and increasing CO_2 and SO_2 intensity of energy consumption. The share of renewable energy remains more or less constant and there is an increase in

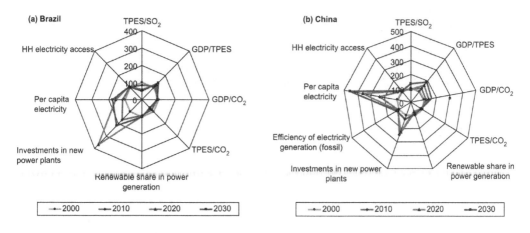

FIGURE 6 Sustainable development indicator projections in the years 2000, 2010, 2020 and 2030 for (a) Brazil, (b) China, (c) India and (d) South Africa for the baseline scenario. An increasing trend over time for any indexed indicator supports SD.

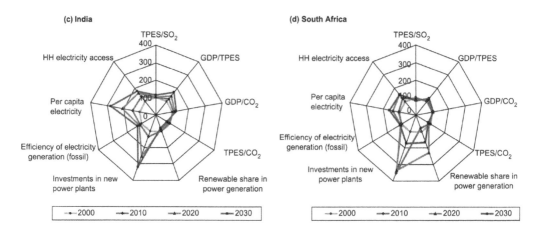

FIGURE 6 Sustainable development indicator projections in the years 2000, 2010, 2020 and 2030 for (a) Brazil, (b) China, (c) India and (d) South Africa for the baseline scenario. An increasing trend over time for any indexed indicator supports SD. *(Contd)*

per capita electricity consumption, especially in the next 10 years, when per household ownership of electricity-consuming appliances such as washing machines and refrigerators increases along with rising incomes. It is noted here that Brazil's per capita electricity consumption at 2,037 kWh/year is already quite high in comparison with other large developing countries like China and India. This is in part explained by a much greater urban population in Brazil than in China and India.

The baseline scenario for China for 2000–2030, shown in Figure 6b, implies an increasing share of renewable energy and a very large increase in per capita electricity consumption (from 1,066 kWh/year in 2000 to 4,872 kWh/year in 2030), while the energy efficiencies of CO_2 and SO_2 emissions improve slightly over 2000–2030. SO_2 emissions show a larger reduction than CO_2 emissions. There is also a high growth in power plant investments, and the efficiency of power production increases by about 20%.

In India, there is a growth in the CO_2 emission intensity of energy consumption, while the SO_2 intensity decreases from the 2000 level (Figure 6c). The energy intensity of GDP also decreases over the period. The per capita electricity consumption increases about threefold, from 557 kWh/year in 2000 to 1,568 kWh/year in 2030, which is still below the present per capita electricity consumption in Brazil, China and South Africa. The lower per capita electricity consumption in India is due to a very high rural population share (73% in 2000), with much lower electricity consumption in rural areas. The rural consumption is projected to increase dramatically in the future with increasing power access. This also reflects the rising investments in the power sector.

South Africa has a particularly high growth in power sector investments from 2000 to 2030 and also some growth in the share of renewable energy in power generation (Figure 6d). The CO_2 intensity of GDP is almost constant throughout the period, while the energy GDP intensity decreases slightly. Per capita electricity consumption is expected to have a relatively modest increase, and this should be seen in the context of the current very high consumption at 4,796 kWh/year.

Several general conclusions can be drawn from Figure 6. There is a tendency for an increase in carbon intensity of energy use in all countries, but this tendency is offset over time by decreasing energy/GDP intensity. Sulphur emissions are generally declining in all countries, which reflects the fact that local environmental policies are becoming increasingly important in these countries. Investments in the power sector are expected to grow fast in the period. In

China and India this implies a large growth in per capita electricity consumption from a present relatively low base. This growth is a high social policy priority in many countries. It is worth recognizing that none of the countries expect very large increases in the share of renewable electricity production in the period, so the major part of new power sector investment is going to be fossil-fuel-based. Although other important indicators on health, employment, import dependency and vulnerability to climate change are not available, the conclusion can be drawn that baseline development in these countries does not lead to a sustainable development in all the focal areas; while a number of economic indicators move in the right direction, GHG emissions still show a high growth.

2.2. Alternative policy scenarios

The next question is therefore: what possibilities exist for alternative policies that deliver development in a truly sustainable development path, including a low-GHG-emission economy and a low vulnerability to climate change?

The Brazil case study of the Development and Climate Programme included an alternative scenario for the power sector, where the electricity generation in 2030 is almost 30% lower due to policies to improve the efficiency of energy use, including demand-side efficiencies of electricity consumption, and where CO_2 emissions are more than 40% lower due to a higher renewable energy share in the power supply (La Rovere et al., 2007; see also Figure 7).

A major policy shift as part of this alternative policy scenario for Brazil is the further development and improvement of biofuel use (bioethanol and biodiesel), which can be used in the transport sector and for electricity generation in remote communities without grid connection. It implies improving Brazil's energy security, its trade balance and its air quality in cities, as well as lowering

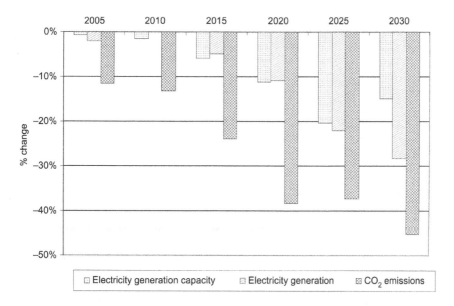

FIGURE 7 Percentage changes in alternative policy scenario over the reference scenario for the power sector in Brazil (La Rovere et al., 2007).

its GHG emissions. The Development and Climate case study includes a detailed assessment of how past and present biofuel programmes have delivered economic benefits and improved air quality in large cities. It concludes that the biofuels programme between 1975 and 2000 has offset 550 million barrels of imported oil, saved US$11.5 billion in foreign exchange, and has avoided 400 million tonnes of CO_2 emissions (Halsnæs and Garg, 2006b).

There are a number of barriers to implementing the alternative policy scenario in Brazil. For example, the existing electricity tariff policies have not strongly encouraged biomass-based electricity production, and in the transportation sector it has been suggested that the efficiency labelling of biofuel-flex vehicles would help to increase the share of biofuels being used.

The alternative policy scenario for China focuses on a strong improvement in the efficiency of electricity production and energy use and a modest increase in the use of renewable and nuclear energy. These policies are motivated by concerns about local air quality (cleaning up coal use and road transport) and energy security (reducing import dependency on oil and diminishing logistical problems with coal supply to the eastern part of China). Compared with the reference scenario, this provides a coal-based energy demand reduction of 120 Mtoe in 2030, a CO_2 emission reduction of 371 Mt in 2030 and a cumulative CO_2 mitigation of over 3% over the reference scenario during 1971–2030 (see Figure 8).

The energy supply structure in the reference and alternative case for the period 2010–2030 is compared in Figure 9, which shows that both coal consumption and natural gas use decrease significantly in the alternative scenario due to the introduction of highly efficient conversion technology in the power sector and in industry, such as supercritical boilers, IGCC, and advanced industrial boilers and kilns (Halsnæs and Garg, 2006b).

The Indian case study of the Development and Climate Programme also included the assessment of a very deep reduction of CO_2 emissions, consistent with a global 550 ppmv CO_2 stabilization scenario. Based on energy economic modelling, it was concluded that India, in a cost-effective

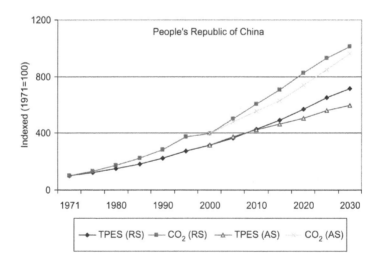

FIGURE 8 Development in total energy demand and CO_2 emissions in China in the reference scenario (RS), and the alternative scenario (AS), 1971–2030 (Kejun et al., 2007).

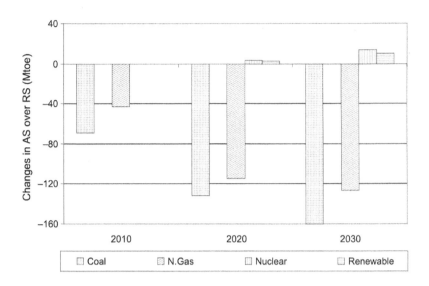

FIGURE 9 Comparison of energy supply structure in China in the reference and the alternative scenario, 2010–2030.

way, could be part of such an international effort if the carbon price were to increase from about zero in 2010 to around US$65/tCO$_2$ by 2100. This carbon price level reflects the carbon price in international models corresponding to a 550 ppmv scenario. The results in terms of the optimum choice of energy sector technologies are shown in Figure 10.

The analysis shows a mitigation of 53% of CO$_2$ emissions in 2095 and 31% in cumulative emissions for 105 years (Figure 10). There are two major insights from this analysis. First, a variety

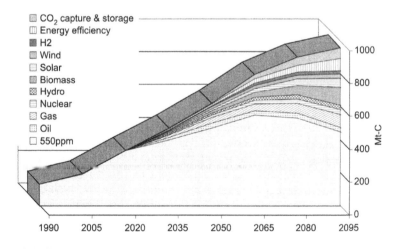

FIGURE 10 A possible portfolio of technologies to achieve mitigation required in India to meet a global 550 ppmv stabilization target (Shukla et al., 2007).

of sources contribute to mitigation. Because mitigation is required in large quantum and spread over the horizon, it cannot be achieved by any 'silver bullet'. Every form of contribution is needed: from wide options including the new and emerging technologies of today such as hydrogen and CO_2 capture and storage. Significant contributions of biomass and energy efficiency in mitigation further imply the kind of efforts required to enable uptake of such choices. The second insight is that most mitigation is going to be achieved by replacement of coal in all possible industries and technologies, as nearly 55% of coal in the reference scenario in 2095 reduces to around 25% in the mitigation scenario. This has very significant implications for energy security concerns and also for the large coal reserves becoming superfluous under such a strong stabilization regime. The sustainability of such a scenario in terms of development benefits will very much depend on how the additional costs of this scenario will be financed, in particular to what extent the financing can be supported by international cooperation.

The India case study of the Development and Climate Programme looked into several alternative energy sector policies that can support SD and climate change jointly. One interesting example with a large potential is the so-called South-Asian Energy Cooperation. South Asia is the most densely populated region in the world, with diverse natural and energy resources. It is also one of the most vulnerable regions to the adverse impacts of climate change. Low incomes and a vast population below the poverty line exacerbate this vulnerability.

Integrating regional energy and electricity markets could provide significant direct, indirect and spill-over benefits via economic efficiency, energy security, water security and environmental integrity, leading to overall economic benefits for each country in the region. Furthermore, individual countries can reduce their respective energy consumptions while maintaining their economic growth rates. This becomes possible due to exploiting the additional and cheaper power generation capacities in individual countries (such as hydro in Nepal and Bhutan) and exporting it to neighbouring countries; sharing cleaner energy resources and technologies; and providing safe passage to imported natural gas (such as through Pakistan, Afghanistan and Bangladesh) for high-demand regions. Over 2010–2030, the benefits include reduced primary energy requirements for South Asia (59 Exajoules), reduced CO_2 emissions (over 5.1 BtCO$_2$), reduced SO_2 emissions (50 MtSO$_2$), increased competitiveness of industry due to lower energy prices, 16 GW additional hydro capacity resulting in flood control and marine production; lower adverse health impacts on populations due to less coal combustion; and a number of social impacts. The cumulative economic value of these benefits over a 20-year period from 2010 to 2030 would be over US$390 billion, i.e. nearly 1% of the region's GDP for the entire period. Realizing such a regional collaboration will, of course, have to overcome a myriad of barriers including many political obstacles as well as capital constraints.

The case study for South Africa examined alternative policy cases with a primary focus on electricity supply, and Figure 11 shows the total CO_2 emissions under alternative scenarios.

The study looked at alternative options with an emphasis on different supply options (nuclear energy, gas, renewables and hydroelectricity). One of the alternative power supply options that might be attractive to South Africa is the import of hydropower-based electricity from the southern African region, and the study includes an assessment of this potential, taking future climate change into consideration. Recognizing huge uncertainties, it is concluded that the hydropower potential is fairly robust, even under conditions of significant climate change. Implementation of cross-border cooperation on hydropower in the South African region, however, will have to overcome many political barriers.

In addition, an alternative scenario with a combination of options was studied. This alternative could deliver a 13% CO_2 emission reduction in 2030, with the largest contribution from nuclear

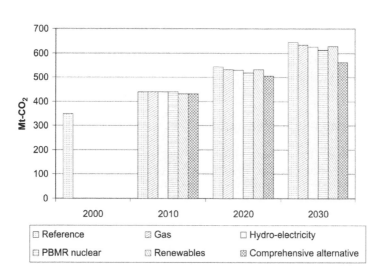

FIGURE 11 CO$_2$ emission projections for South Africa in the reference case and alternative policy scenarios, 2000–2030 (Winkler et al., 2007).

power (see Figure 11). This relatively modest CO$_2$ emission reduction has relatively low costs, but the study emphasizes that the participation of South Africa in international stabilization policies would probably imply significant costs that can have important negative development implications if they are not compensated by international collaboration. These costs, for example, could threaten energy affordability and could demand huge foreign exchange expenditures.

Case studies performed as part of the Growing in the Greenhouse Project also resulted in the identification of significant GHG emission reduction potentials while meeting development goals. This, for example, can be seen in the case study of China on motorization trends (Bradley and Baumert, 2005). As a rapidly growing economy, China is experiencing high growth in vehicle ownership and use. Bradley and Baumert (2005) highlight a strong relationship between GDP per capita and car ownership across countries. This points to the conclusion that vehicle ownership, energy consumption and GHG emissions from the transport sector may increase very fast in China unless alternative policies are introduced.

The study included three alternative scenarios, namely the baseline scenario Road Ahead (RA), and the policy scenarios Oil Saved (OS) and Integrated Transport (IT). The OS scenario is focused on more efficient vehicles and diversification of transport fuels to reduce import dependency of oil through fuel taxes and introduction of CNG fuels. The IT scenario assumes very small gasoline and electric cars and various options to avoid congestion and fuel taxes. These policy options have very great implications for future GHG emissions, but the implementation of these will also require large behavioural changes.

These alternative transport policies could have a very big influence on future GHG emissions. Total carbon emissions from road transport in the baseline scenario are expected to grow from 8.8 Mt C (around 30 MtCO$_2$) in 2003 to 102 Mt C (about 380 MtCO$_2$) in 2020. In the OS scenario, these emissions could be reduced by 50% by 2020, and in the IT scenario the reduction is almost 80% by 2020 compared with the baseline level. The implementation of such extreme GHG emission reductions in road transport will, of course, require a wide range of policies which, according to the study, would include technological standards, taxes, road pricing, public transportation, non-motorized transport and parking charges. Both alternative transport policies serve the purpose of providing the mobility that is essential for social and economic development, and can also help to improve the local air quality.

3. Vulnerability and adaptation options

The Development and Climate Programme has involved a number of national case studies and examples of these are given in this section, including infrastructure studies for India and water scarcity and demand-side management for South Africa.

India is currently in a development phase, where very large investments are made in infrastructure. A study by Shukla (2006) focused on climate variability and extremes related to precipitation and hydrological systems. It is concluded that, despite infrastructure projects being very vulnerable to climate change, the many investments that are currently made in fast-growing economies do not take climate variability and change into consideration.

The Indian study presents an analytical framework in terms of a reverse-impact matrix methodology for climate change impact analysis and a case study of one of the most well-known infrastructure projects in India: the Konkan Railway project. The Konkan Railway was constructed during the last decade and passes through the high-rainfall western Ghat (mountain) region. It is a typical example of a high-value, long-life asset exposed to climate extremes.

The analysis of the project shows that project design and configuration would have been altered if adverse climate impacts had been taken into consideration, and that this already implies large costs. The profit and loss account of the railway company KRCL shows that currently 6% of the annual budget is spent on repair and maintenance and, out of the total repair and maintenance budget, close to 70% goes on the repair and maintenance of permanent components and for bridges and tunnels. As per the estimates of officials at KRCL, about 20% of this expenditure is related to climate-related impacts, and it is clear that any future climate change will definitely increase expenditure on repair and maintenance activities.

The Indian infrastructure study also includes a brief mention of some other recent large-scale projects under discussion in India, namely the 'Linking the Rivers' Project and the development of a national highway network. It is argued that the likely damages from climate change to long-life assets and dependent economic activities could be very high. Furthermore, future climate change vulnerability can be best reduced by adaptation measures that are incorporated into the project design and by operational practices that closely monitor the changing climate as well as future environmental changes. An example of such environmental changes is deforestation around the railway line, which may increase the probability of landslides. In addition, measures to enhance the coping capacity of society to climate change impacts are, for example, the development of insurance markets for sharing and transferring the risks of extreme climate impacts. The analysis shows that the risk of climate change impacts should be internalized within the overall investment framework and the technical design of infrastructure projects.

The South African case study of the Development and Climate Programme focused on future water scarcity as a result of climate change and potential development-related policy options to reduce vulnerability (Mukheibir, 2007). South Africa is expected to be one of the countries that will suffer most from increased water scarcity, and the study includes a detailed assessment of additional water supply requirements in 2035 caused by climate change in the Bresdadorp Municipal Area.

Under a business-as-usual scenario, it is expected that by 2035 planners will need to provide more than 50% more water than without climate change, and this additional supply requires investments 3.5 times greater than the investments without climate change (equal to about US$4.25 million). The unit water costs would increase 2.5 times as a result.

There are several water demand-side management options available that would make sense from the point of view of efficient water use. Some of those with a large potential mentioned in the study are shower-head performance standards, leakage control, washing machine performance standards, and residential and industrial audits and retrofitting. It was considered that implementing a series of demand-side management options could delay water supply investments by 1–2 years up to 2035, which would decrease the additional capital cost associated with climate change by around 8%, which is a significant contribution, but still leaves a huge water supply issue in terms of efficient agricultural water use to be solved.

The OECD project *Bridge Over Troubled Water* (OECD, 2005) included detailed case studies on climate change impacts and development-related proactive adaptation in Egypt, Fiji, Bangladesh, Nepal, Tanzania and Uruguay. The cases demonstrated several examples of how key development objectives might be influenced by climate change, and a significant portion of development assistance is directed at the climate-sensitive sector; this ranges from 50% to 65% in Nepal, and from 12% to 26% in Tanzania. Furthermore, recommendations were given about how many of the projects could be climate-proofed. Despite the vulnerability of many development projects, most activities today routinely overlook climate issues. Some of the recommendations from the OECD study are that climate information, including short-term forecasts and variability, should be made available, and climate-risk screening tools should be developed and applied.

4. Conclusions

This article has provided an overview of a number of research programmes on SD policies and climate change. The activities do not comprehensively cover the full agenda of integrated SD and climate change policies, but they do provide some very useful case examples on synergies between achieving development objectives and dealing with GHG emissions and climate change vulnerability.

The energy sector, in particular, has been studied extensively and it has been demonstrated that there are very strong linkages between alternative economic and energy development scenarios and GHG emissions. For Brazil, China, India and South Africa, it has been shown that current development plans do not lead to a sustainable development pattern since, in all cases, a strong increase in GHG emissions can be expected. It is also shown that there are many good opportunities for alternative development policies to achieve social and economic development goals while resulting in an economy with lower GHG emissions, although not as low as what would be required to meet global stabilization targets at low levels. The plans will require decreasing the energy intensity of GDP and also a tendency to decrease GHG emission intensity over time; however, more efforts in terms of international finance and policy cooperation are needed.

In India, the results of a 550 ppmv study show that technical options are available in the energy sector, including a wide range of renewable energy options, carbon capture and sequestration, advanced fossil fuels, and nuclear power. Furthermore, it was reported that huge economic and GHG emissions savings could be achieved by South Asian regional energy collaboration. The implementation of such options will need support from international cooperation, both regionally and globally, including partnerships in research and demonstration projects, finance, and carbon market development.

In the case of motorization in China, it was demonstrated that more far-reaching climate policy scenarios can actually imply large emission reductions, but this again will require behavioural changes and the use of a wide range of policy options such as fuel taxes, promotion of electric vehicles, CNG fuels, options to avoid congestion such as public transport and non-motorized transport, and road pricing and parking charges. These policies are closely linked to urban planning and also require large investments and lifestyle changes, so the actual policy implementation is likely to meet several financial and social barriers.

Climate change is expected to impose serious impacts on key development sectors in many developing countries, and studies have generated a number of very specific results that demonstrate the high costs of climate change impacts, and opportunities for alternative development policies that could reduce vulnerability. The hydrological system impacts on infrastructure have been studied for railway systems and water regulation in India, and it was concluded that even projects that were established less than 10 years ago are already experiencing large maintenance costs because emerging increased climate variability had not been taken into consideration. Future water regimes will impose increased scarcity in dry areas of South Africa, and it is estimated that an additional 250% capital costs will be needed for water supply in municipal areas due to climate change. Some of these costs can be avoided by demand-side management, but seriously increased water scarcity still remains, and the water unit costs will increase with negative development impacts.

Many of the international study programmes that have been considered in this review originally included ambitions about being able to draw conclusions about how future international policy regimes could build on an integrated SD and climate change framework. However, the studies include relatively few results and concrete recommendations about climate policies, despite the fact that the results clearly demonstrate that specific policy initiatives need to be integrated into national development policies in order to cope with climate vulnerabilities and rising GHG emissions. One could argue that although the programmes have demonstrated the technical and economic potential for joint SD and climate change mitigation and adaptation policies, they have not in practice laid out what policy implementation requires in terms of national and international agreements and regulations.

References

Bradley, R., Baumert, K. (eds), 2005, *Growing in the Greenhouse: Protecting the Climate by Putting Development First*, WRI, Washington, DC.

China Statistics Yearbook, 2005, *China Statistics Yearbook*, National Bureau of Statistics of China [available at www.stats.gov.cn/english/].

Garg, A., 2006, 'Pro-equity effects of ancillary benefits of climate change policies: a case study of human health impacts of outdoor air pollution in New Delhi', paper submitted to *World Development Journal*.

Halsnæs, K., Garg, A., 2006a 'Assessing the role of energy in development and climate policies: conceptual approach and key indicators', paper submitted to *World Development Journal*.

Halsnæs, K., Garg, A., 2006b *Sustainable Development, Energy and Climate: Exploring Synergies and Tradeoffs – Methodological Issues and Case Studies from Brazil, China, India, South Africa, Bangladesh, and Senegal*, UNEP Risø Centre, Denmark.

Halsnæs, K., Garg, A., Olhofff, A., Denton, F., 2006, *Practical Guidance Material for the Development, Energy and Climate Country Studies*, UNEP Risø Centre, Denmark.

IEA, 2000a, *Energy Statistics for OECD Countries*, International Energy Agency, OECD/IEA, Paris.

IEA, 2000b, *Energy Statistics for Non-OECD Countries*, International Energy Agency, OECD/IEA, Paris.

Kejun, J., Xiulian, H., Xianli, Z., Garg, A., Halsnaes, K., Qiang, L., 2007, *Balancing Energy, Development and Climate Priorities in China: Current Status and the Way Ahead*, UNEP Risø Centre on Energy, Climate and Sustainable Development, Roskilde, Denmark.

Kok, M., Verhagen, J., 2007, Kok, M., Metz, B., Verhagen, J., van Rooijen, S., 2008, 'Integrating development and climate policies: national and international benefits', *Climate Policy* 8(2), 103–118.

La Rovere, E.L., Pereira, A.S., Simões A.F., 2006, 'Biofuels and sustainable energy development in Brazil', paper submitted to *World Development Journal*.

La Rovere, E.L., Pereira, A.O., Simões, A.F., Pereira, A.S., Garg, A., Halsnaes, K., Dubeux, C.B.S., da Costa, R.C., 2007, *Development First: Linking Energy and Emission Policies with Sustainable Development for Brazil*, UNEP Risø Centre on Energy, Climate and Sustainable Development, Roskilde, Denmark.

Mukheibir, P., 2007, *The Impact of Climate Change on Small Municipal Water Resource Management: The case of Bredasdorp, South Africa*, Draft Working Paper, Energy Research Centre, University of Cape Town, South Africa.

NSSO, 2001, *Differences in Level of Consumption among Socio-Economic Groups 1999–2000*, Report No. 472 (55/1.0/10), National Sample Survey Organization, Ministry of Statistics and Programme Implementation, Government of India, New Delhi.

OECD, 2005, *Bridge Over Troubled Water: Linking Climate Change and Development*, S. Agrawala (ed.), OECD, Paris.

Shukla, P.R., 2006, *Climate Change Impacts, Vulnerability and Adaptation for infrastructure Assets: Case Studies of Konkan Railway and other selected Infrastructure Projects in India and Lessons for Aligning Development and Climate Policies*, Working Paper, UNEP Risø Centre, Denmark.

Shukla, P.R., 2007, *Development, Energy and Climate Change: India Country Report*, UNEP Risoe Centre, Denmark.

Shukla, P.R., Garg, A., Dhar, S., Halsnaes, K., 2007, *Balancing Energy, Development and Climate Priorities in India: Current Trends and Future Projections*, UNEP Risoe Centre on Energy, Climate and Sustainable Development, Roskilde, Denmark.

WEO (World Energy Outbok) 2006, IEA, Paris.

Winkler, H., Simões, A.F., La Rovere, E.L., Alam, M., Rahman, A., Mwakasonda, S., 2006, 'Access and affordability of electricity in developing countries', paper submitted to *World Development Journal*.

Winkler, H., Mukheibir, P., Mwakasonda, S., Garg, A., Halsnaes, K., 2007, *Electricity Supply Options, Sustainable Development and Climate Change Priorities: Case Studies for South Africa*, UNEP Risø Centre on Energy, Climate and Sustainable Development, Roskilde, Denmark.

climate
policy

■ synthesis article

Brazilian transport initiatives with GHG reductions as a co-benefit

SUZANA KAHN RIBEIRO*, ADRIANNA ANDRADE DE ABREU

PET/COPPE/UFRJ – Federal University of Rio de Janeiro, Transport Engineering Programme, Centro de Tecnologia, Bloco H, Sala 106, Cidade Universitária, CEP: 21945-970, Rio de Janeiro, RJ, Brazil

High oil prices and poor air quality in the urban areas are important factors that motivate efforts to cut consumption of petroleum products. Four public policy initiatives for the Brazilian transport sector are analysed: the adoption of flexfuel technology; the National Biodiesel Programme; the National Vehicle Efficiency Programme; and the Rio de Janeiro State Light Vehicle Inspection and Maintenance Programme. Economic impacts (petrol and diesel avoided) are shown. Significant co-benefits are shown in terms of reduced CO_2 emissions that are often not considered or accounted for by Brazilian policy makers. Lessons from these initiatives for domestic and international policy are presented.

Keywords: biodiesel; Brazil; climate policy; CO_2 emissions; ethanol; flexfuel technology; mitigation; transport sector; vehicle efficiency

Le prix élevé du pétrole et la mauvaise qualité de l'air dans les régions urbaines sont des facteurs importants influençant les efforts de réduction de la consommation des produits pétroliers. Quatre initiatives de politique publique dans le secteur du transport brésilien sont analysées: l'adoption de la technologie des polycarburants; le programme national de biodiesel; le programme national sur l'efficacité des véhicules; et le programme d'inspection et d'entretien des véhicules légers de l'Etat de Rio de Janeiro. Les impacts économiques (pétrole et diesel évité) sont montrés. D'importants gains sont démontrés en terme de réduction des émissions de CO_2 qui ne sont souvent pas pris en compte ou comptabilisés par les décideurs brésiliens. Les leçons tirées de ces initiatives pour les politiques internationales sont présentées.

Mots clés: atténuation; biodiesel; Brésil; efficacité des véhicules; émissions de CO_2; éthanol; politique climatique; secteur du transport; technologie des polycarburants

1. Introduction

Transportation is the human activity that most uses petroleum as an energy resource, in the form of its various refined products. This is the case for Brazil, where in 2006, 40% of final energy consumption came from petroleum derivatives, with the transport sector consuming 61% of these derivatives. Within the transport sector, the most intense use is road transportation, which uses 96% of the country's diesel and 99% of its petrol (MME, 2007).

While the Brazilian transport sector mainly consumes fossil fuels, biofuels also play an important role, ethanol being the most important. In Brazil, ethanol from sugarcane is used as automotive fuel, either pure or blended with petrol. In fact, petrol in Brazil is not used in its pure form, but rather is blended with anhydrous ethanol, ranging from 20% to 25% by volume (called gasohol).

■ *Corresponding author. E-mail:* skr@pet.coppe.ufrj.br

CLIMATE POLICY 8 (2008) 220–240

doi:10.3763/cpol.2007.0431 © 2008 Earthscan ISSN: 1469-3062 (print), 1752-7457 (online) www.climatepolicy.com

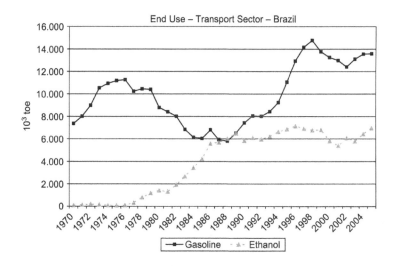

FIGURE 1 Use of petrol and ethanol in the Brazilian transport sector (MME, 2007)

In 1975, in response to the first oil crisis, the federal government decided to encourage the production of ethanol to replace petrol through the Brazilian Alcohol Programme. Figure 1 shows the influence of ethanol in reducing petrol consumption in the Brazilian transport sector in the period from 1975 to 1989.

In Brazil, as well as the factors that normally motivate efforts to cut consumption of petroleum – such as reduction of oil imports for energy security reasons; reduction of foreign currency outflows; and improvement of the balance of trade – policy makers consider the impacts on the environment, along with social motivation, when targeting the transport sector with public policies.

In recent decades, a number of changes in the world context have caused important alterations in the energy planning and use criteria in Brazil. The second oil crisis, in 1979, prompted a series of public policies seeking to decrease the consumption of petroleum-derived fuels and the corresponding cost of importation. In addition, the country's energy planning process began to treat energy efficiency as a parameter for the energy market, using it to make projections for the national energy matrix.

Furthermore, Brazilian policy makers were influenced by social motivations, such as the need to generate jobs and improve the population's health. As for the environmental motivations, Brazilian policy makers only considered the use of renewable fuel and the improvement of air quality and traffic congestion in urban centres.

Finally, efforts in Brazil to cut consumption of petroleum derivatives in the transport sector can be served by diversifying the country's energy matrix and by increasing vehicles' energy efficiency, with the co-benefit of cutting CO_2 emissions, since these emissions are directly proportional to the use of petroleum derivatives.

The main objective of this article is to quantify the potential reduction in CO_2 emissions occurring as a co-benefit of four Brazilian initiatives in the transport sector, in order to increase the limited number and scope of the available studies of mitigation potential and cost. CO_2 emissions reductions are often not quantified or taken into consideration by Brazilian policy makers, since these emissions do not present direct or immediate consequences to transport system customers. Unlike traffic congestion, noise and poor air quality, CO_2 emissions do not indicate that they are excessive by immediately obvious signals.

1.1. Context of the initiatives

This article examines four Brazilian initiatives in the transport sector intended to cut consumption of petroleum derivatives. Two of them originated from the policy to diversify the energy matrix: flexfuel technology (ethanol replacing gasohol) and the Brazilian Biodiesel Programme (biodiesel replacing diesel). The other two are derived from the policy to increase vehicle energy efficiency: the Brazilian Vehicle Efficiency Programme and the Rio de Janeiro Inspection and Maintenance Programme. Figure 2 shows the policies addressed in this work, presenting their objectives, initiatives and driving forces, which have the co-benefit of reducing CO_2 emissions.

Considering practicality, both fuel ethanol and biodiesel have shown, worldwide, that they are practical and complementary alternative options to crude-oil-based transportation fuels. Ethanol, made from sugar or starch feedstocks, can be used directly or blended with petrol and is amply produced in Brazil, the USA and China. Biodiesel, mostly made from the reaction of vegetable oils or animal fats with methanol, can also be used directly or in any ratio with petroleum diesel in most diesel engines. Both are now produced on a large scale. Some 36 million m³ of ethanol was produced globally in 2005, and the year-on-year growth rate was 19%; whilst the global production of biodiesel in 2005 was 3 million m³, though growing at a rate of 60% a year (Worldwatch Institute and GTZ, 2006).

Brazil has been making great strides both in the productivity of sugarcane plantations and the production of ethanol from cane, having reached full maturity in the production of ethanol (Macedo, 2000). Indeed, Brazil is the world leader in production of ethanol from sugarcane, which is a much cheaper and simpler process than making it from other crops, such as corn (in the USA) or beet (in Europe). The country already has installed capacity to produce 18 million m³ of ethanol a year, with room to expand this due to its favourable climate and available arable land (Moreira et al., 2005). Production from sugarcane is more productive in terms of land used than production from corn, with Brazilian ethanol replacing some 150–200 GJ/ha of fossil energy per year as opposed to only 50 GJ/ha of fossil energy replacement accruing to the North American corn-based industry (Quirin et al., 2004, Blottnitz and Curran, 2006, both cited in Botha and Blottnitz, 2006).

While ethanol has been successfully introduced as a partial substitute for petrol in Brazil, there has so far been no equivalent replacement of diesel fuels. Diesel oil is the most important fuel for the transport sector in Brazil (share of 52% for diesel, 26% for petrol, 13% for ethanol, and 9% for others), with an annual consumption of about 38 million m³ (MME, 2007). The National Biodiesel Programme was launched in 2005 and is now under development, using soybeans, castor beans and palm nuts, the main seed crops.

Other major producers of biodiesel, such as Germany, France and Italy, base their production mainly on canola oil, while soybean oil (which also has much potential in Argentina) is the preferred feedstock in the USA. Palm oil (the most productive of the land-based oil crops, with a yield of up to 5,000 L/ha per year) is a significant source too, but is already in high demand for other products, and is contested as being environmentally problematic when primary forest is cleared to make way for plantations. *Jatropha curcus*, another highly productive species producing non-edible oil, is widely discussed and increasingly used in India as well as several African countries, though it is not generally considered viable in the Americas (Botha and Blottnitz, 2006).

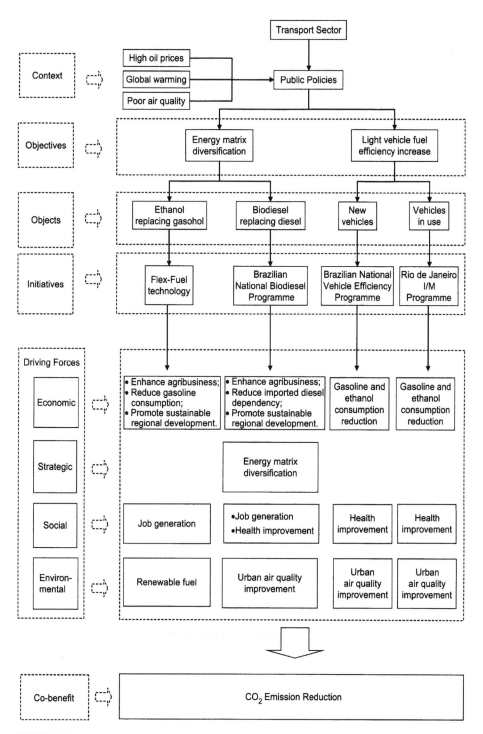

FIGURE 2 Synthesis of the transport sector initiatives chosen for this work

The Brazilian Programme aims to generate employment through the production of biodiesel, especially in the northeast of Brazil, making this more of a social than energy programme *per se* (Macedo and Nogueira, 2004; NAE, 2005). An official national standard for biodiesel is already available. Recently, the National Petroleum Agency (ANP) issued a set of regulatory documents to prepare the downstream oil industry to deal with biodiesel implementation. Since 2005, the government has allowed the blending of 2% of biodiesel in regular diesel. This amount will be adjusted annually.

The Brazilian energy efficiency policy, 'National Policy of Conservation and Rational Use of Energy', was created only in 2005, due to the increase in oil prices. This action was underpinned by the fact that automobile fuel economy standards have proven to be one of the most effective tools in controlling oil demand from the transportation sector in many countries around the world. While fuel economy standards for light-duty vehicles have been largely stagnant in the USA over the past two decades, other areas and jurisdictions – especially the EU, Japan, and more recently China and California – have moved forward, establishing or tightening them.

Inspection and Maintenance (I/M) measures to control emissions from in-use vehicles are an essential complement to improving fuel economy. For several decades, important initiatives have been developed in Brazil to reduce energy waste and vehicle emissions, consolidating an increasingly broad legal framework (CONPET, 2005). Besides the purely economic motivation, environmental aspects also play a role, mainly the need to improve air quality in urban centres and to improve public health. The implementation and improvement of the National Vehicle Efficiency Programme and the Rio de Janeiro Light Vehicle I/M Programme have been the subject of a good deal of discussion in the country in recent years (Ribeiro and Abreu, 2003, 2004; CONPET, 2005; Szwarcfiter et al., 2005).

2. Flexfuel technology

Flexfuel technology manages car engines to allow them to use gasohol, ethanol, or any mixture of the two, with a single fuel tank and system. While, in the USA, flexfuel vehicles evolved from petrol-burning vehicles, Brazil took advantage of its previous experience with ethanol-burning vehicles, which have engines with higher compression ratios, allowing the use of up to 100% ethanol.

In Brazil, the studies for application of the flexfuel technology began in 1990 in an attempt to replace cars running on pure ethanol, which at that time were quickly falling from favour, representing only 0.8% of new car sales in 2000, after peaking at 89% of light vehicle sales in 1987 (ANFAVEA, 2006).

With the presentation of a flexfuel prototype in early 2002, made by Ford's Brazilian subsidiary, associated with growing interest for new incentives to expand the use of ethanol, the government's interest in the technology increased. This stimulated the federal government to announce, late that same year, that flexfuel vehicles would have the same favoured tax treatment as pure ethanol vehicles (tax reductions in the range of 15–28%). This decision and the heightened interest in the use of ethanol in other countries, such as India and China, motivated automobile manufacturers to adopt the flexfuel technology. In 2003, the first Brazilian flexfuel vehicle was officially launched on the market.

In 2003, flexfuel vehicles in the Brazilian market corresponded to 4% of total sales of light vehicles (passenger cars and light-duty vehicles). In 2004, 2005 and 2006, the sales reached 22%, 52% and 78%, respectively (Figure 3) (ANFAVEA, 2006).

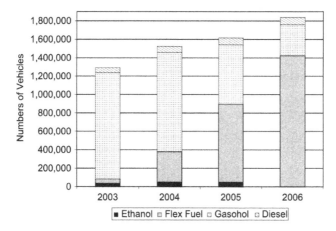

FIGURE 3 Sales of light vehicles in Brazil according to fuel type (ANFAVEA, 2006).

Although the efficiency of flexfuel vehicles in terms of km/L is lower than those only burning gasohol, the ethanol prices during most of the year make the use of ethanol more economically advantageous to consumers. Besides this, the fact that they have the option to use both fuels according to their needs or desires (savings, environmental concerns, vehicle performance) has made the technology a success.

2.1. Economic impacts

To quantify the economic results of this initiative, we calculate the potential gasohol consumption avoided by the use of hydrous ethanol to replace 95% of the gasohol in the Brazilian flexfuel light vehicle fleet. We considered this percentage because this is the figure that has already been achieved in São Paulo, Brazil's largest state in terms of population and industrial output, and expectations are that the other states can also reach this figure. The methodology developed here is in accordance with a case study developed by Ribeiro and Abreu (2006b).

To develop the methodology, the period from 2003 to 2006 was selected, because the sale of flexfuel vehicles only began in 2003.

The estimated number of light vehicles fitted with flexfuel technology sold in the Brazilian market each year during the assessment period is presented in Table 1 (line (B)).

Based on these figures, the average number of kilometres driven by each vehicle in the fleet sold that year through to the end of 2006 was calculated (Table 1, line (C)). This calculation is based on the average number of kilometres travelled annually, classified by vehicle age (Table 2), as adopted by the São Paulo State Environmental Agency (CETESB) for its Annual Air Quality Reports.

Then the accumulated number of vehicle-kilometres through year-end 2006, for each year of sale, was determined by multiplying the number of vehicles sold in each year of sale by the respective accumulated average kilometres driven through 2006 (Table 1, line (D)).

The next step consisted of calculating the ethanol consumed by the flexfuel vehicles during the assessment period, by multiplying by 95% (percentage of ethanol replacing gasohol) of the accumulated number of vehicle-kilometres through 2006 for each year of sale by the vehicles' fuel efficiency (L/km). As the fuel efficiency varies according to the technical characteristics of the vehicle (capacity, compression ratio and weight), minimum and maximum fuel efficiencies were

TABLE 1 Summary of the methodology for quantifying gasohol consumption that would have been avoided through flexfuel technology

	Assessment period				
Year of sale (A)	2003	2004	2005	2006	Total
Automobiles and light vehicles sold (B)	48,178	328,379	812,104	1,525,943	
Average accumulated kilometres driven through to 2006 by each vehicle [km] (C)	73,000	58,000	41,000	22,000	
Vehicle-km accumulated through to 2006 (D)	3,516,994,000	19,045,982,000	33,296,264,000	33,570,755,152	89,429,995,152
Minimum hydrous ethanol consumption [litres] (E)					11,327,799,386
Maximum hydrous ethanol consumption [litres] (F)					13,070,537,753
Minimum gasohol avoided [litres] (G)					7,929,459,570
Maximum gasohol avoided [litres] (H)					9,149,376,427

Vehicle age [years]	Average annual kilometres driven [km]	Vehicle age [years]	Average annual kilometres driven [km]
1	22,000	7	14,000
2	19,000	8	13,000
3	17,000	9	13,000
4	15,000	10	13,000
5	14,000	+11	9,500
6	14,000		

applied in order to obtain an ethanol consumption range for the entire flexfuel fleet. This calculation considered 0.1333 L/km (7.5 km/L) as the maximum and 0.1538 L/km (6.5 km/L) the minimum fuel efficiency, based on average results presented in D'Agosto (2004). The findings are presented in Table 1 (lines (E) and (F)).

Finally, the avoided gasohol was calculated based on the amount of ethanol consumed and the equivalence of 1 L of hydrous ethanol to 0.7 L of gasohol (Macedo et al., 2004) (see Table 1, lines (G) and (H)).

In this form, we obtained the potential consumption of gasohol avoided for the period from 2003 to 2006, within a range of 7.9–9.1 G litres. These results correspond to 42–49% of the road-mode gasohol consumption in 2006.

2.2. CO$_2$ emission reduction co-benefit

The use of ethanol in Brazil has contributed to reduced CO$_2$ emissions. This is due to the carbon capture during sugarcane growth and the use of sugarcane bagasse to produce electricity to run the plant and also to the power grid. Consequently, the energy balance of Brazilian ethanol indicates that, for each unit of energy invested in sugarcane industry dedicated to ethanol production, roughly 8.3 units of renewable energy are produced. In contrast, in the USA this ratio is only 1.3 because of the use of fossil fuels to run the corn mills (Macedo et al., 2004). Positive results are also observed regarding air quality because of the elimination of lead additives and aromatic hydrocarbons, which are particularly toxic; and the reduction of sulphur and carbon monoxide (CO) emissions (Moreira et al., 2005).

Recent analyses from the IEA and others (IPCC, 2007) reported that the mitigation potential for reducing CO$_2$ emissions by ethanol use in the transport sector by 2030 is between 500 and 1,200 Mt CO$_2$. In order to quantify the CO$_2$ emissions that could have been avoided by the use of flexfuel technology, Ribeiro and Abreu (2006b) developed a methodology based on the ethanol consumption.

This calculation is done by multiplying the minimum and maximum hydrous ethanol consumption (calculated in Section 2.1) by the avoided emissions factor due to substituting gasohol by this fuel. The avoided emissions factor applied was 1.97 kgCO$_2$/L of hydrous ethanol, which is the one used by the São Paulo State Environmental Agency (Macedo et al., 2004).

Consequently, through the data presented above, we conclude that significant quantities of CO$_2$ – a minimum of 22.3 Mt and a maximum of 25.7 Mt – would not have been discharged into the atmosphere through the substitution of gasohol by hydrous ethanol in the Brazilian fleet fitted with flexfuel technology.

2.3. Policy lessons

The most relevant policy issue in the case of the undeniable success of the flexfuel vehicle in Brazil was the merging of private and governmental interests. After a huge ethanol shortage in Brazil, the consumers no longer bought vehicles powered by ethanol. The sales of the ethanol-running vehicles had a drastic fall from 90% to 1% within a period of few years. Due to this scenario of big losses, the sugarcane industry demanded an urgent solution from the Brazilian Government. The answer was to put into practice the idea of a flexfuel vehicle with prices similar to the gasohol vehicles. The demand for ethanol rose enormously, reaching almost 80% of flexfuel vehicles sold within the total sales of light vehicles.

Another positive aspect that followed the increased demand for ethanol was the consequent increase in sugarcane bagasse production. This became increasingly used in systems of co-generation (heat and power), representing a new opportunity for renewable energy generation.

The Brazilian experience with ethanol use and the introduction of a new flexfuel technology supports these findings:

- Despite the advantages of sugarcane in both primary energy productivity and high conversion efficiency, land requirements are high. In order to make a significant impact on the country's fuel consumption, it will require large amounts of land.
- Being an agricultural product, long-term planning is required to prevent shortages in supply. The logistics for fuel storage and distribution is crucial after ethanol is produced, due to its agricultural cycle.

- In Brazil the success of biofuels was tied to the rural economy. Encouraging smaller, locally owned, bio-refineries and creating new, more flexible, markets for agricultural crops offers great potential for countries that might be poor in fossil fuels but rich in terms of biomass resources.
- To enable biofuels to expand, policy makers should accelerate the commercialization of cellulose-to-ethanol plants. To achieve this, much more research is needed as well as the necessary conditions to accelerate its development. The production of ethanol from cellulose is welcome not only for economic reasons but also as a way to guarantee low carbon emissions from renewable energy.

In short, the main lesson obtained from this initiative is that the private sector has an important role to play in making some policies succeed.

3. The National Biodiesel Programme

The second initiative analysed in this work is the National Biodiesel Programme. Biodiesel is an alternative fuel to regular diesel oil, obtained from a chemical process called transesterification of oils or fats,[1] which can be new seed oils or cooking oils left over from deep-frying.

In 2004, the Brazilian government established the National Biodiesel Programme, which will gradually increase the amounts of biodiesel added to petroleum diesel. Initially, the figure was 2%, which will be authorized up to 2008 and obligatory thereafter. (It is expected there will be biodiesel production capacity by then to supply the entire country with enough biodiesel for the 2% admixture). It will then rise to 5%, which will be mandatory as of 2013.

The development of this programme was initially prompted by economic, strategic and social motivations. The substitution of diesel with biodiesel implies less need to import diesel and thus an improved trade balance. Imported diesel in the period from 1995 to 2005 represented 14% of the diesel consumed in the country. As well as this, there were agricultural factors, particularly the desire to provide a greater market for soybeans, along with potential expansion of the market for other vegetable oils, such as castor oil and palm oil, to encourage sustainable regional development.

Regarding the social aspects of the National Biodiesel Programme, the expectation is that it will generate jobs, both in agriculture and the industrial and logistical phase. According to the Ministry of Mining and Energy (NAE, 2005), the use of 5% biodiesel (1.5 million tonnes) added to diesel will generate 200,000 jobs (direct and indirect).

In Brazil, the main seed crops are soybeans, castor beans and palm nuts. Table 3 illustrates the area needed and the volume of vegetable oil produced, in all Brazilian regions, to supply biodiesel replacing 5% of diesel (NAE, 2005). For comparison, the total harvested area of main crops (for food and fuel) in Brazil covers 65 million ha (Moreira et al., 2005). The area of possible expansion for grains is evaluated (NAE, 2005), in the low-density savannas, as around 90 million ha; in Amazonia the suitable area for palm oil covers about 70 million ha, with about 40% of this being capable of high yields. The same evaluation states that 20 million ha is already deforested and without current use in Amazonia, and 2.5 million ha of the land already has the appropriate infrastructure. It is important to emphasize that the above-mentioned potential areas for cultivation are already degraded lands.

From an environmental standpoint, besides being a renewable fuel, biodiesel promotes better air quality, since it reduces the main tailpipe emissions associated with diesel (Table 4). In addition, it is nontoxic and biodegradable (US-EPA, 2002).

TABLE 3 The area needed and the volume of vegetable oil produced to supply biodiesel replacing 5% of diesel in Brazil (NAE, 2005)

Region in Brazil	Volume of vegetable oil [1,000 m³]	Crops	Area[1,000 ha]
South	7,200	Soybeans	600
Southeast	15,840	Soybeans	1,320
Northeast	5,400	castor	600
North	3,240	Palm nuts	35
Central-West	4,320	Soybeans	360
Total	36,000		2,916

TABLE 4 Tailpipe emissions reduction due to biodiesel admixtures (US-EPA, 2002; and McCormick, 2005)

Percentage biodiesel	Percentage emissions reduction		
	Older engines (until 1997)		Newer engines (2004 compliant)
	PM and CO	HC	PM and CO
5%	5	5	7
20%	12	20	25
100%	48	65	75

3.1. Economic impacts

Quantification of the economic impacts of this initiative is done by calculating the potential consumption of petroleum diesel that would have been avoided by adding 2% biodiesel, as of 2005, in the transport sector.

We adopted the premise that all the diesel used by road transport (lorries and buses, since passenger cars are not allowed to burn diesel in Brazil) in 2005, 2006 and 2007 contained 2% biodiesel made from soybeans and methanol.

Based on the amount of diesel consumed by the road transport sector in 2005, 2006 and 2007 (MME, 2007)[2] we calculated the quantity to be replaced by biodiesel – each litre of petroleum diesel requires 1.1 litre of biodiesel in substitution (US-DOE, 1998) (Table 5). The following potential results were derived for the 2005–2007 period: 2.0 million m³ of biodiesel consumed and 1.9 million m³ of diesel avoided (equivalent to an 18% reduction in diesel imports in the same period, representing US$1.5 billion saved). There is no additional cost to the consumer because biodiesel is not taxed, in an effort to make the production cost equal to that of mineral diesel.

3.2. CO$_2$ emission reduction co-benefit

IPCC (2007) reports mitigation potentials between 100 and 300 MtCO$_2$, for reducing transport CO$_2$ emissions by biodiesel use for 2030. To estimate the potential CO$_2$ emissions avoided by the use of biodiesel replacing petroleum diesel in road transport in Brazil, we conducted a case study

TABLE 5 Summary of the methodology for quantifying CO_2 emissions that would have been avoided through 2% of biodiesel admixture

Year	Petroleum diesel consumed in road transport	Petroleum diesel avoided	Biodiesel consumption
2005	30,429,000 m³	608,580 m³	669,438 m³
2006	30,899,000 m³	617,980 m³	679,778 m³
2007	32,580,000 m³	651,600 m³	716,760 m³
Total	93,908,000 m³	1,878,160 m³	2,065,976 m³
Energy consumption [TJ]		66,639	67,166
Carbon content [tC]		1,346,114	1,335,257
Carbon stored [tC]		0	534,103
Net carbon emissions [tC]		1,346,114	801,154
Actual carbon emissions [tC]		1,332,653	793,142
Actual CO_2 emissions [tCO_2]		4,886,394	2,908,189
Potential CO_2 emissions avoided [tCO_2]			1,978,205

considering the results presented in Section 3.1 and the IPCC (1996) methodology to develop National Greenhouse Gas Inventories.

As there is no avoided CO_2 emission factor for Brazilian biodiesel replacing petroleum diesel, we calculated the potential CO_2 emissions avoided by this replacement. CO_2 emissions that would have occurred from the consumption of biodiesel were subtracted from the volume of petroleum diesel avoided. To do this calculation, we applied the IPCC methodology in six steps (Table 5):

1. *Energy consumption*: converting the diesel volume to a common energy unit by the conversion factor of 0.777 toe/m³ (biodiesel) (US-DOE, 1998) and 0.848 toe/m³ (petroleum diesel) and using the equivalence of 41.841×10⁻³ TJ = 1 toe (MME, 2007).
2. *Carbon content*: multiplying the energy consumption in TJ by the carbon emission factor of 20.2 tC/TJ (petroleum diesel) (IPCC, 1996) and 19.88 tC/TJ (biodiesel) (IVIG and CENPES, 2002).
3. *Carbon stored*: for this study, the petroleum diesel volume is used for energy purposes, so carbon stored equals zero. For biodiesel, the fraction of carbon stored reaches 40%, representing the quantity sequestrated through biomass renewal (NAE, 2005).
4. *Net carbon emissions*: the amount of carbon stored subtracted from carbon content.
5. *Actual carbon emissions*: multiplying net carbon emissions by fraction of carbon oxidized (0.99).
6. *Actual CO_2 emissions*: multiplying the actual carbon emissions by 44/12.

In this form, assuming that the roadway fleet running on petroleum diesel had used biodiesel (2%) in 2005, 2006 and 2007, a total of 1.98 million tonnes of CO_2 emissions would have been avoided.

3.3. Policy lessons

It is a necessity that the economic rationale should never be ignored when establishing a policy. This is illustrated in the following example. The driving force of the implementation of the Biodiesel Programme in Brazil was job generation, mainly in rural areas through small farms. Nevertheless, biodiesel from soybean proved to be much more competitive than the biodiesel produced by small farmers. The soybean industry is already strongly established in the country, having a high level of mechanization, capacity for storage and good logistics. Therefore, the majority of biodiesel in Brazil comes from soybean. To increase biodiesel production on a small scale by farmers would demand a programme of incentives and subsidies that would not be well accepted by the Brazilian economy.

4. Vehicle Efficiency Programme

In 2005, the Technical Committee on Vehicle Efficiency was established, responsible for initiating and developing a strategy to improve the energy efficiency of light vehicles in Brazil.

Users of light vehicles have limited access to figures on the energy efficiency of their vehicles when making purchasing decisions, which does not happen with the purchasers of commercial vehicles, to whom the relevant data is readily available.

The Brazilian automobile industry is not obliged to publicize the fuel efficiency of their vehicles. Comparing the specific consumption levels of more modern cars, which should be more efficient due to better technology, with the levels of cars made over 20 years ago, Figure 4 shows that there has been a 15% increase in the specific consumption of gasohol cars and 38% for ethanol vehicles, due to power and weight increases (CONPET, 2005).

Because of this potential to increase the fuel efficiency of light vehicles, the Brazilian government, through the Technical Committee on Vehicle Efficiency (CONPET, 2005), has established four steps for implementing a Brazilian Vehicle Efficiency Programme, to start in 2008:

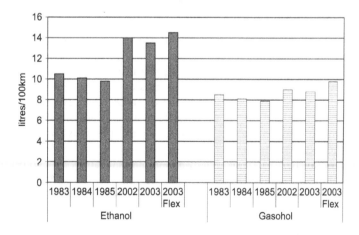

FIGURE 4 Evolution of specific consumption of Brazilian light vehicles
(Branco et al., 2004, cited in CONPET, 2005).

1. Definition of standardized procedures for the testing of light vehicles
2. Dissemination of vehicle efficiency indicators to encourage consumers to think of efficiency as an additional valuable feature of their cars and consider it in their buying decisions
3. Introduction of comparative and voluntary vehicle labelling, showing the classification of the vehicle in comparison with others in its class, and its ranking on an absolute efficiency scale
4. Definition of maximum specific consumption limits and compulsory energy performance targets.

4.1. Economic impacts

As this initiative is still being formulated, the National Vehicle Efficiency Programme has not yet produced benefits that can be quantified. Nevertheless, Ribeiro and Abreu (2006a) calculated the potential saving that could be attained through this initiative. They assessed the past potential that might have been achieved if a vehicle labelling system had been implemented in São Paulo municipality considering the gasohol consumption that would have been avoided by the automobile fleet in that municipality. São Paulo was chosen due to its importance as Brazil's largest city, with its largest vehicle fleet.

For this calculation, a vehicle labelling system was used as reference based on energy efficiency categories, similar to the European system (EVA, 1999, cited in Ribeiro and Abreu, 2006a). The hypothesis was that the labelling system would be introduced in 2000 and assessed over the period 2000–2004.

Based on the fleet distribution by age, for each year of the assessment period, the target fleet for the case study was defined, assuming that the vehicles had their energy efficiency enhanced through adopting energy efficiency labels, which in turn fostered petrol savings. The following assumptions were used: (i) in 2000, only vehicles manufactured in 2000 would be in circulation, sold with energy efficiency labels; (ii) in 2001, vehicles manufactured in 2000 and 2001 would be in circulation, sold with energy efficiency labels; (iii) in 2002, vehicles manufactured in 2000, 2001 and 2002 would be in circulation, sold with energy efficiency labels; and so on.

After that the number of vehicle-km was calculated (based on Table 2), corresponding to each year of manufacture, for each year of the assessment period (Table 6, columns (B)). Then the share held by vehicles in the target fleet of total gasohol consumption was weighted. As the gasohol consumed does not depend only on the number of vehicles in circulation, but also the distance covered by each of them, this was carried out as a function of the number of vehicle-km calculated previously.

Taking each year of the assessment period separately, a percentage share was calculated for each year of manufacture of the target fleet, dividing the number of vehicle-km for that year of manufacture by the total vehicle-km (Table 7, columns (A)).

Having calculated the percentage shares held by the target fleet in gasohol consumption, the gasohol consumed by the target fleet was calculated (Table 7, columns (B)). This calculation was carried out by applying the percentages calculated in the previous stage to total gasohol sale volumes at service stations in São Paulo (Table 7).

Finally, the gasohol saved by the target fleet was computed by applying a consumption reduction percentage to the volume of gasohol consumed by the target fleet. For this percentage reduction, a potential figure of 4.7% was adopted (on average, due to the introduction of the vehicle labelling system proposed for the EU by the European Community Commission (EVA, 1999, cited in Ribeiro and Abreu, 2006a)).

This led to the conclusion that in a period of just 5 years the consumption of 0.141 million m^3 litres of gasohol could have been avoided in São Paulo municipality.

TABLE 6 Distribution of the registered gasohol-fuelled automobile fleet and vehicle-km by year of manufacture (CETESB, 1994; DENATRAN, 2006)

São Paulo Municipality

Assessment period

Year of manufacture	2000		2001		2002		2003		2004	
	Registered fleet (A)	Vehicle-km (B)	Registered fleet (A)	Vehicle-km (B)	Registered fleet (A)	Vehicle-km (B)	Registered fleet (A)	Vehicle-km (B)	Registered fleet (A)	Vehicle-km (B)
pre-1989	743,92?	7,067,248,130	742,408	7,052,874,294	733,645	6,969,628,400	723,576	6,873,969,059	708,924	6,734,777,695
1989	34,939	331,916,210	34,662	329,286,692	34,126	324,199,958	33,521	318,453,933	32,770	311,312,919
1990	72,012	684,113,476	71,449	678,767,152	70,321	668,050,919	69,117	656,609,049	67,555	641,776,376
1991	72,776	946,089,939	72,055	684,523,898	70,807	672,664,325	69,532	660,551,717	67,905	645,097,542
1992	62,349	810,540,278	61,658	801,551,175	60,603	575,730,991	59,522	565,456,075	58,150	552,428,284
1993	96,675	1,256,778,261	95,660	1,243,586,416	93,988	1,221,840,847	92,282	876,676,284	90,142	856,348,992
1994	147,008	2,058,109,337	145,357	1,889,639,477	142,768	1,855,978,000	139,943	1,819,258,944	136,431	1,296,092,478
1995	207,699	2,907,789,843	204,995	2,869,932,671	200,764	2,609,927,135	196,300	2,551,895,698	190,774	2,480,060,094
1996	215,232	3,013,245,810	212,269	2,971,772,987	207,542	2,905,592,496	202,680	2,634,845,940	196,714	2,557,288,341
1997	260,430	3,906,449,569	256,718	3,594,057,665	251,002	3,514,022,363	244,997	3,429,954,999	237,747	3,090,716,306
1998	194,852	3,312,489,683	192,486	2,887,293,534	188,052	2,632,732,413	183,345	2,566,827,065	178,019	2,492,266,811
1999	153,68?	2,919,931,181	152,307	2,589,225,313	149,323	2,239,847,440	145,588	2,038,231,648	141,126	1,975,766,612
2000	164,310	3,614,818,064	189,503	3,600,558,590	187,058	3,179,991,332	183,110	2,746,645,888	177,482	2,484,753,768
2001			172,025	3,784,540,667	196,410	3,731,794,935	193,929	3,296,795,522	189,065	2,835,968,265
2002					149,636	3,291,985,256	173,050	3,287,943,470	170,234	2,893,981,048
2003							140,298	3,086,547,364	156,322	2,970,120,062
2004									126,547	2,784,027,477

TABLE 7 Summary of potential economic results due to the Vehicle Efficiency Programme in São Paulo Municipality

São Paulo Municipality

Assessment period – Total fleet

	2000	2001	2002	2003	2004
Total gasohol sold at service stations [L]*	2,491,400,233	2,533,174,605	2,419,711,060	2,171,796,319	2,114,270,891

Assessment period – Target fleet

Year of manufacture	2000		2001		2002		2003		2004	
	Share in total gasohol consumption (A)	Gasohol consumed [L] (B)	Share in total gasohol consumption (A)	Gasohol consumed [L] (B)	Share in total gasohol consumption (A)	Gasohol consumed [L] (B)	Share in total gasohol consumption (A)	Gasohol consumed [L] (B)	Share in total gasohol consumption (A)	Gasohol consumed [L] (B)
2000	11.01%	274,325,017	10.29%	260,762,340	8.74%	211,426,691	7.34%	159,450,675	6.61%	139,708,876
2001			10.82%	274,086,828	10.25%	248,114,215	8.81%	191,388,440	7.54%	159,456,419
2002					9.05%	218,872,782	8.79%	190,874,553	7.70%	162,718,272
2003							8.25%	179,182,932	7.90%	166,999,298
2004									7.40%	156,535,974

	Gasohol [L]	Gasohol [L]	Gasohol [L]	Gasohol [L]	Gasohol [L]	Total [L]
Consumed	274,325,017	534,849,168	678,413,688	720,896,601	785,418,840	2,993,903,314
Potential avoided	12,893,276	25,137,911	31,885,443	33,882,140	36,914,685	140,713,455

* *Note:* ANP (Petroleum National Agency), personal communication.

4.2. CO₂ emission reduction co-benefit

The improvement of energy efficiency allows an excellent opportunity for transport GHG mitigation. Carbon emissions from new light-duty road vehicles could be reduced by up to 50% by 2030 compared to currently produced models, assuming continued technological advances as well as policies ensuring that technologies would be applied to increase fuel economy rather than increase horsepower and vehicle weight. The total potential mitigation of the energy efficiency options applied to light-duty vehicles would be around 0.7–0.8 Gt CO_2-eq in 2030 (IPCC, 2007).

For the purpose of quantifying the co-benefit that could be obtained by the National Vehicle Labelling Programme, we developed a methodology that calculates the avoided CO_2 emissions, based on the amounts of gasohol that could be saved during each year of the assessment period of the case study presented in Section 4.1.

The potential avoided CO_2 was calculated by multiplying the potential avoided consumption of gasohol (141 million litres) by the emission factor, which considers direct and indirect CO_2 emissions: 2.82 kg CO_2/L gasohol (Macedo, 1998).

This calculation led to the conclusion that in the period from 2000 to 2004, through implementation of the National Vehicle Labelling Programme, similar to that used in Europe, the discharge of 0.4 million tonnes of CO_2 could have been avoided in São Paulo municipality.

4.3. Policy lessons

A programme such as the National Vehicle Labelling Programme should be supported by car manufacturers and governments. However, in Brazil, the car industry has been resistant in implementing this kind of programme, even though it would bring great profits not only in terms of fuel economy but also in terms of GHG emissions, as shown above. An important lesson is that if a policy is to be successful, then it has to involve sectors other than the policy maker.

Nevertheless, with the rising price of oil and increasing consumer awareness of global warming and other environmental issues, it is expected that the programme will be able to go ahead once a sufficient number of consumers are worried about energy consumption and its consequent environmental impacts. The demands of society can be decisive for the implementation of a policy.

5. Rio de Janeiro State Light Vehicle Inspection and Maintenance Programme

Brazil and other developing countries (as well as in developed ones) have restrictive pollutant emissions standards for all new vehicles. However, the maintenance of this low-emissions profile is only possible if the emission control systems and engines are working properly.

Furthermore, even if the automobile's engine and emission control systems are initially perfect, they will naturally decay over time. The amount of pollutants from a vehicle increases with the vehicles's age. Therefore, I/M programmes aim to ensure that the vehicles stay 'clean' during their useful lives. The implementation of an I/M programme will identify high-polluting vehicles and, as a consequence, force the owner to perform correct maintenance in order to pass inspection. The identification of vehicles with maintenance problems, followed by adequate repair, can lead to a 16–44% reduction in carbon monoxide (CO) emissions, a 9–37% reduction in hydrocarbon (HC) emissions, and a 3.5–19% reduction in fuel consumption (Faiz et al., 1996).

Rio de Janeiro has a distinctive role, on a national scale, in pollution control of vehicles, as it was the first Brazilian state to implement an I/M programme in 1997 (based on those established by the US Environmental Protection Agency – US EPA) in order to minimize the costs generated by the effects of pollution on the environment and on the health of the population, since vehicle emissions are one of the main pollutants that degrade air quality and cause respiratory and cardiovascular diseases.

5.1. Economic results

For this study we considered the potential economic result to be the gasohol consumption that could have been avoided. Based on the study of Ribeiro and Abreu (2003), we developed a method to calculate the potential gasohol consumption avoided with the implementation of the Rio de Janeiro State Light Vehicle I/M Programme.

Considering 2002 as the study year, we obtained the number of vehicle-km for each year of manufacture (based on Table 2) and then defined an average specific consumption (calculated for the Brazilian fleet from the total gasohol consumed in 2002 and total vehicle-km in 2002 (Abreu, 2007)) of 0.1018 L of gasohol/km (9.82 km/L), for the entire fleet, thus obtaining the total consumption.

From the standards of the US EPA for the implementation of I/M programmes, we applied the percentages of reduced consumption estimated for the fleet of light vehicles running on gasohol in the Rio de Janeiro metropolitan region. Applying a percentage reduction of 3.5% for a low-performing quality programme, and 6% for a high-performing quality programme (Faiz et al., 1996), we obtained a minimum and maximum potential amount of gasohol avoided of 74.6 million litres and 127.9 million litres, respectively (Table 8). In 2002, the Rio de Janeiro I/M Programme

TABLE 8 Summary of economic results due to Rio de Janeiro State Light Vehicle I/M Programme

Manufacture year	Gasohol light vehicle fleet	Vehicle-km
1968–1992	681,605	6,475,247,500
1993	60,093	781,209,000
1994	75,253	978,289,000
1995	106,405	1,383,265,000
1996	106,469	1,490,566,000
1997	115,264	1,613,696,000
1998	99,233	1,389,262,000
1999	82,473	1,237,095,000
2000	94,592	1,608,064,000
2001	101,383	1,926,277,000
2002	93,503	2,057,066,000
Total vehicle-km		20,940,036,500
Total consumption [L]		2,131,695,716
Minimum consumption avoided [L]		74,609,350
Maximum consumption avoided [L]		127,901,743

employed 716 people in 33 inspection stations. The cost for consumers is an annual tax of US$25 paid together with the annual vehicle registration renewal (MMA, 2002).[3]

5.2. CO_2 emission reduction co-benefit

In OECD countries, vehicles consume 10–20% more fuel per km than indicated by their rated efficiency. It is estimated that a 5–10% reduction in CO_2 emissions can be achieved by stronger I/M programmes, adoption of on-board technologies, more widespread driver training, and better enforcement and control of vehicle speeds (IPCC, 2007). For the purpose of quantifying the co-benefit obtained by the Rio de Janeiro State Light Vehicle I/M Programme, we calculated the potential avoided CO_2 emissions, based on the potential gasohol saved during the assessment year (2002) of the case study presented in Section 5.1.

Then we calculated the potential avoided CO_2 emissions by multiplying the minimum and the maximum avoided consumption of gasohol by the emission factor 2.82 kg CO_2/L gasohol (Macedo, 1998).

This calculation led to the conclusion that in a period of just one year (2002), the discharge of from 0.21 million tonnes to 0.36 million tonnes of CO_2 could have been avoided in the greater Rio de Janeiro metropolitan region.

5.3. Policy lessons

As previously mentioned, the I/M programme was not fully implemented. This is due to the fact that this initiative adversely affects the low-income populace, who possess older and badly maintained vehicles, and therefore was avoided by politicians. Large campaigns clarifying the benefits of the programme would help public acceptance. For this, urban planners and government agencies engaging the State and the Municipality should cooperate not only in expanding current programmes but also in developing new ones for the future.

Although I/M programmes are linked to vehicle registration renewal, there is still a need for stricter measures to ensure compliance by reducing evasion. There is also the problem that the existing I/M programmes do not always encourage long-term repairs. These programmes can be weakened when owners of excessively polluting vehicles can obtain 'quick fixes' that allow them to pass inspection but do not ensure lasting emissions reductions.

6. Conclusions

The importance of mitigating GHG emissions needs to be acknowledged as one of the criteria to be considered when formulating transportation policies, and treated directly instead of indirectly through synergies with other problems and in the form of co-benefits. The direct focus in policies formulated for the Brazilian transport sector needs to be on reducing GHG emissions.

The analysis of the potential impact of measures aimed at reducing GHG emissions, and the adoption of these measures in practice, is increasingly acknowledged as an urgent necessity. However, an accurate evaluation of the potential mitigation of GHG emissions by the Brazilian transport sector is hampered by the small number of studies in this area, and the limited scope of the studies that have been published, generally focusing only on renewable fuels. Therefore, there is a shortage of supporting data for implementing other measures to reduce GHG emissions besides using renewable fuels.

TABLE 9 Summary of results from the different initiatives

Initiative	Assesment period	Fleet considered	Potential economic and strategic result[G litres]		Potential CO_2 emission reduction co-benefit [Mt CO_2]
Flexfuel Technology	2003–2006	Flexfuel light vehicles all over Brazil	Avoided gasohol 7.9–9.1	Ethanol consumed 11.3–13.1	22.3–25.7
Brazilian National Biodiesel Programme	2005–2007	Heavy duty vehicles all over Brazil	Avoided diesel 1.9	Biodiesel consumed 2.0	1.3
Brazilian National Vehicle Efficiency Programme	2000–2004	Light vehicles in São Paulo Municipality	Avoided gasohol 0.141		0.4
Rio de Janeiro I/M Programme	2002	Light vehicles in Rio de Janeiro State	Avoided gasohol 0.075–0.127		0.21–0.36

A brief analysis of four initiatives in the Brazilian transport sector (motivated by economic, strategic, social and environmental questions, but not by concern for climate change) indicated reduced CO_2 emissions as a co-benefit. A summarized quantification of the results is presented in Table 9.

Although this is a simplified, and thus imprecise, analysis, it is fundamental to recognize the importance of quantifying the GHG emissions that can be avoided in the Brazilian transport sector. Such quantification can serve as a basis for policy makers to use GHG emissions as one of the factors in formulating public policies in Brazil. This quantification can give further support for increased utilization of biofuels and spur the implementation of new measures along the lines of the National Vehicle Efficiency Programme, and foster the extension to the entire country of the Rio de Janeiro Inspection and Maintenance Programme.

In each of the initiatives analysed in this article, cooperation with the private sector is the key to success (flexfuel technology) or failure (Energy Labelling Programme) of the initiative. Another factor is the economic sustainability of the measure to be implemented (biodiesel). Cooperation is vital at all levels of government, along with the commitment of the population as a whole (I/M programme).

Notes

1. A chemical reaction between triglycerides (ester formed from glycerol) and methanol or ethanol, producing glycerine and ester (biodiesel).
2. By linear regression from 1983 to 2006 data.
3. 2007 US$.

References

Abreu, A.A., 2007, *Medidas de Eficiência Energética como Instrumento de Mitigação do Aquecimento Global no Setor de Transportes Rodoviário Brasileiro*, COPPE/UFRJ, Universidade Federal do Rio de Janeiro, Rio de Janeiro.

ANFAVEA, 2006, *Anuário da Indústria Automobilística Brasileira – 2006* [available at www.anfavea.com.br].

Botha, J.J., Blottnitz, H. von, 2006, 'Practical complementary options to crude oil transport', in: *Electronic Proceedings of the XVI International Symposium on Alcohol Fuels* (ISAF), Rio de Janeiro.

CETESB, 1994, *Inventário das Emissões Veiculares – Metodologia de Cálculo Departamento de Tecnologia de Emissões de Veículos*, Companhia de Tecnologia de Saneamento Ambiental, São Paulo.

CONPET, 2005, *Promovendo a Eficiência Energética nos Automóveis Brasileiros*, CONPET, Ministério de Minas e Energia, Brasília.

D'Agosto, M.D.A., 2004, *Análise da Eficiência da Cadeia Energética Para as Principais Fontes de Energia Utilizadas em Veículos Rodoviários no Brasil*, COPPE/UFRJ, Universidade Federal do Rio de Janeiro, Rio de Janeiro.

DENATRAN, 2006, *Tabelas Estatísticas: Departamento Nacional de Trânsito*, Estatísticas de Frota de Veículos, Brasília [available at www.denatran.gov.br/frota.htm].

Faiz, A., Weaver, CS., Walsh, M.P., 1996, *Air Pollution from Motor Vehicles: Standards and Technologies for Controlling Emissions*, The World Bank, Washington, DC.

IPCC, 1996, *Revised 1996 IPCC Guidelines for National Greenhouse Gas Inventories: Workbook Volume 2*, NGGIP Publications.

IPCC, 2007, *Climate Change 2007: Mitigation. Contribution of Working Group III to The Fourth Assessment Report of the Intergovernmental Panel on Climate Change*, B. Metz, O.R. Davidson, P.R. Bosch, R. Dave, L.A. Meyer (eds), Cambridge University Press, Cambridge, UK and New York.

IVIG and CENPES, 2002, *Viabilização do Uso do Biodiesel*, International Virtual Institute of Global Change, Petrobras Research Centre, Rio de Janeiro.

Macedo, I.C., 1998, 'Greenhouse gas emissions and energy balances in bio-ethanol production and utilization in Brazil (1996)', *Biomass and Bioenergy* 14(1), 77–81.

Macedo, I.C., 2000, 'Commercial perspectives of bioalcohol in Brazil', in: *Proceedings of the 1st World Conference on Biomass for Energy and Industry*, Sevilla, 2001, James & James (Science Publishers) Ltd, London, 35–47.

Macedo, I.C., Leal, M.R., Silva, J.E., 2004, *Balanço das Emissões de Gases do Efeito Estufa na Produção e no Uso do Etanol no Brasil*, São Paulo State Environmental Secretariat, São Paulo.

Macedo, I.C., Nogueira, L.A.H., 2004, 'Biocombustíveis', *Parcerias Estratégicas (Brasília)* 19, 255–310.

McCormick, B., 2005, *Effects of Biodiesel on Pollutant Emissions*, National Renewable Energy Laboratory, Clean Cities Informational Webcast on Fuel Blends, Golden, CO.

Moreira, J.R., Nogueira, L.A.H., Parente, V., 2005, 'Biofuels for transport development, and climate change: lessons from Brazil', in: R. Bradley, K.A. Baumert (eds), *Growing in the Greenhouse: Protecting the Climate by Putting Development First*, World Resources Institute, Washington, DC.

MMA, 2002, *Avaliação do Programa de Inspeção e Manutenção de Veículos em Uso do Rio de Janeiro*, Ministério da Meio Ambiente, Brasília.

MME, 2007, *Balanço Energético Nacional*, BEN 2007, Ministério de Minas e Energia, Brasília.

NAE, 2005, *Biocombustíveis*, Cadernos NAE, Número 2, Núcleo de Assuntos Estratégicos da Presidência da República, Brasília.

Ribeiro, S.K., Abreu, A.A., 2003, 'O Potencial de Redução das Emissões de Monóxido de Carbono, Através da Implantação de Programas de Inspeção e Manutenção – O Caso do Estado do Rio de Janeiro', in: *Proceedings of XVII ANPET: Congresso de Pesquisa e Ensino em Transportes*, Vol. 1, ANPET, Rio de Janeiro, 375–386.

Ribeiro, S.K., Abreu, A.A., 2004, 'A comparative analysis between the I/M programme of Rio de Janeiro and the one in Phoenix', in: *Electronic Proceedings of the 11th CODATU Conference*, Bucharest.

Ribeiro, S.K., Abreu, A.A., 2006a, 'A Etiquetagem Veicular Como Indutora de Redução de Consumo de Gasolina: O Caso do Município de São Paulo', in: *Proceedings of the IV Rio de Transportes Congress*, Rio de Janeiro.

Ribeiro, S.K., Abreu, A.A., 2006b, 'Evaluation of potential reductions in carbon dioxide emissions through the introduction of flex-fuel technology in Brazil's light vehicle fleet', In: *Electronic Proceedings of the XVI International Symposium on Alcohol Fuels* (ISAF), Rio de Janeiro.

Szwarcfiter, L., Mendes F.E., la Rovere, E.L., 2005, 'Enhancing the effects of the Brazilian program to reduce atmospheric pollutant emissions from vehicles', *Transportation Research Part D: Transport and Environment* 10(2), 153–160.

US-DOE, 1998, *Life Cycle Inventory of Biodiesel and Petroleum Diesel for Use in an Urban Bus*, US Department of Energy Office of Fuels Development and US Department of Agriculture Office of Energy, National Renewable Energy Laboratory, Golden, CO.

US-EPA, 2002, *A Comprehensive Analysis of Biodiesel Impacts on Exhaust Emissions*, Draft Technical Report (EPA420-P-02-001), Environmental Protection Agency [available at www.epa.gov/OMS/models/biodsl.htm].

Worldwatch Institute and GTZ, 2006, *Biofuels for Transportation: Global Potential and Implications for Sustainable Agriculture and Energy in the 21st Century* [available at www.worldwatch.org/pubs/biofuels].

For Product Safety Concerns and Information please contact our EU
representative GPSR@taylorandfrancis.com Taylor & Francis Verlag GmbH,
Kaufingerstraße 24, 80331 München, Germany

Batch number: 08158490

Printed by Printforce, the Netherlands